Holy Anime!

Japan's View of Christianity

Patrick Drazen

Hamilton Books
Lanham • Boulder • New York • Toronto • Plymouth, UK

Copyright © 2017 by Hamilton Books
4501 Forbes Boulevard, Suite 200, Lanham, Maryland 20706
Hamilton Books Acquisitions Department (301) 459-3366

Unit A, Whitacre Mews, 26-34 Stannary Street,
London SE11 4AB, United Kingdom

All rights reserved
Printed in the United States of America
British Library Cataloguing in Publication Information Available

Library of Congress Control Number: 2017933588
ISBN: 978-0-7618-6907-8 (pbk : alk. paper)—ISBN: 978-0-7618-6908-5 (electronic)

Cover image: "Tamagawa River in Musashi Province", number 27 from Katsushika Hokusai "36 Views of Mount Fuji" (c. 1830-1832)

Contents

Acknowledgments	v
1 Introduction: Why This Book	1
2 History of Christianity in Japan: It's Complicated	11
3 Christianity in Japanese Popular Culture through the Lens of Said's *Orientalism*	31
4 Christian References in the Manga of Tezuka Osamu	39
5 Crucifixion in Manga and Anime: The Good, The Bad and The Unreal	65
6 The Exorcists	77
7 Jinguru Beh! Christmas in Manga and Anime	89
8 Christian Weddings in Japan: Just Like in the Movies	99
9 Clergy	105
10 Nuns in Anime/Manga: Sisterhood Is Not So Powerful	117
11 *Witch Hunter Robin*: Love and Fear and a Side-Trip to Barack Obama	127
12 Japan's Most Famous Christian Martyr: Amakusa Shirō	133
13 Angels and Other Metaphors	139
14 The "Not Safe" Chapter	161
Atogaki (Afterword)	175
References	179
Index	185

Acknowledgments

This book owes its existence to quite a few people who haven't had much to do with Japanese popular culture, but without them in my life it would have been a very different book—if it had come to be written at all.

First, most of the first draft of this book was written in the summer of 2015 while living with my brother Daniel. I had been living with in-laws following the death of my wife, but they went their separate ways by the spring of 2015 and I was welcomed into a spare room. As long as I had a bed, a place to set up my computer, and a way of reviewing my collection of manga and anime, I threw myself into this book. Daniel's hospitality allowed me to focus on the book to the exclusion of almost everything else.

Most importantly, though, I acknowledge the quarter-century I was married to Carla Inara Clarke. She took the pen name Carlos as a teenager (actually, it was thrust upon her, but that's a long story) and shifted her goals from playwright to journalist to historian to scholar; however, there was always a common thread in her life. That thread was to communicate with others, to reach out to them, to listen to them tell their stories and to tell other stories in return. Her verbal skills were, I think, driven by the compassion she had for others—a compassion driven in turn by spending most of her life with physical disability. Although her growth was a work in progress, cut short when she died, her example moves and inspires me still.

When she died, she was in the process of writing her doctoral dissertation, which is how I met her dissertation advisor, Lennard Davis. You could call him a college professor, which would be accurate, but he was so much more than that to Carlos, and to the countless students and readers he's influenced through his students, his memoirs, his analysis of disability issues, his activism, and other writings. Yet he has never been an imposing figure; Carlos has always referred to him as Lennie, which is how I—and many others, I'm sure—think of him, with no disrespect and great admiration.

Lennie's background includes a faculty position at Columbia University, where he not only helped to guide a student named Barack Obama, whom you may have heard of, but also as a colleague of someone whose work is not only central to this book but has been a great influence on the world even beyond his own death. Edward W. Said was born in Jerusalem in 1935; since Jerusalem at that time was in the patch of land called Palestine, Said was a Palestinian—a word that now conjures up images of the only Palestinian many in the west ever knew: the short, swarthy, unshaven Yassir Arafat. Said had the good looks of a matinee idol, on the other hand, but also the interests of a historian and the compassion of a thoroughgoing humanist, as so many of his writings demonstrate. He is best remembered for one of those writings: a study of the western world's writing about the East, whether as escapist prose or as government policy. That 1978 book *Orientalism* is a landmark study and a true eye-opener; in my case, certainly, it explained and expanded on traits I had seen in others—and in myself—but had not been able to put into diagnostic words so succinctly.

I've been writing for decades—small works and large, fact and fiction—but saw my first book published at the end of 2002: *Anime Explosion: The What? Why? And Wow! Of Japanese Animation.* I'm forever grateful to Stone Bridge Press and to its publisher Peter S. Goodman for taking a chance on an unpublished guy who wanted to say a few things about Japanese cartoons.

Once I stepped over that threshold, I found myself among names I'd regarded as scholars high up a mountain; ladies and gentlemen so accomplished that I didn't realize for some time that I was among them. That roster of names, of writers and scholars who share my interest in Japanese popular culture, is a lengthy one, and they include, but are surely not limited to: Frederick Schodt, Martha Cornog, the late Timothy Perper, Frenchy Lunning, Marc Hairston, Helen McCarthy, Mikhail Koulikov, Thomas LaMarre, Susan Napier, Charles Dunbar, Gilles Poitras, Brian Ruh, Tony Levi... the list is endless.

Also endless is the list of artists, writers, composers, cinematographers and others who create the postwar phenomena of Japanese comics and animation. They have given the entire world, not just Japan, something to read, to watch, to listen to, to write about, and to think about, especially in the west where their work would in the past have been relegated to the Kids' Table. I can only start to mention the giants, living and deceased: Tezuka Osamu, Ishinomori Shotaro, Matsumoto Reiji, Takahashi Rumiko, Hagio Moto, Ikeda Riyoko, Miyazaki Hayao, Rin Taro, Obata Takeshi, Shiina Takashi, Arakawa Hiromu, Hatori Bisco... with new names being added to the list almost daily.

And the same applies to the fans, of high school age or younger, and college age or older, who come to conventions and watch the videos and write the fanfiction and create the music videos and read the manga, sometimes on the page and sometimes online; they give the creators and scholars someone to create for, but their questions and enthusiasm feed energy back to the creators and scholars, providing a reason to do even better tomorrow, because we know somebody is out there listening and reading, grasping what we think and building on what we say, and especially enjoying it, and keeping it all going on.

In that spirit, I dedicate this book to all of the above, named and unnamed, with a line from poet Nikki Giovanni:

One ounce of truth benefits like a ripple on a pond

PD

Chapter One

Introduction

Why This Book

In January of 1992, during the same trip to Japan in which he vomited onto Prime Minister Miyazawa, President George H. W. Bush committed another faux pas. Visiting a Shinto temple during the New Year holidays, Bush interrupted two priests playing a traditional ball game. Without inquiring as to the rules or the object of the game, Bush proceeded to bounce the ball off of his head, soccer style. This particular mistake went largely unnoticed in the American press, for the simple reason that the reporters covering the incident knew as little about the game as did President Bush.

This is emblematic of the superficial approach toward Japan that many Westerners, even those with the best intentions and with an education in the ways of the Japanese, still sometimes take. It perhaps should not be surprising that American political, business and farming interests seem to be under the impression that there is no difference between negotiating with Americans and with Japanese. The apparent mentality at work is that, since Japanese businessmen wear suits and ties and eat Kentucky Fried Chicken, they understand and may prefer, if given the choice, the Euro-American way of doing things. Obviously, this assumption leaves a great deal of the Japanese approach to life out of account.

Westerners who study Japan can often come to widely divergent conclusions by interpreting only superficial data of Japanese behavior, to the neglect of the broader cultural and historical context, or, in studying Japanese culture, by focusing almost exclusively on Japan's "high culture" at the expense of the popular culture and its reflection of contemporary day-to-day life and the beliefs of the people. Even the most carefully documented and researched evidence can be misinterpreted for various reasons, some having nothing to do with the subject.

Japan's cultural context, as broad a topic as that may be, is not so broad that it cannot be studied by the west. Furthermore, such a study is imperative if the west is to truly understand the Japanese—not only what they do and say but why they choose to do and say it in a particular manner. Finally, it is my belief that one of the clearest ways to examine this cultural context is through an analysis of both the high culture and the popular culture of Japan, in this case, perhaps the most pervasive of the popular media, comic books (manga) and their animated versions on television, in movies and for home video (anime).

The case for the study of popular culture in general has been made by a host of incisive and insightful commentators, from Marshall McLuhan to Susan Sontag to James Baldwin. A study of the pop culture of Japan may be especially critical for the simple reason that, unlike the "serious" writings of Tanizaki, Kawabata, Akutagawa, Mishima, Oe, Endō and many others, these works do not seek to call attention to themselves or their creators as upholding a classic Japanese literary tradition, or interpreting that tradition in terms understandable to those familiar with the classic Western literary tradition. Popular culture is one product that was never designed for the export market. William W. Savage, Jr., has pointed out that "culture functions to systematize values and has an internal orientation." (p. 15) The popular culture, in this case anime and manga, can give us, as it were, Japan at home, without the suit, stretched out spread-eagled on the floor, arms and legs wide apart, "dai no ji ni natte (like the sign for the word "big")" in the words of Katei's verse. (Blyth, p. 165)

The preface to Blyth's volume on senryu offers one of the most focused rationales for a study of Japanese pop culture as well as Japan's higher literary and graphic art. Blyth called for a parallel study of both haiku and senryu, a more down-to-earth, folkish style of poetry similar to, yet distinct from, haiku. "The two together give not only a fairly complete idea of the nature of the Japanese people, their spirituality and idealism on the one hand and thoroughgoing realism on the other, but embrace within them the two attitudes of the human spirit, the constructive and the destructive." (p. i) Perhaps it would be more succinct to say that high art celebrates a more idealized vision of a culture's most cherished values and beliefs than the pop culture, which seeks to have those values and beliefs immediately ratified by public consumption. Similar to Blyth, Gregory Barrett's study of archetype in Japanese cinema states its thesis early on: "The traditional "high culture," . . . is certainly important in the evaluation of Japanese film. Still, our understanding must be insufficient, if we ignore traditional 'low culture,' as well as modern popular culture (admittedly Americanized to some extent)."

(p. 15) While there are American components to Japanese popular culture, they have generally been introduced on Japan's terms, not the west's.

In any event, this dichotomy—between an idealized view of a culture through its high art and the reflection of the same ethos at work through its popular culture—has baffled many observers of many cultures, not only Japan's.

Two books published in the West offer glimpses of Japanese comics through Western eyes, and horrified glimpses at that. Travel writer Paul Theroux tells of his encounter with a Japanese comic magazine on the bullet train to Aomori. Theroux was "upset" at this point, having read the short stories of Taro Hirai, whose pen-name Edogawa Rampo is a punningly Japanese reworking of Edgar Allan Poe and whose stories are even more dependent on the grotesque and depraved than the works of his namesake. Theroux, "driven to distraction" by the stories and unable at this point to reconcile "the agonized Japanese spirit" in literature with the placid surface of Japanese people, has the following encounter:

> There was a young girl seated beside me. Very early in the trip I had established that she did not speak English, and for nearly the whole time since we had left Ueno Station she had been reading a thick comic book. When we arrived at the far north of Honshu, at Noheji Station (fifteen seconds) on Mutsu Bay, . . . (t)he girl rose, put her comic down, and walked the length of the car to the toilet. A green TOILET OCCUPIED light went on, and while that light burned I read the comic. I was instructed and cautioned. The comic strips showed decapitations, cannibalism, people bristling with arrows like Saint Sebastian, people in flames, shrieking armies of marauders dismembering villagers, limbless people with dripping stumps, and, in general, mayhem. The drawings were not good, but they were clear. Between the bloody stories there were short comic ones and three of them depended for their effects on farting: a trapped man or woman bending over, exposing a great moon of buttock and emitting a jet of stink (gusts of soot drawn in wiggly lines and clouds) in the captors' faces. The green light went off. I dropped the comic. The girl returned to her seat and, so help me God, serenely returned to this distressing comic. (Theroux, pp. 277-278)

Theroux cannot be faulted for his shock that Japanese comic books (or young Japanese girls, for that matter) are not what he expected them to be. It also may not be improper to suggest that the shock of discovery was intensified by Theroux's furtive mode of examination; had he purchased the magazine outright at a newsstand and thumbed through it at leisure, rather than hastily trying to avoid being seen by the child whose magazine it was, he may have come away with a different impression. In an ironic way, Theroux seems to have played the protagonist in, and the whole scene could well have come out of, a short story by Edogawa Rampo.

Someone who should have known better than to fall into the same trap, however, was Edward Seidensticker. He has produced numerous writings on Japan, notably two concise histories of 20th century Tokyo: *Low City, High City* about the 1923 Kantō earthquake, and a companion volume on the city after the quake, *Tokyo Rising*. The latter devotes a few paragraphs to comics, discussing them in the context of television and of their supposedly non-comic content:

> Television scenes speed by at such a great rate that no one has time to say much of anything, and there is very little room indeed for what may be called distinguished language. Manga dispense with words almost entirely. They are frighteningly popular. In 1987 one and two-thirds billion copies of manga magazines were sold. The word manga is generally rendered "comics," but it is not a good rendition. The big Japanese-English dictionary has among its definitions "cartoon," which is better. There is little humor in these magazines. The cartoon, humorous and bloodcurdling, has a venerable history in Japan. Of recent years the latter has come to prevail, along with the erotic. Such words as there are to slow the devotee down on his gallop through a manga magazine tend strongly toward the imitative or onomatopoetic. They do not convey a meaning so much as an immediate physical experience. They cut through the descriptive functions of language, and splash and splatter and otherwise seek, like Aldous Huxley's feelies, to strike immediately at the senses.
>
> The Japanese language has always been rich in such words. The argument has been made that because of them it is uniquely suited to such anti-rational modes of belief and conduct as Zen. They bear a much larger share of the burden in manga than in ordinary language. Some of them are rather amusing. A newspaper article in 1970 listed these: za-she, for cutting someone's face open; zuzu-u-u zuzu-u-u, for slurping noodles; chu chuba, for a kiss; pattan, for a punch in the jaw; murereri murumuru, for the impatience of a young lady awaiting her young gentleman. They are many of them sounds that would convey nothing at all independently of their manga, which is to say that they are outside of and beyond language. (Seidensticker, pp. 335-336)

It seems strange that someone who was so well versed in Japanese culture could miss the humor of manga, unless his comments were born of disapproval of some of the bloodcurdling, earthy and erotic content rather than ignorance or a lack of humor. It also is surprising that Seidensticker should commit such a massive error as to dismiss manga, and claim a deleterious effect on the Japanese language, because of the use of sound effects. Onomatopoetic devices, as Seidensticker himself noted, were part of the spoken Japanese language long before comics were developed. As we shall see, this is just another example of a long-standing Japanese cultural tradition being sustained within a contemporary, apparently anarchic medium; it also shows someone from outside that culture casually, or even willfully, insisting on viewing the outsider culture in terms of something more familiar. The word for this view is Orientalist, and chapter 3 takes a deeper look at how it works both on and by the Japanese culture.

Additionally, while some manga rely on their graphics to convey the bulk of the story, manga can also go to the other extreme and, Seidensticker to the contrary, rely to a great degree on the written word. There are pages of manga that contain no words, and conversely (sometimes within the same story) pages with massive blocks of text that drive the plot. I think Theroux, Seidensticker and many other western commentators on Japanese culture have on some topics "missed the boat."

The use of manga and anime to provide an inner glimpse of the Japanese mind can be especially beneficial in a study of the Japanese approach to religion in general, and toward Christianity in particular. One factor that often stymies sociologists seeking to study the religious component in the life of typical Japanese is that the entire concept of religion in Japan does not match that of the West, so the ground rules begin with a significant difference. In the 19th century, when Christian missionaries returned to Japan after being banned for centuries, the Japanese had to create a word for "religion" (*shūkyō*—the teachings or doctrine of a sect) to accommodate the western view of the matter, which was (and is) that there was such a thing as the One True Church, and that, according to Ian Reader, even today "the word conjures up bad images of being disturbed on Sunday mornings by ladies ringing one's doorbell and asking awkward questions." (p. 14) The religious impulse, when expressed in Japan, tends toward religions that have historically been part of the culture; other religions have been absorbed into Japan, but usually within the context of a belief that was already there. The tendency for Japan is to look for a sense of collective belonging, which can encompass a family, a neighborhood, or even a nation, rather than the western "personal god". Perhaps the most notorious statistic in this regard was the 1985 finding that membership in Japanese religious organizations (Buddhist temples, Shinto shrines, plus Christian churches and various "new religions") totaled 223 million—when Japan's population was 121 million. (p. 6). Reader continues that:

> most religious organisations in Japan in submitting their figures are liable to provide inflated and optimistic evaluations of their strength. Common practice includes counting every member of a household as a member when one person joins,[1] and not removing from membership registers those who have long ceased their affiliation, which is particularly common among Buddhist temples. New religions also have a penchant for signing on anyone who attends their events and meetings, whether they become active members or not. (pp. 6-7)

However, the main numerical discrepancy noted above is almost totally accounted for by the two main religions, Shinto (115 million) and Buddhism (92 million). These numbers suggest that both Shinto and Buddhism are an integral part of the Japanese identity, and more than a personal theology. Add to this the desire to second-guess the interviewer and say what s/he wants to hear, and the refraction of the image turns into an outright distortion. Further add the tendency for Western students of religion to impose their own culture's assumptions about the "naturalness" of monotheism and denigration of spirit-worship as "pagan", factor in the occasional hidden agenda of proselytizing for the One True Faith so that the Japanese may be "saved", and take into consideration the most obvious and fundamental differences between the two philosophies—common cultural assumptions about the myth of resurrection in the West and the myth of reincarnation in the East—and the various errors, substantial enough in and of themselves, add up to one giant miscalculation—one which the West seems to persist in making.

This persistence has gone on for centuries, and not merely in regard to Japan. In his 1978 book *Orientalism*, Palestinian Edward W. Said examined the ways in which European cultures viewed the lands east of the Mediterranean. This portion of the earth, running from Egypt to China and also including both Saharan and sub-Saharan Africa, has been collectively dismissed for centuries as "the Orient", filled with undisciplined dark-skinned people of no cultural significance. Japan has proven to be one of the cultures most resistant to general "civilizing", and specifically to Christian outreach from the west.

This raises the question of why Westerners would want to influence the Japanese attitude toward religion in general and Western religion in particular. Part of it may be simple egoism, the American desire to be liked in all other parts of the globe, and hence to try to determine if we really are liked. We quiz the Japanese directly in an attempt "to see ourselves as others see us," not realizing that the direct approach may not be the most fruitful in this case. It is as critical for us to realize that Japanese culture is fueled by fundamental assumptions of its Shinto-Buddhist heritage as it is for us to recall that certain fundamental tenets of Judeo-Christianity underlie Western culture. These assumptions act on their respective cultures at a profound level, even a mythic level in the Carl Jung/Joseph Campbell sense of that word. Unless and until we attempt to understand the various mythic components that underlie all cultures, including our own, we will only be able to communicate with others in the world on a superficial level that would leave both sides open to misinterpretation and misunderstanding. The value of complete communication should be self-evident. The humanism that informed most of Said's writings certainly points toward a more productive model of cross-cultural communication.

Of course, the process would be simpler, and this book would be shorter, if the Japanese held only one or two attitudes about Christianity. There is, and has been, a range of opinions on the subject, from approving to skeptical to xenophobic, all of which are reflected, to one extent or another, in Japan's popular culture. A survey of these varying depictions can serve as a barometer to the observer outside the culture who wishes to determine something of the attitudes within.

For all of these reasons I believe that the study of Western religious images as reflected in Japanese popular culture, wherein the Japanese are speaking to themselves and unconcerned about pleasing the gaijin—the word, a shortened form of "gaikokujin", literally means foreigner, but in Japanese is generally taken to mean Americans, particularly white Americans—can provide a much truer picture of Japanese impressions than can a formal historical or quantitative study. The pop culture provides the truer mirror.

As for the use of "comic books and cartoons" to discuss religious attitudes, a blog titled "Beneath the Tangles" illustrates Christian sermonizing with allusions to anime regardless of the creator's intent or even the original storyline. This work will avoid that technique, and will examine the manga and anime of a variety of postwar artists; if attention is paid exclusively in chapter 4 to the work of Tezuka Osamu, it is necessarily because he was Japan's premier manga artist and a bellwether for most if not all of the major developments of the medium in postwar Japan, to such an extent that his influence continues to be felt decades after his death. Nor will the analysis of Christianity in Japanese pop culture be used to attempt to deduce the individual attitudes of the artists and writers; where such attitudes can be documented, and where these attitudes are relevant to the finished product, they will be considered. This study will approach the manga and anime directly, as a Japanese media consumer would, and in doing so downplay the influence of the artists and writers, except in such a forum as a fan would be exposed to (forewords/afterwords to collected editions, marginalia, fan mail, etc.) The primary concern of this book will be the examination of the depictions of Christianity in manga and anime, with an eye to determining cultural attitudes from these depictions.

Speaking of a manga as being "by" a particular artist or writer involves a convention. Although there are some four-panel gag manga which are produced, beginning to end, by a single artist, it is, especially for the longer serialized stories, a deadline-conscious mass medium which requires mass output. Usually the principal artist will create pencil roughs of the pages of the story, and it will be left to apprentices and assistants to finish the page by inking and toning (Schodt, pp. 142-143). Some studios are more open to creative input from the assistants than others. Generally, however, inasmuch as assistants do not have significant creative input into the content of the story, often saving these ideas until they try to break into the business on their own, a manga can still be safely said to be "by" one or two people.

Theroux, Seidensticker and other nervous gaijin to the contrary, manga and anime are funny. The humor ranges from elaborate puns to low slapstick to Dadaesque absurdity, much as the humor of Shakespeare can encompass farce, four-letter words and sophisticated banter. The differences, however, are more noticeable because the Japanese sense of humor admits to a more open approach to sexual and scatological humor than has been traditional in the West.

This is to say that, in dealing with manga depictions of Christianity, the researcher must take precautions against over-interpreting some of the presentations. These may be primarily or solely for humorous effect, and it would be a misrepresentation to read broader cultural meaning into what was intended to be nothing more or less than a gag. This book will attempt to stay clear of taking punch-lines involving Christianity as always completely meaningful, and yet will examine such punch-lines if their *consistent* appearance suggests a particular cultural perception of western religion.

Similarly, in the analysis of both Japanese religion and popular culture, some examples carry more weight than others. Historically, Japanese religions are no more monolithic than their western counterparts, and over the centuries Shinto and Buddhism have occasionally shown signs of evolving into a belief system that would remind western observers of more familiar beliefs and behaviors. There was, for example, a conscious decision to reorganize some native religious services in the 19th century, after the return of Christianity to Japan, along the lines of Protestant Christian church services. Similarly, some Japanese religions have seen offshoots that have evolved theologically into something more closely resembling the western worship of a "personal God"; one example would be the variant of Japanese Buddhism known as Soka Gakkai. These offshoots should not be given more than their due weight, and the Western observer must resist the Orientalist temptation to consider beliefs and practices that seem to mirror those of the west as somehow more "natural."

There is one additional cautionary note. Simply because a work was created for the popular culture of a given nation does not mean that the work will be limited to the parent culture or nation. American popular culture has, at this stage in history, become a component of Japanese popular culture. In the same synergistic spirit with which they approach western religion, the Japanese have taken select bits and pieces of western pop culture and either used them as such or modified them or parodied them. By the same token, some western pop culture icons can be adopted into the Japanese way of doing things without understanding their function in the west at all. There is a famous photo of a Japanese crèche scene in which the infant Jesus is being adored by Walt Disney's Seven Dwarfs; perhaps because the scene in the Disney movie with the dwarfs around the body of the "dead" Snow White seemed reminiscent of a crèche scene, or perhaps in the belief that these dwarfs were somehow related to the Seven Chinese Gods of Good Luck. (Certainly Dopey's pendulous ears would be regarded as an Oriental harbinger of blessings, regardless of Disney's original intent). On an earthier note, Bornoff observes that several call-girl rings in Japan took to calling themselves YMCA after the song of the same name by the Village People became popular in Japan; as can be seen from its use in this case, "the gay innuendo in the lyrics was entirely lost in Japan"—not to mention the Christian association with that name. (p. 283)

This cross-cultural adoption can be illustrated by a throwaway gag in one of the stories in Tezuka Osamu's 1980 manga series *Don Dracula*. (3 vols. Tokyo: Akita Shoten) This series was based on the Bram Stoker vampire novel and, indirectly but no less definitely, on the host of films that were based on the book. The Bela Lugosi vehicle directed by Tod Browning in 1931, based largely on Hamilton Deane and John Balderston's 1927 stage adaptation of Stoker's novel, is perhaps the best-known, but there have been many others. This particular manga, however, was directly inspired by the 1979 American parody Dracula film *Love at First Bite*, released in Japan under the title *Dorakyura Miyako e Iku (Dracula Goes to Town)*. ("Hajime ni (Introduction)", *Don Dorakyura* vol. 1, pp. 4-5) In the manga episode titled "Dorakyura Sono Henshin (Dracula in Disguise)," patrons in a restaurant see the Count turn into a bat and fly out the window, prompting this exchange: "Tori ka? Hikooki ka?" "Iya, Battoman da!" ("Is it a bird? Is it a plane?" "No, it's Batman!") (vol. 2, p. 148) This is a conjunction of no less than four examples of Western pop culture: the Stoker "Dracula", the film versions of Stoker, the "Superman" comic book and the "Batman" comic book, recombined simply to produce a laugh on the way to the next page.

This book will focus on religious attitudes as expressed in the pop culture of Japan, allowing that a Japanese take on western pop culture may be one of the ways these ideas are expressed without filters or self-editing. This survey will begin with a historical overview of the history of Christianity in Japan, a history less than five centuries old and marked by a societal ambiguity over the years about whether and how to tolerate this religion's presence in Japan. This will be followed by a discussion of Said's *Orientalism*, since this way of thinking about other cultures has been used in the west to critique Japanese literature and was also used in Japan to critique the west. Literature on Japanese attitudes toward Christianity will also be examined, illustrated by a look at the manga and anime themselves, particularly the work of Tezuka Osamu, which set the tone for others to follow. Christianity seldom appears in manga or anime in a Biblical context, and is usually shown indirectly by focusing on issues as varied as Christmas, exorcisms, crucifixions and weddings.

NOTE

1. This is a reference to the fact that, when Portuguese Catholics introduced Christianity to Japan in the 16th century, it was not uncommon for a feudal lord or headman to order his underlings to convert, regardless of their feelings. This essentially medieval approach will be examined in greater detail in chapter 2.

Chapter Two

History of Christianity in Japan

It's Complicated

THE KNOCK ON THE DOOR

Christianity in Japan is not yet 500 years old, and actually encompasses only about half of that time. This history begins with the first contact between Japan and Europe. "In 1541 some Portuguese drifted ashore in Kyushu, the southernmost of the main islands of Japan, and two years later other Portuguese came, largely by accident, to Tanegashima, a small island lying off the southern tip of Kyushu." (Reischauer, p. 5) The relationship was all about trade until 1548, and the arrival of Francis Xavier (1506-1552) in Manila, capital of the Portuguese colony of the Philippines. Locals told Xavier of the existence of the Japanese islands to the north which had never known Christianity; he decided that they needed the missionary work of the Church and specifically his Society of Jesus, now known as the Jesuits. "(T)he warring, feudal conditions of sixteenth-century Japan reminded (the missionaries) so much of home. The Jesuits in particular, with their special liking for martial order and discipline, could readily appreciate the rigorous life-style of Japan's ruling samurai class." (Varley, p. 127)

Describing 16th century Japan as "warring" and "feudal" may, if anything, be an understatement. The period from roughly 1467 to 1573 is known as the "Sengoku jidai" (Warring States Period) in Japanese history, during which scattered fiefdoms overseen by a distant emperor gradually coalesced (by force of regional warlords and one nation-building shogun or another) into approximately the nation of Japan that exists today. This was an era in which political power in Japan shifted with the rise and fall of various warlords. However, this was also the time in which one of these warlords, Oda

Nobunaga (1534-1582), would go a long way toward establishing a centralized seat of government for the emperor.

By 1568 Nobunaga had established a major power-base in Kyoto and allied himself to the present shogun, Ashikaga Yoshiaki. This alliance did not last, however; Nobunaga proved to be a ruthless tyrant, and the shogun worried about the stability of his new ally. He was right to worry; in 1573 Nobunaga moved against the shogun and, from that time until his death in 1582, he attacked all other warring clans which posed a threat to his rule. For their first decade, the Jesuits were limited to ports on the southern island of Kyushu already visited by Portuguese ships, and neither the sailors nor the missionaries were considered a threat. (*Ibid.*)

It is not clear whether the practice of crucifixion in Japan predated the arrival of Christian missionaries, but Nobunaga took to it quite readily. He did not hesitate to use it as one means among many to achieve power. Nobunaga abused friend and foe equally, but the blow that sealed his fate was the murder of the mother of Akechi Mitsuhide, another warlord who had allied himself to Nobunaga after the latter's arrival in Kyoto, serving thereafter as the general of Nobunaga's forces.

During one battle in 1579, Mitsuhide had sent his mother to serve as a hostage to convince the enemy to negotiate with Nobunaga; protocol at the time was that the negotiators were safe in the enemy camp during peace talks. When the enemy negotiators arrived at the parley, however, Nobunaga, ignoring his own terms, had the hostages crucified; Mitsuhide's mother was killed in retaliation. General Mitsuhide decided to bide his time. In June of 1582, Mitsuhide was ordered to lead his forces in an attack on the Moori clan; instead, his men turned on Nobunaga. Trapped in a temple in Kyoto, Nobunaga committed suicide. At that time, he controlled about one-half of Japan. (Hane 1972, pp. 130-134)

At first Nobunaga welcomed the Christian missionaries. "One apparent reason for this cordiality was his hope that the Jesuits might be useful in combatting . . . those Buddhist sects of the capital region that opposed his advance to national power." (Varley, p. 127) As we have seen, while Nobunaga may have welcomed Western contact in general and Christian missionaries in particular, this was not because he professed to believe in the Christian ideals.

"One of the most prominent of the Christian daimyos was Ōmura Sumitada, who in 1570 opened the harbor of Nagasaki in his domain to Portuguese commerce and ten years later ceded it as a territorial possession to be administered by the Jesuits." (*Ibid.*, p. 128) Ōmura also decreed at one point that only Christians could live in Nagasaki. Of course, this was a time when a warlord or headman could order those under him to convert to the new religion; the idea of free will and individual action was still alien to Japan (and the rest of the civilized world) at that time for the most part.

The death of Nobunaga "was speedily avenged by another general, (Toyotomi) Hideyoshi, who . . . within eight years, brought [most of] the remainder of Japan under his control." (Varley, p. 126) The establishment of the modern nation of Japan was largely completed within the first few years of the Tokugawa Shogunate which succeeded Toyotomi after his death in 1598.

Hideyoshi had approached Jesuit missionaries in 1586 with a request to charter two Portuguese galleons which he could use to invade the mainland. In return, Hideyoshi offered to build Christian churches in China and to force the conquered people of the mainland to convert to Christianity. (Hane 1972, pp. 136-7) He did not trust the Catholics to act in Japan's best interests; he considered himself too much of a realist to think that. Toyotomi therefore set out to either suppress or co-opt the Catholics:

> [I]n 1587, without warning or intimation, Hideyoshi declared the "nationalization" of Nagasaki[1] and ordered the Jesuit missionaries to leave the country within twenty days. Hideyoshi never fully implemented his decree. . . . Yet, the fact that he issued it at all suggests a growing anti-Christian feeling in Japan's ruling circles. (Varley, p. 128)

"Hideyoshi was also . . . keenly interested in foreign trade and, through courtesies extended to the missionaries, sought to lure an ever greater number of Portuguese ships to Japan." (Varley, pp. 127-128) The Jesuit missionaries were, at first, well received. "Conversions came slowly at first but soon in increasing numbers, until, by the end of the century, there may have been as many as 300,000 Catholics in Japan." (Reischauer, pp. 5-6) However, many of the converts tried to incorporate Western civilization in general, and Catholicism in particular, into their culture on their terms. The Japanese focus on the tangential trimmings of the faith, even at this early stage, was documented in a letter from a Jesuit father:

> (Hideyoshi) has become so enamored of Portuguese dress and costume that he and his retainers frequently wear this apparel, as do all the other lords of Japan, even the gentiles,[2] with rosaries of driftwood on the breast above all their clothing, and with a crucifix at their side, or hanging from the waist, and sometimes even with kerchiefs in their hands; some of them are so curious that they learn by rote the litanies of Pater Noster and Ave Maria and go along praying in the streets, not in mockery or scorn of the Christians, but simply for gallantry, or because they think it is a good thing and one which will help them to achieve prosperity in worldly things. In this way they order oval-shaped pendants to be made containing reliques of the images of Our Lord and Our Lady painted on glass at great cost. (cited in Boxer, pp. 207-208)

The Jesuits also encouraged converts to keep votive pictures to display in their homes. "So great was the demand . . . the Jesuits were obliged to instruct Japanese artists in Western-style painting." (Varley, p. 132) Very few of these works survived the banning of Christianity by the Tokugawa shoguns in the 17th century.

Given this interest in things Christian in Japan, Toyotomi's working relationship with the Jesuits earlier in the decade, and the fact that at the beginning of his reign he let stand the special favors granted Christian missionaries by Nobunaga, the 1587 banning order came with little or no warning. Furthermore, the order was not aimed solely at foreign missionaries; nobles who had already converted to Christianity were forbidden from ordering their underlings to convert, and samurai of the nobler houses who wished to become Christians could not do so without official permission. Although a single incident may have touched off Toyotomi's anger—a Christian peasant was ordered to renounce his religion and refused—he embodied many of the anti-Christian prejudices felt in Japan at the time.

Just before the ban, Toyotomi granted an audience to a monk named Coelho, and asked several revealing questions about Christian behavior, among them: why the Portuguese bought and sold Japanese people as slaves, why the Portuguese have a preference for eating beef, and why the missionaries persecuted Buddhist monks and destroyed their temples. As to the first of these questions, there was no simple answer. The Jesuits were opposed to the Portuguese slave trade, and in 1571 had persuaded the king to issue a decree against the practice. However, there was no practical way to enforce the decree, especially thousands of miles from home. As a result, Portuguese sailors during the 16th century purchased or kidnapped a number of Japanese women and children to work as slaves in South and Central America. The Jesuits, like the king, were essentially powerless to prevent it.

There was also no great love between the Shinto lords of Japan at this time and the Buddhists of the nation; the former mistrusted the latter as a potential political foe. However, persecution of Buddhists by Christian missionaries was another crime that could be laid at the Europeans' doorstep. Toyotomi could express concern about the Buddhists without seeming hypocritical. Meat-eating was not commercially viable in Japan given the absence of open range land except in the far northern island of Hokkaido, but this escalated into another contentious issue between Toyotomi and the Christians. Sex, or specifically monogamy, was another such issue; it was not unusual for upper-class Japanese men to turn to concubines, or even to young boys, as sex partners over and above their wives. The Jesuits could not condone the practice, while the Japanese elite found monogamy an alien concept—mainly because they could afford to be polygamous.

Toyotomi's main concern, however, was Christianity's threat to his power. His servant's refusal to renounce Christianity marked the religion as a destabilizing influence, which could lead to open rebellion in the future. Not that Hideyoshi felt absolutely secure about non-Christians; he could remember how Mitsuhide's forces disobeyed Nobunaga's orders and turned against him. If Christian allegiance could not rest in the warlord, but arose from within the believer (or came down from the Vatican), Japanese Christians could not be counted on to serve. As in the early Roman Empire, Christianity in 16th Century Japan was, although a hobby of the nobility, eagerly adopted by the lower classes.

This was especially so beginning in 1593, when the first Franciscan missionaries arrived in Japan. Unlike the Jesuits, who enjoyed creature comforts and spent much of their time among the nobility, with whom they shared an essentially top-down vision of society and power, the Franciscans sought out the humbler members of Japanese society—those whom the Jesuits dismissed, the "blind, halt, burned, deaf, dumb, lame." Considering also that the Franciscans were predominantly Spanish, while the Jesuits were predominantly Portuguese, Christian infighting in Japan, as in Europe, was inevitable. (Hane 1972, pp. 144-146)

Although Toyotomi's 1587 order for Christian missionaries to leave Japan was not enforced, it was never rescinded; everything changed in 1597, when Hideyoshi "inaugurated some four decades of persecutions that led to the virtual extirpation of Christianity from Japan," with an act now known as the Martyrdom of the Twenty-Six.

> In 1596, at the height of the Jesuit-Franciscan rivalry, a Spanish galleon was shipwrecked on Shikoku Island and its cargo confiscated by Hideyoshi's officials. Evidently the pilot of the galleon, angered by the loss of the cargo, warned the Japanese officials that military conquest by Spain would soon follow based on the spy work being done by the Franciscans in Japan. The Franciscan version of the story was that the Jesuits, not the pilot, concocted the story about spying and conquest. In any case, Hideyoshi promptly ordered the rounding-up of Franciscan missionaries for execution. Six missionaries of the central provinces were arrested and they, along with twenty of their Japanese converts, were paraded to Nagasaki where, early in 1597, they were crucified and became the first Christian martyrs in Japan. (Varley, p. 147)

It should be noted that, in fact, three of the martyred Christians were not Franciscans but Jesuit lay brothers, caught in the dragnet. (Hane 1972, p. 147) This emphasizes the fact that, as far as Toyotomi was concerned, the sectarian difference between Christians was immaterial.

A NEW REGIME

The Tokugawa Shogunate was established in 1600, characterized by:

> the policy of national seclusion which the shogunate adopted during the late 1630s. . . . They pursued their seclusion policy for essentially two reasons: first, the fear, smoldering since Hideyoshi's day, that Christianity was by its

nature antithetical to Japan's traditional social order and religious beliefs; and second, the apprehension that the daimyos of western Japan, who had been the leading opponents of the Tokugawa before the battle of Sekigahara, might ally themselves with the Europeans and attempt to overthrow the [Tokugawa] regime. (Varley, pp. 146-147)

Varley's analysis leaves the fear of colonialism out of account altogether, which would have been a driving force for Toyotomi, whether alone or coupled with fears of sectarian violence.

The sectarian differences between Jesuit and Franciscan were bad enough for Christianity's image in Japan, but the arrival in the 1600s of Protestants from England and the Netherlands only gave the new shogun more reason for suspicion. In 1610 the Dutch stadtholder sent a message to Tokugawa Ieyasu warning that the secret aim of the Catholic missionaries was to sow "political dissention and civil strife." Ieyasu could also point to "unsavory behavior by some Japanese Christian officials," which Hane does not specify (Hane 1972, p. 147). Ultimately, on January 27, 1614, Ieyasu banned Christianity outright, in an edict that also required the Japanese to register at a Buddhist temple where they lived. Thus the primary competitors with Shinto for Japanese hearts and minds were either suppressed or absorbed into the bureaucracy.

Tokugawa Ieyasu died in 1616, but his successor Hidetada was just as merciless toward Christians who chose to remain after the 1614 edict. In September of 1622, fifty-five Japanese Christians, including women and children, were burned or decapitated at Nagasaki. The following year, Hidetada died and was succeeded by Iemitsu, who was, if anything, more ruthless and relentless than his predecessors. Torture of Christians, and those who protected them, expanded, and Iemitsu often took part in the proceedings. The torture was designed to force converts to abandon Christianity; interestingly, the higher-class, Jesuit-influenced samurai were more ready to abandon the faith than were the Franciscan-oriented peasants, perhaps because the latter felt that they had nothing to gain under a change in political dynasties, while the former could hope to be reinstated in the court of some daimyo or other. Toyotomi had stressed that a live apostate could do more in the long run to dissuade Japanese Christians than a dead martyr.

JAPAN'S HOLY WAR

The closest that Japanese Christians came to actively rebelling against their repression by the Tokugawa shogunate came in the Shimabara Rebellion of 1637-1638. It started in October 1637 as a tax revolt against the Shimabara Daimyo, who was installed in 1633 and proceeded to levy extreme taxes, torturing those who could not pay. The rebels began by resisting only the daimyo, but attackers soon began shouting the names of Jesus, Mary and Santiago during their raids. When the movement spread to the nearby island of Amakusa, the Christian rebels chose as their leader a 16 year old boy named Masuda Shirō, who later took the name Amakusa Shirō. He could offer the rebels little practical military advice, but this was supplied by several ronin who joined the rebellion. However, the rebels were driven off Amakusa and back to Shimabara. The rebel force, numbering about 37,000 and including women and children, were besieged in a castle for three months during the winter of 1638; before the surviving rebels surrendered, 13,000 of the 100,000 warriors of the Bakufu[3] had also died. (Hane 1972, pp. 148-149) Chapter 12 will include some of the modern interpretations of the young rebel leader and martyr.

This was the last mass move against Christianity by the emperor. For the remainder of the Tokugawa Shogunate, there would be the occasional sweep, and any Christians found would be persecuted. Persecution included tribunals in which believers were offered the chance to demonstrate their renunciation of the Christian faith through the practice of *fumie*; stepping on an image of Jesus. These *fumie* images were among the few Christian relics allowed to exist by the Tokugawa Shogunate. In addition, a system of regulating families through membership rolls in local Buddhist temples, a system known as *terauke seido*, was created in 1635; building on the 1614 edict by Tokugawa Ieyasu, its several purposes were to create a kind of civil service roster of the community while keeping watch for Christian or other undesirable influences while giving Buddhists responsibility for enforcement. (Suter, pp. 19-20)

A continuing intent to rein in Christianity during the Tokugawa Shogunate, when covert Christians had gone into hiding and overt Christians were strictly controlled, is evidenced in a 1760 document in which local civil authorities acknowledge their duties, under pain of death, to keep accurate records of the heretical elements in the community; "If mistakes in the *[terauke seido]* register are found, or if there are any omissions from the register, we admit the fault and will accept any kind of punishment." (cited in Robert Smith, p. 39)

Official mistrust of Christians must have had several contributing factors, including in no small part the fear of following the Philippines and becoming just another colony of a larger power—if not China then Spain or Portugal—but it is likely that the Christian missionaries and converts themselves were a contributing factor. Among the Catholics, the Jesuits and Franciscans were openly at daggers drawn with each other, and by the beginning of the Tokugawa Shogunate, when Dutch and British ships introduced Protestantism, the sectarian fights aflame in Europe at that time could be witnessed in microcosm in Japan. The earlier fear that Christians may have formed a nucleus around which Buddhists could rally against Shinto must have lessened, with the realization that the Christians themselves were fragmented and far from unified. This very character of disunion (or, if you will, diversity) would, however, provide its own reason to reject Christianity as a destabilizing influence on Japanese culture. The Shinto-Buddhist split was bad enough; the apparent inability of any two Christian sects to get along would have made the Tokugawa court hesitant. "By 1638 direct Japanese contacts with the West had been reduced to one closely supervised Dutch outpost, which was moved three years later to the tiny island of Deshima in the harbor of Nagasaki." (Reischauer, p. 6)

NOTES FROM UNDERGROUND

> The faith was preserved, however, as a supreme treasure in many Christian families and transmitted from generation to generation within the relatively narrow confines of some farming and fishing villages in northwestern Kyūshū. . . . Isolated Christian families or even groups of families were particularly susceptible to a loss of faith from inadequate instruction, from intermarriage with non-Christians, or from the fear of consequences of exposure. Corruption of faith also occurred in varying degrees through syncretistic adaptations (apparently unconscious)[4] or debasement into magical practices. In those areas, however, where all or most of the inhabitants of the village remained Christian, Catholic faith and practice were better preserved. (Drummond, p. 113)

Ironically, the hidden Christians of the Tokugawa were able to project Christian values onto non-Christian artifacts in their home shrines, thus being assured, even with the surveillance of Buddhist priests during the active persecution of Christians, the privacy which they needed to pursue their faith in a hostile environment:

> A strong devotion to the Virgin Mary was maintained by the hidden Christians. Because the possession of Christian devotional objects was strictly forbidden, only a few images of the Virgin were preserved. Christians, however, frequently used small statues of Kannon (Chinese: Kwan-yin), the Buddhist goddess-symbol of mercy, especially those which, made of white porcelain and imported from China, represented the goddess with a child on her arm similar to the Madonna and Child. Certain representations of Kannon bore the mark of a swastika on her breast that resembled a cross. These statues, which are now known as Mariya Kannon, could be venerated by Christians without unduly arousing suspicion. Very few other devotional objects were preserved. (Drummond, p. 116)

LaFleur mentions that, among the other objects that survived, "(t)eacups had hidden crosses in their designs." (p. 131)

As time went on, the desire to persecute Christian adherents became less important; there were too many other, more important concerns. As for the hidden Christians, they had developed a *modus vivendi* that allowed them to practice the faith. There was no need to do more than that; life would continue without change until 1853.

During the late Tokugawa period, with open membership in the Christian religion suppressed, imagination took the place of reality regarding the foreigners and their faith. An anonymous book titled *Kirishitan monogatari (Tales of the Christian)* painted this unlikely portrait of a European Christian for an audience which was increasingly unlikely ever to have seen either:

> an unnamable creature, somewhat similar in shape to a human being, but looking more like a long-nosed goblin. . . . His eyes were as large as spectacles, and their insides were yellow. His head was small. On his hands and feet he had long claws. His height exceeded seven feet, and he was black all over; only his nose was red. His teeth were longer than the teeth of a horse. (Suter, pp. 24-25)

THE TIMES THEY WERE A-CHANGING

Japan's policy of isolation from the rest of the world (Sakoku) was not absolute but it was severely governed by the court in Edo. "(T)he only European influence permitted was the Dutch factory at Dejima in Nagasaki. Trade with China was also handled at Nagasaki. Trade with Korea was limited to the Tsushima Domain (today part of Nagasaki Prefecture). Trade with the Ainu people was limited to the Matsumae Domain in Hokkaidō, and trade with the Ryūkyū Kingdom[5] took place in Satsuma Domain (present-day Kagoshima Prefecture). Apart from these direct commercial contacts in peripheral provinces, trading countries sent regular missions to the shogun in Edo."(Wiki)

This policy did not receive its historical name until it was almost over: "The term Sakoku [locked country] originates from the manuscript work Sakoku-ron written by Japanese astronomer Shizuki Tadao in 1801. Shizuki invented the word while translating the works of the 17th-century German traveller Engelbert Kaempfer concerning Japan." (Gunn, p. 151)

The Tokugawa Shogunate's policy of isolation cracked in 1853 with the arrival in Japan of Commodore Matthew Perry of the United States Navy. He had been dispatched by President Millard Fillmore to attempt to open commercial and diplomatic relations with Japan. It is likely that America did not particularly want trade with Japan as such, but was interested in establishing a "listening-post" close to China. That Asian nation, after all, had been defeated by the British during the Opium War of 1839-42, (Varley, p. 203) and, in spite of the negotiated end to the War of 1812-1814, relations between Great Britain and the United States would remain tense throughout the century. Fillmore, among other American presidents, would want to keep track of this major move in the Orient by the British Empire.

Since at the time Edo was not an open port, Perry's fleet was originally directed by the shogunate to sail to Nagasaki, hundreds of miles to the south, to the only port officially open to the outside world. A bombardment of Edo by Perry's cannons made it clear that they would not comply. This was a major part of Japan's decision to resume dealings with the rest of the world.

> At the beginning of the Meiji era in 1868, when the ban on Christianity had not been lifted, it was discovered that some Japanese families had secretly continued their practice of Christianity for two hundred years. These "hidden Christians" were severely punished by the Japanese government, and this news travelled rapidly to Western countries. When representatives of the Japanese government toured Western countries in order to study modern social and political conditions in these countries and develop better ties with them, they encountered hostility because of the recent suppression of hidden Christians. This helped persuade the government to remove the ban on Christianity in 1873. (Earhart, p. 42)

The issue was completely tangential as far as Japan was concerned, yet it seemed to be of supreme importance to the Westerners. Part of this is because the West was predominantly Christian, and would focus on the repression of its own preferred theology. But there was another factor of which Japan could not have been aware because of its isolation from the evolution of western philosophical thought: the fact that, while Japan had tried to prevent social change during the Sakoku, Europe had experienced the Age of Enlightenment, during which science rose in importance as governments became increasingly secular.

> Ideas are the glue that holds a culture together over time. Individual governments, economic systems, and even religions themselves (in the sense of ecclesiastic institutions) may come and go, but this substrate of ideas remains and evolves. . . . Humanism, democracy, natural rights, capitalism: each relies on a particular understanding (one that is so fundamental that it often does not need to be expressed) of individual human dignity. This includes even the right *not* to believe in God. (DuBois, p. 9)

When Japan wasn't looking, the western world had made a quantum leap beyond its own Holy Wars, such as that waged by Cromwell against the Irish Catholics in the 17th century. The Age of Enlightenment didn't stop war altogether, but it influenced WHICH wars were fought and WHY they were waged. The west was moving beyond the Machiavellian embrace of power for its own sake and beginning to weigh the consequences of power against the benefit to the people. And the people themselves were being redefined not merely as peasants and potential soldiers in some noble's army, but as "endowed by their Creator with certain unalienable rights".

Japan was still caught up in its non-democratic imperial tradition, and came to realize during the Meiji period that this way of thinking would have to become a casualty of the demise of the Bakufu. Unlike the knights of medieval Europe, who could eventually become landowners, samurai swore allegiance to higher lords, who rewarded their services with agricultural tributes from the peasants under their control. Authority was central and regional, but not until the advent of western democracy after the Sakoku was the idea put forward that any kind of attention should be paid to the Japanese people themselves—that they too were endowed with unalienable rights. This radical notion did more to change the nature of Japanese life and government than did the cannons of Commodore Perry.

SECOND CHANCE

> The first missionaries to reenter Japan were Americans, and three American Protestant denominations, the Episcopalians, Presbyterians, and Dutch Reformed, started formal missionary work in Japan in 1859. Among the first American missionaries to come to Japan were such great figures as Dr. Guido Verbeck, who was an influential advisor to the Japanese government and played a large role in the development of the institution which was to grow into Tokyo University, and Dr. J. C. Hepburn, who has left his name on what is still the most widely used romanization system. (Reischauer, p. 13)

"One field in which the missionaries performed especially valuable service was education. While the government concentrated on developing a national system of primary education, foreign missionaries and prominent Japanese independently established private schools to provide much of the higher training essential to Japan's modernizing program. Among the well-known private colleges founded about this time were the Christian University, Dōshisha, in Kyoto, and Keiō University and Waseda University in Tokyo." (Varley, p. 219)

> The missionaries from the start concentrated on education and in cooperation with native believers built up many of the pioneer schools both for boys and girls, founding no less than forty-three schools for girls in the first two decades of the Meiji period. For several decades American missionary schools, particularly at the secondary level, were in the forefront of the educational movement in Japan, and only in the twentieth century did they gradually drop behind in prestige and facilities to the government institutions. . . . Because of the consistent emphasis on education in the missionary movement, Japanese Christians are almost exclusively from the better educated classes. They constitute far more than one half of 1 per cent of Japanese leadership, and few among the educated classes of Japan have not felt the influence of Christianity in one

form or another. . . . It is no accident that there is a disproportionately high percentage of Christians in the present [1965] Japanese Diet or that one of Japan's postwar premiers was a Protestant Christian. Right up to the outbreak of the recent war, the strongest of all American influences in Japan was probably that exerted by our Christian missionaries there. (Reischauer, pp. 13-14)

Reischauer's assumption, that Japanese Christians are better educated and therefore tend to gravitate to positions of political power, needs to be reexamined as an example of Orientalist thinking. Reischauer wrote these words in 1965, midway through the lengthy success of Japan's Liberal Democratic Party (LDP) in monopolizing national politics. From the Occupation until about 1995, the Diet was almost always controlled by the LDP, which in spite of its name was a fairly conservative political clique, opposed to the policies of the socialist/left opposition and very friendly with Japanese business. In fact, they were too friendly; in 1988, various kickback scandals began surfacing, implicating high-ranking LDP members in a variety of lucrative sweetheart deals. Most notable of these was the Recruit scandal, in which shares of stock were given to politicians in return for preferential legislation. Other scandals also began surfacing, including links of the LDP to organized crime through Yakuza control of the delivery company Tokyo Sagawa Kyubin. (Jones 1992) It seemed as if no major member of the LDP was untouched by the taint, which ended the absolute control the party had on the Diet.

In October 1994, reports surfaced which confirmed what had long been a rumor: that the LDP was also connected to the U.S. Central Intelligence Agency. (Weiner) Apparently the CIA had been close to the LDP since the Occupation, supporting the LDP in limiting any attempts at socialist or pacifist legislation in the Diet. The LDP-CIA collaboration included trying to finance a dissident faction of the Japanese Socialist Party. CIA involvement with Japanese politics may well have begun during the Allied Occupation; with the Communists under Mao Zedong in control of China in 1949, the new plan was to make Japan "a revitalized bastion of the Free World in the struggle to contain the spread of Communism in Asia." (Varley, p. 269) The United States government confirmed some details of the plan in 2006, decades after the fact. (Japan Times)

This puts Reischauer's quote in a different light. It may well be that Japanese Christians did not rise to positions of power because their faith—by intent or by coincidence—made them better educated. The possibility must be considered that the LDP, conscious of the CIA's involvement in Japanese politics, tended to offer important positions to Christians to impress the CIA. Until the full facts come out, we cannot simply accept Reischauer's assertion that Christianity was the cause, or even a cause, of the apparently disproportionate success of Japanese Christians; it may well have been an effect of a different cause.

> Many of the youths most strongly influenced by Christianity were samurai from domains that had been on the losing side of the Restoration. Restricted in the opportunities open to them in the new government, these youths sought alternate routes to advancement through the acquisition of Western training. When brought into direct contact with foreign Christian teachers, they were particularly impressed with the moral caliber and fervid personal commitment of most of these men. To the young and impressionable Japanese, the foreign teachers seemed to possess qualities of character very similar to the ideal samurai and Confucian scholars of their own traditional background. Indeed, many Japanese who converted to Christianity in the 1870s and 1880s seem to have viewed it as a kind of modern extension of Confucianism.
>
> For their part, the American missionary and lay Christian teachers who came to Japan in the 1870s also responded with high enthusiasm toward their Japanese students. The faith of these men, who were imbued with the religious spirit of late nineteenth-century New England, was rooted in the belief that God's work on earth was to be carried out by individuals acting in accordance with a high moral code and the dictates of their Christian consciences. They were not particularly concerned with questions of dogma and abstract theology but wished to build strong characters; and *they were quick to appreciate the features of good character, derived from the samurai code of conduct, that they detected in many of their students.* (Varley, pp. 219-220, emphasis added)

Morioka writes of a Congregational church founded in 1878 in Annaka, in the western part of Gumma Prefecture.

> Of the first forty-four adherents of this church, thirty-seven were probably clansmen of the Annaka clan and members of their families. These clansmen had a Bible-reading society even prior to the foundation of the church, so it seems that there was some sort of congeniality between them and Christianity.
>
> There were two reasons for this congeniality. The first is that samurai were the largest literate class in Japan at the time and were able to gain a rough understanding of Christianity from reading a Chinese version of the Bible and such parts of a Japanese version as already existed. The second reason is that, deprived of their economic, political, and social privileges after the abolition of the clan system in 1871 (which led to a brief but futile resistance by young samurai), they were looking for a new guiding principle to replace the old morality; inflation had disorganized samurai domestic finances and, in addition, the disappearance of the feudal servant-master relationship had led to an internal crisis. . . . Organizing a group of Christian converts was a new movement on the part of the Annaka clansmen in response to the days of suffering. However, as the economic situation of the samurai declined and inflation spiraled, more and more samurai left Annaka so that the church acquired fewer converts from among them. (Morioka, pp. 119-120)

Reischauer records that "Fukuzawa Yukichi, the founder in 1858 of a school which was to grow into Keiō University in Tokyo, accompanied the first Japanese diplomatic mission to the United States in 1860 and, after a trip to Europe two years later, again visited America in 1867. Joseph Niishima, the founder in 1875 of Doshisha, one of Japan's earliest Christian educational institutions, and perhaps its most distinguished, secretly left Japan in 1864 to complete his studies in the United States." (Reischauer, p. 12) Morioka, who romanized the name as Niejima, cites Joseph as the Annaka clansman who introduced Christianity to that village. (Morioka, p. 120)

While there were Japanese educators such as Fukuzawa and Niishima who were influenced by the West, it is safe to say that, at first, they were outnumbered by the Westerners:

> Dr. David Murray of Rutgers was brought to Japan in 1873 to serve as the educational advisor of the Ministry of Education, and during his fruitful stay in Japan he profoundly influenced the whole Japanese educational philosophy and structure. Between 1880 and 1885 the Japanese even attempted to follow the American educational system before returning once more to European models. . . . The Harvard zoologist, Edward Sylvester Morse, who arrived in Japan in 1877, was responsible for introducing the Japanese to the fields of zoology, anthropology and archaeology.[6] Ernest Fenollosa of Boston, arriving in Japan the next year, became an influential teacher of Occidental philosophy and inspired the Japanese to take renewed interest in their own art. (Reischauer, pp. 12-13)

Fenollosa found his Japanese students willing to study some writers who would have been suspect in a Western/Christian curriculum; notably, Hegel and Spencer. Morse found the Japanese eager to read and discuss Charles Darwin, and commented that it was "delightful to explain the Darwinian theory without running against theological prejudice as I often did at home." (Fields, p. 147) It is not known whether his students were Christian converts or Buddhist/Shinto believers, but it is possible that the Japanese Christians of this period could have studied both the Bible and Darwin at once with no internal disharmony. We do know, however, that Inouye Enryo, a student of Fenollosa's and a Pure Land Buddhist priest, paradoxically cited western writers such as Darwin and Hegel to argue that Christianity was less apropos to Japan than Buddhism. (*Ibid.*)

> (I)n 1889, the Meiji constitution formally gave Japanese citizens relative freedom of religion "within limits not prejudicial to peace and order, and not antagonistic to their duties as subjects." . . . Christianity gained a small number of converts and made some important contributions to Japanese society, especially in education and social welfare. But from about 1890, with the heightened nationalism accompanying the Sino-Japanese War (1894-95) and the

Russo-Japanese War (1904-05), the Japanese turned more to their native traditions and did not enter Christianity in significant numbers. (Earhart, pp. 42-3)

TWO-WAY STREET

While Christian missionaries re-entered Japan, Buddhist missionaries sometimes left Japan and moved to American controlled territory. A priest of the Jodo Shinshu (Pure Land) sect named Kagahi traveled to Hawai'i, where Japanese day-laborers—more than two thousand by 1890—had been working the sugar cane fields for several years. While Kagahi's establishing of the first Buddhist temple in Hawai'i—in Hilo in 1889—was meant to bring spiritual comfort to the Japanese laborers, it was taken as a provocative act by the white American plantation owners, who perceived the Japanese as more "arrogant" than Chinese laborers, in wanting to be treated as equals. Toward that end, the Japanese dressed in Western clothes, and studied English at Methodist church schools.

In 1892, Queen Liliuokalani had been approached by the Meiji government with the notion of a political union of Hawaii and Japan. Before any such steps could be taken, however, the queen was deposed by United States Marines, supporting the interests of the plantation class. The United States government maintained that it had no responsibility for the coup, but, in 1898, the United States annexed the Hawaiian Islands. (Fields, pp. 80-81)

SEXUAL REVOLUTION

As happened in the United States during the Industrial Revolution, social dislocation attended the rapid industrialization of Japan in the late Meiji era. Samurai found themselves masterless, and Christian missionaries went looking for converts among this class. Another likely pool was among women. "The plight of the young girls and women in the silk filatures and textile plants became a matter of urgent concern for reform-minded social and political leaders, especially Christian humanitarians. Many socialists and communists got their start as social critics and many reformers as Christians." (Hane 1988, p. 18)

However disparate radicals and Christians may seem in Twenty-First Century America, they were aware of their common cause in early Twentieth Century Japan and would occasionally join forces.

> Sakai Toshihiko, a socialist, Kōtoku Shūsui, an anarchist, and Uchimura Kanzō, a Christian reformer, formed the Heiminsha (Commoners' Society) in 1903 and began publishing the Heimin Shimbun (Commoners' News) in late 1903. Despite government interference, they managed to keep their publica-

tion in print until 1905. A number of women activists joined the Heiminsha circle, including Kanno Sugako, Fukuda Hideko and Itō Noe. (*Ibid.* p.19)

"The group that became the major rival of the anarchists and communists in the labor field was the moderate socialists who had come out of the earlier Christian reform movement. Among the earlier activists in this group were Kagawa Toyohiko, who devoted his life to helping the poor, especially the urban slum-dwellers, and Suzuki Bunji, another Christian social worker." (*Ibid.*, p.24) However, this phase did not last long. Some Christian groups became forces for maintenance of the status quo, leaving the communists, socialists and anarchists as the primary agents for social change.

Christians seemed to be most interested, as far as social reform in Meiji Japan was concerned, with the elimination of legal prostitution and the keeping of mistresses. This is not to belittle the cause by suggesting that prostitution became an issue only because of Western Christian sexual attitudes; the hardships of life for the sex workers in the Yoshiwara district of Tokyo were real enough. The girls, from 3,000 to 5,000 in Meiji-era Tokyo alone, were often sold into "voluntary servitude" by a culture which on the one hand presumed the inferiority of females and on the other hand discouraged women from asserting their rights, depicting this as an insult to the clan. Hane (1972) cites this description by a Swiss official of an ill-run house:

> (the girls were) publicly exposed like animals on display, to be freely scrutinized by all comers. After first examining the goods, they are purchased and used by the first man who sets the price. The impression I got of these unfortunate creatures was one of utmost misery. (p. 343)

"Among the early fighters against (the Yoshiwara tradition) was Yajima Kajiko (1833-1925), a Christian educator who formed the Fujin Kyōfūkai (Women's Moral Reform Society) in 1886 to carry out her campaign against public brothels and male promiscuity." (Hane 1988, p. 10)

> Efforts to end this practice and free the girls were spearheaded by Christians as early as 1882, but to no avail. In 1899-1900, however, a movement led by a missionary, U. G. Murphy, forced the courts to recognize the right of prostitutes to leave the brothels. The girls were still obliged, however, to repay the money that had been advanced to their families for their services. The movement to free the prostitutes was joined by the Salvation Army and Christian journalists and for a short period their efforts were rewarded. Some houses of prostitution went out of business, but this was only a temporary victory. The system survived until the end of the Second World War. (Hane 1972, p. 344)

This was the extent of Christian activism in Japan on behalf of women's rights and social reform. Itō Noe, a prominent activist of the left, "derided the Christian reformers who were seeking to abolish public brothels, because they were unwilling to get at the root cause of the institution, poverty." (Hane 1988, p. 23) A prominent turn-of-the-century Japanese Christian educator, Nitobe Inazō, showed a continuing male bias in spite of Christianity's supposed liberalism:

> (A woman's) surrender of herself to the good of her husband, home and family was as willing and honorable as the man's self-surrender to the good of his lord and country. Self-renunciation, without which no life enigma can be solved, is the keynote of the loyalty of man as well as the domesticity of woman. (Hane 1988, p. 7)

Activist Yamakawa Kikue wrote of an appearance in a Kanda textile plant by the Salvation Army during Christmas 1908:

> Directed by the lecturer and accompanied by an organ, the girls sang a Christmas carol that was written out on the blackboard. Then Mr. Yamamuro got up to speak. He told the girls that Our Lord, Jesus Christ, was a laborer just like them. Labor is sacred. "You too must become good workers, just like Our Lord Jesus. You must be grateful that you are able to work every day in good health. Then God will answer your prayers." Mr. Yamamuro was followed by Kawai Michiko, and she also spoke of the sacred nature of work and in a highly emotional voice intoned a lengthy prayer. The meeting closed with a psalm. All during the ceremony I was seated on the platform but hated being there. I was filled with shame and anger. The girls had worked all night beside roaring machines. They were pale and bloodless. How could they be told that the life they led was due to God's blessings and that they should view this kind of slave labor as sacred and holy? (*Ibid.* p. 167)

THE BIG ONE AND THE DAYS AFTER

Ironically, the first staging area for Christian entry into Japan became the last theater of the war with the atomic bombing of Nagasaki on August 9, 1945. The epicenter of the nuclear bomb blast was within 400 yards of Urakami Cathedral; most of the nuns of the St. Francis Convent were destroyed in the blast. "(O)ver 6,000 Catholics in the Urakami Valley died in that . . . instant." (Chinnock, p. 108)

> After experiencing its share of wartime suppression, local Christianity enjoyed a sudden boom in membership and church attendance, and a proliferation of several denominations including Catholic, Seventh Day Adventist, and Holiness. This pro-Christian enthusiasm turned out, however, to be little more than a postwar fad which reached its peak around 1948-1949. (Lebra, pp. 18-19)

Whether the "fad" was inspired by Christianity itself or by the fact that it was the religion of the Allied Occupation Forces is unclear. However, a percentage of the postwar conversions can surely be attributed to a desire to curry favor with the occupying troops, who after all were predominantly Christian. Another percentage can be attributed to what might be called the "sympathetic magic" aspect of Christianity; there were surely some converts in the 1940s who turned to Christianity solely because it "worked" for the side that won the war. Another percentage would include true believers, or at least those who sincerely started out to embrace the religion. Those adherents who later decided to reject Christianity after having joined Christian churches generally were not able to make the religion work for them; i.e., they could not fit Christianity into their previously well-defined Japanese life.

Speaking of fads, one way that Christianity has found a home in modern Japan is in the popularity of a Christian wedding ceremony. The reason for the popularity is simple: a Christian wedding in modern Japan contains all of the glamour and none of the religious commitment. It is literally all for show. Chapter 8 will take a deeper look at this unique religious transplant.

Christianity has also entered into Japanese political battles, as it has in other countries. According to William LaFleur's *Liquid Life: Abortion and Buddhism in Japan,* Japan is a culture that has long practiced abortion (certainly long before its legalization in 1948) and yet espouses Buddhist doctrines of pacifism and reverence for life.[7] One of Japan's so-called New Religions, the Seichō no Ie, or House of Life (also translated as "House of Growth"), has no such conflict, openly advocating the recriminalization of abortion. This religion has elements of both Christianity and Shinto, especially the militarist Shinto of the period from the Meiji to the end of World War II, in which a Japanese woman's patriotic duty was to bear as many children as possible. (LaFleur, p. 161)

The prophet of Seichō no Ie, Taniguchi Masaharu, studied, in his college days at Waseda in Tokyo, Western writers as diverse as Schopenhauer and Poe, Baudelaire and Oscar Wilde, as well as the Omoto sect. Yet many of his teachings were derived from the writings of Fenwicke Holmes, a New Thought writer whose philosophy was in turn based on American Transcendentalism of the 19th century. (Ellwood, 153-155) Although there is a heavy admixture of Buddhist elements, and even some Shinto, Seichō no Ie remains philosophically the most Western of Japan's New Religions, and in spite of its history of pantheistic stress that all are manifestations of God and its interest in what can only be called psychic phenomena, the use of Seichō no Ie for political purposes by Christians, especially after Taniguchi's death, is not surprising.

Having looked at Christianity in Japan's past, this book moves to the present and the future: to Christianity in Japan during the era of Soft Power (Otmazgin) and Gross National Cool (McGray); an era governed in large part by popular media, including cyberspace. Christianity appears in manga and hours of movies and television programs, live and animated. Sometimes it's a plot point, and sometimes it's window dressing. Almost all of these portrayals, however, present Japan with a Christianity that bears little or no resemblance to what they can find among the (admittedly few) adherents to the faith in their own country. Christianity in Japan exists alongside its more fanciful media version, and the media version by its nature gets greater exposure.

The difference between the fantasy and the reality of Christianity in Japan, and the reasons for those differences, is examined by a theory presented in chapter 3 that described what happens when cultures collide. The cultures examined in Edward Said's *Orientalism* aren't Japan and Christianity, but the principles laid out in Said's book are very helpful, and should seem familiar to the observer of the intersection of politics and popular culture.

NOTES

1. Hideyoshi could not assert any control over the city until he appointed a deputy to take control from the Catholic Church. (Hane 1972, p. 146) This illustrates the autocratic, top-down approach to Christianity in feudal Japan. Yet it was seen as perfectly normal in the context of the Warring States period's approach to politics; the Emperor (or his surrogate) proposes and the populace disposes. It was part of the medieval, Machivellian worldview that did not allow for the sense of individual human dignity—a concept which would not be seen as a behavioral norm until the 18th Century.

2. The letter used the Portuguese word "gentios" to refer to non-Christians; the word evolved into the Japanese loan-word "zencho". (Suter, p. 96)

3. The term refers broadly to the feudal military dictatorship that had governed Japan for centuries, in which power flowed down from the shogun through the warlords and samurai under the shogun to the people.

4. The phrase "apparently unconscious" reflects the cultural bias of the author; as shall be seen later, the syncretistic view of Christianity by the Japanese has been, and is, often both conscious and deliberate.

5. The group of islands between Japan and Taiwan, presently known as Okinawa.

6. Conversely, he also introduced concepts of Oriental architecture to the West, in a reasonable and non-biased manner, in books such as *Japanese Homes and their Surroundings* (1886) and *Glimpses of China and Chinese Homes* (1902).

7. One way of distancing the fetus is to refer to it as a *mizuko*—literally a water child. Regarding it as different from, and not quite, a human avoids the debate about fetal personhood.

Chapter Three

Christianity in Japanese Popular Culture through the Lens of Said's *Orientalism*

Until February 5, 1597, when six European Catholics and twenty of their Japanese followers were crucified in Nagasaki, then and now perhaps the most Christian city in Japan, Catholic Christianity was a foreign curiosity, tolerated at first as eccentric but later perceived as a threat to Japanese society and a potential forerunner of European colonialism. Fearing a foreign takeover of Japan as had happened in the Philippines, the shogun Hideyoshi Toyotomi had earlier banned Christianity outright, although the ban wasn't enforced for years. The ban was lifted after 250 years, at which time it was found that some Japanese families still practiced a version of the religion in secret.

Since then, Christianity has become a small but less threatening part of Japanese life and culture. Christian institutions have established universities, hospitals and charitable organizations in Japan, and a few individuals, such as novelist Endō Shusaku, gained fame both as believers and representatives of the faith. However, it remains a very minor part of Japanese life.

This raises a follow-up question: if the Japanese have little or no exposure to Christianity directly, how do modern-day Japanese learn of Christianity at all? Formal education has to walk a fine line in telling the history: providing information without being seen as crossing over into advocacy. In fact, education in the United States faces a similar dilemma, except that the question is not how to teach the minority religion of Christianity to Japan, but how to teach the minority religion of Islam to America.[1] (The word "minority" is relative to the particular country, and not globally.) A sensible and thorough examination of the latter question can help us to answer the former question, and such a sensible and thorough work was written by a Palestinian scholar and published in 1978.

Edward Said's study *Orientalism* traced the evolution of western (meaning first European, then American) perceptions of, and attitudes toward, the world east of the Mediterranean—what the West has come to call the Middle East and the Far East or generically combining the two into "the Orient".[2] Said's analysis—as informed by fact and fiction, literature as well as the politics of colonialism—focuses on Western reactions to Islamic cultures. However, for science to be science it must be replicable. Said's approach does not have to be tied specifically to western European colonialist thought; the essential components of what he called Orientalism can be applied to other encounters and relationships between different cultures. Said himself wrote that "Orientalism is better grasped as a set of constraints upon and limitations of thought." (p. 42)

A review of Said isolates three such necessary constraints:

- A distinction must first be established between the two cultures involved, disregarding their similarities and focusing instead on their differences, defining the foreign culture as the Other. "Orientalism was ultimately a political vision of reality whose structure promoted the difference between the familiar . . . and the strange." (p. 43)
- To approach the Other is the job of particular scholars, experts (usually self-proclaimed) in the ways of the Other; these experts can draw on literature, legend, or legitimate research and exploration, but always resulting in work that supports a particular point of view, which is adopted by the culture at large. Again quoting Said: "What inevitably goes with such work, however, is a kind of free-floating mythology of the Orient, an Orient that derives not only from contemporary attitudes and popular prejudices but also from what Vico called the conceit of nations and of scholars." (p. 53)[3]
- That point of view serves to trivialize, even infantilize, the Other, compared to the Experts' own culture. According to Said, "an assumption has been made that the Orient and everything in it was, if not patently inferior to, then in need of corrective study by the West. The Orient was viewed as if framed by the classroom, the criminal court, the prison, the illustrated manual." (pp. 40-41)

One interesting aspect of Orientalism was touched on by Said in passing, since he focused on the most formally influential messages from the "Experts" about the East. Said wrote that "until the mid-eighteenth century Orientalists were Biblical scholars, students of the Semitic languages, Islamic specialists, or, because the Jesuits had opened up the new study of China,

Sinologists." (p. 51) However, it would not remain the private property of academics. There would also be:

> a kind of second-order knowledge—lurking in such places as the "Oriental" tale, the mythology of the mysterious East, notions of Asian inscrutability—with a life of their own . . . a genre of Orientalist writing as exemplified in the works of Hugo, Goethe, Nerval, Flaubert, Fitzgerald and the like. (pp. 52-53)

This version of the East was "not so much the East itself as the East made known, and therefore less fearsome, to the Western reading public." (p. 60) It is likely that government studies of reality in the Middle East of the 19th century were not as widely read as the story of Haydee Tebelen, the orphaned daughter of Ali, the Pasha of Yanina, whose story was part of the plot woven against Edmund Dantes in Alexander Dumas' *Count of Monte Cristo,* and yet it became, for many of that novel's readers, a picture of Oriental reality.

The principles and pitfalls of Orientalism in action, as it were, are illustrated nicely in the film *Topsy-Turvy*, a retelling of the partnership of W. S. Gilbert and Arthur Sullivan. In 1884, the men seemed likely to end their partnership as, respectively, the writer-director and composer of comic operas when Gilbert was inspired by a Japanese trade exhibition. The exposure to various aspects of Japanese culture (including kabuki theater and martial arts) inspired Gilbert to write the book for *The Mikado;* the rest of the film is about preparing the premiere production. This included bringing three women from the trade exhibition to a rehearsal, during which Gilbert used the women to assert his own expertise. Gilbert tries to tell the three Japanese women to walk downstage, which they do in three completely different manners (one nervous woman shuffling, another trying to imitate the choreography she had seen earlier). Gilbert, however, loudly declares that the three women had just walked downstage "in the Japanese manner!"

In fact they had done no such thing, but Gilbert—who couldn't speak a word of Japanese—could not have seen that. In a purely Orientalist manner, he had asserted his credentials over the choreographer, who had, according to the film, originally had the "three little maids from school" doing a cakewalk. None of the members of the company could speak Japanese, although the pianist tried to communicate in Italian. The scene is structured to be funny, but plays out the way western cultures have tried to "correct" foreign cultures for centuries.

This second-order knowledge is alive and well today. One fascinating case story was H. Bruce Franklin's book *M.I.A.: Mythmaking In America.* Franklin focused on one event that took place after America's withdrawal from Vietnam. Reports circulated, and kept circulating, that some American servicemen had not actually died in combat in Southeast Asia, but were being kept alive as Prisoners of War, in secret camps in North Vietnam or Cambodia or especially Laos, about which almost nothing was known and therefore a place in which virtually anything could happen. The POW Flag continues to fly at public buildings and private residences, despite the fact that any POWs would have been held for four decades at this point, and despite accounts in Franklin's book stating that military personnel occasionally reported those killed in action as Missing and Presumed Captured because it would increase the cash benefit to the soldiers' families. Despite the existence of absolutely no evidence at all of secret POWs in Southeast Asia, the flag still flies, in part because Hollywood made movies about POWs held in secret camps in Asia.[4] This, too, is Orientalism in the age of pop culture and cyber communication.

At its most benign, Orientalism is a marker of differences in cultural evolution. Unfortunately, it most commonly has been used to identify cultural differences as a pathology, with the familiar culture being viewed as a biological norm, and with the Other characterized as not merely different but an inconvenient or even dangerous mistake.

This is not to say that Said's work endorses a particular political or religious view. Said was, after all, a thoroughgoing and compassionate humanist, as his other writings and interviews illustrate. However, when a scholar develops a thesis that makes others nervous, for whatever reason, the first instinct has been to put the scholar personally on trial. This literally happened to Galileo because of his theory that the earth orbited the sun, and a similar reaction happened to media theorist Marshall McLuhan, who defended his work by saying that he was "describing and not prescribing." Galileo's view of the solar system turned out to be correct, and McLuhan does seem to have anticipated our mediated society long before personal computing and multi-purpose communication devices were invented.

The west has subjected Asian and Middle Eastern cultures to this paradigm for centuries, and Japan is no exception. William George Aston (1841-1911) was regarded as the authority on Japanese prose and poetry—at least, the expert of explaining it to Anglophones who didn't study Japanese themselves. Author of *A History of Japanese Literature*, published in 1899, it was said "time has not diminished his standing as a Japanese scholar."

The *History* is detailed and at times ponderous, going back to the earliest extant Japanese writings (seventh century A.D.). The good news: he recognizes the best of Japan's writings, from *The Tale of Genji* to Sudō Nansui's "satirical" novel *The Ladies of New Style* written during the Meiji Era.

Aston, unfortunately, sees everything through a Meiji-era western lens, including the Japanese themselves. He describes Japan's "national mind" thus:

> a brave, courteous, light-hearted, pleasure-loving people, sentimental rather than passionate, witty and humorous, of nimble apprehension, but not pro-

found; ingenious and inventive, but hardly capable of high intellectual achievement; of receptive minds endowed with a voracious appetite for knowledge; with a turn for neatness and elegance of expression, but seldom or never rising to sublimity. (p.4)

Aston was a CMG (Companion of the Order of Saint Michael and Saint George) and seems to have followed the British colonial line. The stunning description above reduces Japan to a stereotype of every other Pacific or Polynesian culture Britain encountered in the 1800s. He faulted Japan for borrowing literary, religious and other influences from China. He criticized the Meiji concept of proper literature, as if by "proper" one meant a non-fantastic narrative that can be taken as "real life" as in Britain. Aston described such "proper" literature as emphasizing traits such as "the gradual growth of the sentiment (of love) in man or woman, the ennobling influence of a pure love, and all the more delicate shades of feeling" (p. 362) which were absent from Chinese classics but present in Victorian romantic literature. Ironically, there are many examples of modern manga that meet Aston's definition, especially in seinen (grown-up) or josei (housewives) manga, such as Takahashi Rumiko's *Mezon Ikkoku*, which scans like a Jane Austen novel set in modern-day Tokyo.

Finally, he dismisses the Japanese culture as inherently non-aggressive: "things happen, rather than are done; the tides of fate are far more real to them than the strong will and the endeavour which wrestles with them." (p.31) It's a pity that he couldn't contemplate the medieval character of the Warring States period a bit more deeply, or jump into the future and witness the half-century of Japanese imperial militarism that began with the 1894-1895 war against China.

Aston's view of Japanese literature is similarly critical. His judgment of non-Chinese-influenced writing is that the Japanese texts are "not very important as literature. It consists chiefly of lives of the Buddhist saints, and of edifying tracts and stories all addressed to the more ignorant classes, and highly seasoned with a thaumaturgic element." (p.344) Would he have dismissed medieval lives of the Christian saints as magical or miraculous—the meaning of "thaumaturgic"? Were they not also addressed to "the more ignorant classes"?

A fascinating comparison is to see how Aston describes a work versus how a Japanese reader describes the same work. In this case, it is Bakin's massive tale *Hakkenden (The Eight Dog Warriors)*. Aston:

> I can only express my amazement at its extraordinary popularity in Japan. It is full of physical and moral impossibilities, and, worse still, is often pedantic and wearisome. . . . (H)is faults are as glaring as his merits are conspicuous. (Bakin) constantly overleaps the bounds of possibility to an extent which tries the patience of the most indulgent reader. (pp.361-362)

For counterpoint, we have Sugimoto Etsu, whose memoir *A Daughter of the Samurai* was published in 1925. Born in Nakaoka, Niigata Prefecture, Sugimoto immigrated to America, eventually becoming a Japanese instructor at Columbia University. She writes:

> To me, *Hakkenden*, with its wonderful symbolism, was one of the most inspiring books I had ever read. It was written in the 18th Century by Bakin, our great philosopher-novelist, and so musical is the literature, and so lofty the ideals, that frequently it has been compared, by Japanese of learning, to Milton's *Paradise Lost* and the *Divine Comedy* of Dante. (p. 133)

She did not neglect to mention that western readers—or at least those who were told about *Hakkenden* without actually reading it—were scandalized by the notion of a woman bearing eight magical children sired by a dog, and begotten in the magical but highly sexual metaphor of a bullet which pierced the dog, then settled in the body of the woman, killing them both. Before they died, however, eight shining lights rose from the woman's body and scattered to different places. These were the eight dog children of the title, who would be born of eight different mothers, grow up, find each other, and then heroically return to their mother's original family.

Sugimoto understood that her American boarding-school mentors disapproved of *Hakkenden*, after confiscating her copy and "saying they were not proper books for me to read." (p. 133) However, she could not make sense of why such writings were frowned upon in America, except by employing a type of Orientalism:

> I could not understand why this miracle-story, filled with lofty symbolism, could be more objectionable than the many fables and fairy tales of personified animals that I had read in English literature. . . . I concluded that thoughts, like the language, on one side of the world are straightforward and literal; and on the other, vague, mystical, and visionary. (p. 135)

Like the Experts, she divided the world not merely into cultures but into entire hemispheres. In this she seems to follow her traditional grandmother, who becomes an imagined character in her book. To this elderly woman, the Japanese were "the children of the gods" while the westerners were "the red barbarians." (pp. 312-314)

In this example Aston, the expert on Japanese literature, passes judgment on a major work by trivializing and belittling it, for the purpose of arguing that this state of affairs must change and Japanese letters must be made to more closely resemble Victorian literature. This covers all three parts of Said's formula. But this process also works in reverse: by having a Japanese expert comment on the Other as she saw it. Sugimoto was neither the first nor the only Japanese national to comment, sometimes in a belittling, sometimes in a trivializing manner, that the Japanese way of doing things is equal to, if not better than, the western ways held up as a model since 1853 with the arrival of Commodore Perry.

This book will focus on Christianity, a subject far older than America, and introduced to Japan in Elizabethan times. It will feature modern examples from Japan's popular culture: manga and anime. Before we can do that, however, we need to briefly look at why Christianity in Japan was—and is—as marginalized as Islam was, and is, in the west, and what pop culture has to do with any of it.

The full history of Christianity in Japan would take a semester to teach, or maybe two, and has already been touched on in chapter 2. But the passage of half a millennium has resulted in the status of Christianity in Japan being, as Facebook would say, complicated. If it can be summed up succinctly, it would be in this statement from composer/pianist Kanno Yoko: "Japanese don't believe in one God, but in gods everywhere in plants and animals. That's right. In Japan, Christianity has a wonderful image. People enjoy the image of Christ and Christianity in picture books, but not as a religion."

There were problems from the beginning of Christianity in Japan, above and beyond cultural differences. In part because of language difficulties, some Christian concepts proved impossible to translate to Japanese whose only point of reference was the mix of Shinto and Buddhism that still characterizes Japan today.

Chapter 2 of this book quoted from a letter from a Jesuit father, which described Japanese, whether or not they had converted to Catholicism, wearing European dress and walking "with rosaries of driftwood on the breast above all their clothing, and with a crucifix at their side, or hanging from the waist," phonetically repeating "the litanies of Pater Noster and Ave Maria and . . . praying in the streets." (Boxer, pp. 207-208) Such early devotees of the surface details of Christianity have a modern equivalent in the use of English words on Japanese clothing, even if a native English speaker would find the use of the words incongruous or even offensive. It is done, as was the wearing of rosaries centuries ago, to be *kakkoo ii*—to be cool.

This particular look at Orientalism is a two-way street. While Said's work was about western writers and politicians reacting to the Orient, this will be more than just Japan taking the same approach to Christianity in reality and in the popular culture. We also get to see what happens when some of these Japanese interpretations of Christianity find their way to the Christian west, and how they are dealt with to make them tamer, more acceptable.

The Japanese Media Christian is its own creation in many respects, even if some of its ground rules were laid out five centuries ago. Keeping this is mind, we turn to the Japanese postwar visions of Christian imagery in the pop culture, beginning with the career—covering nearly half a century—of the man known as Manga no Kamisama (the God of Comics)[5]: Tezuka Osamu.

NOTES

1. Since the recent increase of politicized Islam with groups such as al Qaeda and ISIS, western mistrust of Islam has turned in some quarters to outright fear and loathing. In one extreme reaction in Virginia, "Riverheads High School teacher Cheryl LaPorte's lesson on Friday, Dec. 11, [2015] brought a deluge of "profane" and "hateful" messages from around the country. Those messages ... led to the decision to lock down Riverheads High School Wednesday and Thursday—meaning 'all doors were locked and monitored' once students had entered the buildings. Security was also increased at other county schools. ... Some parents were upset after learning that Riverheads High School teacher Cheryl LaPorte had students in her class complete an assignment that involved practicing calligraphy and writing a statement in Arabic. The statement translated to: "There is no god but Allah and Muhammad is the messenger of Allah." During a forum Tuesday night at the Good News Ministries church in Greenville, parents discussed the lesson and some expressed outrage over what they called indoctrination." (Crimesider Staff)

2. The definition has also come to include all of Africa.

3. Eighteenth century historian and philosopher Giambattista Vico (1668-1744) argued, among other points, that a nation/culture is mistaken if it seeks to glorify its own accomplishments by claiming preeminence in the development of civilization. Instead of this conceit of nations, he maintained that there was a process of separate but similar development among all nations, evolving from worshipping the divine (poetic imagination) to recognizing the role of humankind in shaping its own destiny (rational thought). The conceit of scholars for Vico, who lived in and was an example of the Age of Enlightenment, is the false presumption that the way a nation/culture thinks now is the same as the way it thought in the past. He also stated that a culture can backslide from rational thought to past patterns of mythic thought, repeating the cycle.

4. They include, but are not limited to, *Missing in Action, Rambo: First Blood, Part Two*, and countless sequels and imitations.

5. This very title for Tezuka is subject to Orientalism to the extent that it can refer to a man as a god; even the alternate translation of "Lord of Manga" is considered too close to the edge of blasphemy for some in the west. A video advertisement for an anime based on Tezuka's manga version of the Fritz Lang film *Metropolis* (2001) referred to Tezuka as the "Godfather of Manga". People in the west still get nervous about the word "kami", as we will see in chapter 5 looking at the English dub of Miyazaki Hayao's *Kaze no Tani no Naushika*.

Chapter Four

Christian References in the Manga of Tezuka Osamu

Manga evolved out of single-panel and four-panel comic strips appearing in American and British newspapers and magazines, which served as models for Japanese journalists in the Meiji era. Both the style and content were heavily influenced by their Western counterparts, although the originals didn't have much of a run as such. A Japanese translation of George McManus's *Bringing Up Father* began appearing in the *Asahi Graph* weekly in November 1923; two months later, a Japanese analogue began appearing in the *Hōchi* newspaper: Asō Yutaka's "Nanki na Tōsan (Easygoing Daddy)." This was not a translation of McManus, nor a copy of the artwork, but an adaptation of western source material for Japanese tastes, commissioned for a specifically Japanese purpose: to bring some gentle humor to a newspaper still filled with tales of tragedy and horror from the Great Kantō Earthquake that devastated Tokyo in September 1923. (Schodt 1983, pp. 45-48).

TEZUKA: THE MAN

Modern manga did not appear until after World War 2, since Japanese publishing was dominated in the previous decades by politics and militarism. In 1947, a medical student named Tezuka Osamu (1927-1989) turned to cartooning as an alternative to medicine, having been told after getting through medical school that Japan's main health issue after the war was malnutrition. Tezuka grew up watching European films and Disney animation, and later applied cinematic techniques to his manga. The result was a revelation: other artists looked at Tezuka's work for inspiration on how to create their own manga, and a publishing phenomenon was born.

Tezuka's innovations were of both form and substance. His artwork was among the first, but certainly not the last, to be influenced by Western cinema. Tezuka credits his upbringing with this influence; his father, an executive with the Sumitomo Corporation, was a movie buff who regularly had the most recent French and German films screened in his home, as well as Walt Disney animated films. The pages of Tezuka manga are brimming with panning shots, extreme close-ups, montages and other cinematic devices.

The content likewise departed from the model of domestic comedy. The four hundred plus volumes of Tezuka's collected works range from romance to science fiction,[1] from children's adventures to adult contemplations of war, from a comic retelling of the Chinese legend of the monkey who went to the West to a melodramatic version of the life of the Buddha, from a juvenile version of Dostoevsky's *Crime and Punishment* to the notorious series *Aporo no Uta (The Song of Apollo)*, exploring psychosexual perversions. Tezuka created figures of such popularity and complexity that he transcended the title of "Japan's Walt Disney". As Frederik W. Schodt noted, "This is someone who, if you're interested in Cool Japan or anime or manga and how that came to be, if you trace back the roots, you'll always go back to Tezuka." (Davidson) His work became templates for other manga and anime creators to follow, on a wide range of subjects, including Japanese uses of, and reactions to, Christianity.

Tezuka has for many years been better known in the United States through animated versions of his work, rather than through his manga. One of the first anime to be screened in the west was ostensibly based on Tezuka's parody adaptation of the Chinese classic text *Saiyu-ki (Journey to the West)* written in the 16th century by Wu Cheng-en; the manga treatment, *Boku no Son-Goku (My Son-Goku)* was a blatant parody which included the Buddha, Popeye the Sailor Man, and a sequence in which Tezuka was kidnapped and forced to enter the comic to take over for the Buddhist monk searching for sutras. The parody element was completely missing from the film version, which was only nominally based on the Tezuka manga. Because of his name recognition at the time as a manga artist, Toei Studios credited Tezuka as director of the film. From this point, however, Tezuka created his own animation studios (first Mushi Pro, then Tezuka Pro).

The animated version of *Tetsuwan Atomu (The Mighty Atom)*, renamed *Astro Boy*, was, along with *Speed Racer*, among the first examples of Japanese animation on American television. Although seldom broadcast since its 1963 American television premiere, the black-and-white *Astro Boy* series is still nostalgically remembered by many "baby boomers", has been remade every few years with modern animation technology by both Japanese and western studios, and even the original has been revived on home video. Tezuka's two animated TV versions of *Janguru Taitei*, renamed *Kimba the White Lion* and *Leo the Lion* for the American market, included the first color animation produced for Japanese television in 1965. In the United States *Leo* was broadcast as recently as 1986, when the Reverend Pat Robertson's Christian Broadcasting Network carried it. ("Leo the (Buddhist) Lion") The animated series based on *Ribon no Kishi* was broadcast on Spanish language stations in America as *La Princessa Caballero*.

THE MANGA

Boku no Son-Goku

From 1952 to 1959 Dr. Tezuka drew *Boku no Son-Goku (My Son-Goku)* for *Manga-O* magazine. This was a deliberately humorous, idiosyncratic retelling of the Saiyu-ki legend, employing many unusual elements, not the least of which was Tezuka's including himself as a reluctant character in his own manga (not for the last time). When the golden-haired Son-Goku is born from a boulder, his arrival is duly noted by an angel, an old man with a halo, no wings but (we can only see it in one panel) a cross on his chest. He announces the birth to the Emperor of Heaven, a decidedly Chinese character. His attendant angel has wings, is dressed in European Baroque costume and also sports a halo. Other residents of Heaven include the Roman god Mercury, Mahatma Gandhi and, as leader of the army of Heaven, Popeye the Sailor Man who speaks in English word-balloons. The comic context of the story mitigates what some would consider blasphemy; this is just another example that the Japanese do not insist on Western definitions of blasphemy. It should be noted, however, that, consistent with Orientalism, an overall sense of propriety is maintained, since the only one who can subdue Son-Goku's early rampages is the Sakyamuni Buddha.

Co-directed (according to Toei Studio) by Yabushita Taiji and co-written by Uekusa Keinosuke, *Boku no Son-Goku* was a conjunction of two of Tezuka's manga projects. Most of the material came from the Chinese legend of the monkey who went from China to India with a Buddhist priest in search of sutras (Buddhist scriptures). A romantic subplot was introduced to the film by adding the character of a female monkey, Rin Rin-chan, the subject of her own Tezuka manga.

The film's experience in the United States was emblematic of the early problems encountered in trying to bring pop culture material from one culture to another. According to one account, James H. Nicholson, one of the heads of American International Pictures, a studio notable for producing low-budget teen-oriented horror and science-fiction films in the 1950s, visited Japan and stumbled into a local movie house on a rainy day; *Saiyu-ki,* one of the first feature length anime, was playing.

He thought that marketing (*Saiyu-ki*) in the United States would be very profitable, since beside Disney's, there were few animated features. He bought rights to the film's foreign release and promptly Americanized his product. Six minutes were cut from the original print and the entire score was altered. By dubbing the film the whole story line was changed. Lou Rusoff wrote a new screenplay and changed the Japanese religious myth theme that ran throughout the film, providing a whole new "be good to your neighbor" theme. Under the title *Alakazam the Great!*, the film, whose plot now bore only the slightest resemblance to the original, was not the moneymaker Nicholson had hoped it would be, causing the studio to back out of a deal distributing two other Japanese animated features. (Medved and Dreyfuss, pp. 21-25.)

That this bit of Orientalism is not an isolated occurrence can be seen in comparison viewings, in English and Japanese, of other Japanese animated features that were released to the American market decades later, with the advent of home videotape machines. The 1979 film based on Matsumoto Leiji's manga *Ginga Tetsudoo 999 (Galaxy Express 999)* has about ten minutes of material missing in its English incarnation as *Galaxy Express*. Many of the missing scenes feature a member of the crew of an interstellar ship designed to look like a steam locomotive, the titular Galaxy Express. This crewman appears to be a naked woman whose entire body is made of glass.

The English voices are also treated as comic in an otherwise serious story about the implications of humans abandoning flesh and blood bodies for everlasting machine bodies. One character fighting against the robot conversion is given a broad comic Scandinavian accent, while the character of the space pirate Captain Harlock is made to sound like John Wayne. Similarly, about twenty minutes—most of them crucial to the ecological subplot—were deleted by Roger Corman's New World Pictures in turning Miyazaki Hayao's film *Kaze no Tani no Naushika (Nausicaä of the Valley of the Wind)* into *Warriors of the Wind*. At least Tezuka learned his lesson from the *Saiyu-ki* experience, and translations of his subsequent animated projects, including two features on the character Unico and one based on the Phoenix, were faithful to the original.

The same could not always be said for his manga. In the case of *Astro Boy*, the name and image were licensed to the West, but the stories were not. The stories that appeared in American *Astro Boy* comics had little to do with the original Japanese manga. In spite of the interest in translated manga in the 1980s, at first only a few of Tezuka's manga appeared in complete form in English; the exceptions included Frederik Schodt's translation of the manga based on Fyodor Dostoevsky's *Crime and Punishment*.

Schodt, who translated part of one of the *Hi no Tori* books for his *Manga! Manga!*, also wrote a two-part article, "Black and White Issues," on the depictions of racial characteristics in manga; specifically, the tendency to westernize Japanese characters (which Schodt attributed to, in part, the influence of Tezuka's girls manga) while exaggerating the characteristics of other non-white peoples. (*Mangajin #15 & 16*) Brian Covert took this one step further in "The Tezuka Controversy" (*Mangajin #19*, August 10, 1992, pp. 6-10). This article also played up the black caricatures that occur in some early Tezuka manga, from *Janguru Taitei (Jungle Emperor)* to the early chapters of *Kirihito Sanka (Ode to Kirihito)* in 1970, and generally complained about the political incorrectness of some of the depictions of blacks, to the extent that they borrowed the American caricatured approach of the time to drawing Africans. Tezuka was sensitive to the criticism and changed his style accordingly in the 1970s, rendering later African characters more realistically.[2]

Crime and Punishment

In 1954 Tezuka created a youth-oriented manga retelling of Fyodor Dostoevsky's novel *Crime and Punishment (Kei to Batsu)*. Some of the devices in this version are cinematic in inspiration, some adhere to manga conventions, and some are drawn from a staging of the novel in Osaka at the Asahi Kaikan; Tezuka, a student at the time, played a comic-relief house-painter. There is Christian imagery in the sequence (pp. 36-39) about a magazine article which describes the "superior man," a Nietzschean figure for whom normal social rules do not apply. These scenes are illustrated with crude silhouettes, a "slide-show" technique that can be found in other Tezuka manga as well as his anime. In this case, the man who rises above the level of ordinary humanity is first seen with a cross on his collar. In the next panel, however, the silhouette is that of a Napoleonic military leader; the text anachronistically lists Hitler, Stalin and Eisenhower along with Napoleon in this class of superior men. The fact that such a man may be ahead of his time is illustrated in the final two panels. One shows the superior man tied to a cross and being stoned by an angry crowd; the following panel shows two people kneeling and praying to an image of the crucified man.

Ribon no Kishi[3]

In the Tezuka epic *Ribon no Kishi*, Satan puts in an appearance, but it amounts to little more than that. The antagonists are of both this world and the otherworld—in fact, of different otherworlds. We have as the main supernatural antagonist Queen Hell, who desires to steal the heart from Princess Sapphire in order to give it to her daughter Hecate, a rambunctious tomboy who is dressed according to the era of the reader, rather than of the story, in a sweater and toreador pants. Queen Hell reacts to the sight of a crucifix the same way that a vampire would, but there is little else vampiric (apart from a shape-shifting ability) about her.

God, like Satan, only puts in a token appearance in the prologue. This prologue takes place in a corner of Heaven where the souls of children are waiting to be sent to Earth to be born. God, represented as an old man in a robe with a mustache and pince-nez, doles out pink hearts for girls and blue hearts for boys; swallowing the heart determines the child's personality, not its gender. This reinforces the traditional notion (not exclusive to the Japanese) that certain behaviors are gender-specific. A not too competent angel named Chink takes some initiative and thrusts a boy's heart into one child's mouth, only because "you look like a boy." The child, however, is actually to be Princess Sapphire of Goldland, where by law only a male could be heir to the throne. Her subsequent tomboyish behavior allows her to dress as a male and pass as a prince; the bulk of the story involves others' attempts to reveal her true gender, with an eye to usurping her throne. God does not take part in these battles; he is represented by Chink, whose mistake (the instilling of unconventional behavior into the soon-to-be Princess Sapphire) precipitated the story in the first place.

In one interesting episode of the story (chapter 8, "Ribon no Kishi Toujou (The Ribbon Knight Arrives on the Scene)", Chink, at his wits' end as to how to retrieve the male heart from Princess Sapphire, prays to a roadside shrine, asking his Heavenly Father for a suggestion. He sleeps, and dreams of an insect orchestra in a sequence influenced by American animation. This inspires Chink to carve a wooden flute whose music can subdue Princess Sapphire. Unfortunately, his playing catches the princess in the middle of a swordfight in which she has been holding her own against three assassins. The music causes her swordplay to deteriorate. The assassins overwhelm her, and only when Chink stops playing does she rally to defeat them. Chink sadly realizes that the flute will not serve his purpose, and throws it into the river. (vol. 1, pp. 135-150) There is room for several interpretations here (that the dream and the prayer were unconnected, or that Chink, already established as a flawed cherub, misinterpreted the dream) but the overall message of this episode would seem to be that divine revelation through dreams is not infallible.[4]

About two-thirds of the way through the story, Tezuka abandons connections with Judeo-Christianity altogether, introducing Venus, Mount Olympus and other elements of the Greco-Roman pantheon.

Futago no Kishi

There is a similar theological mix in the story's sequel, *Futago no Kishi*, which was serialized between January 1958 and June 1959 in the girls manga magazine *Nakayoshi* and drawn in a style based on both Disney animation and the Takarazuka theater. Sapphire and her Prince Charming (whose name was Franz Charming!) have become the parents of twins: a boy and a girl. To determine which shall be heir to the throne, the king prays to God. In answer to the prayer, Chink returns and advises that chance should decide the successor. The heir turns out to be the boy, Prince Daisy. The Duchess Dahlia, who favored the Princess Violet for the succession, arranges to have Daisy kidnapped and left in the woods to die. To cover the disappearance, Violet must grow up in the footsteps of her mother, appearing at times as a male and at times as a female.

Daisy is found by a deer named Papi who asks the Forest Goddess, a fairy who dwells in a pond, for help in protecting him. In the syncretistic mix of this story, there is no apparent conflict between God in Heaven and the Forest Goddess in the pond; each has its own part to play. The fairy grants Papi the ability to turn into a human, but only at night. In this way she raises the prince as her younger brother in a cabin in the woods.

The prince grows to become a hunter and one day shoots a deer, which he takes back to the cabin. When the sun sets, the deer is transformed into his sister. It is in this shape that she dies and is buried beneath a cross. Shortly after the burial, a wildcat named Zubora starts digging up the grave. The prince (even though he had vowed at the funeral never to kill again) kills Zubora by pushing a shovel into the cat's mouth and forcing him off a cliff. In the cell showing the dead cat, the handle of the shovel, still sticking out of Zubora's mouth, melds with the cross that marks Papi's grave.

This example is one of a series of usages of the cross by Tezuka in manga of the late 1950s, perhaps suggested by the spate of Biblically inspired Hollywood films of the time,[5] in which the cross served two distinct purposes for Tezuka. On the one hand, it was a death marker, denoting or even forecasting the death of a character. In addition, it would be used to signal the just conclusion of a story or sequence. That just ending might involve the death of the villain, or it may mean the avenging of the death of a sympathetic character by the arrest of the responsible party.

There is a somewhat different usage in a later episode of *Futago no Kishi*. In "Ookami no Yama" (Wolf Mountain), a mother wolf dies protecting her pups, and is buried beneath a cross. Unlike Papi, the wolf was not anthropomorphized at all; the reader was intended to view her as a wolf. Topping her grave with a Christian symbol was done partly as a sign of respect, honoring the mother who died protecting her children, thus conforming to traditional human gender expectations. The wolf, in other words, may not have been human, but she was behaving appropriately. The definition, however, is from the culture of the comic's reader, and not from that of the characters' fantasized European culture.

There is also a religious sense in which the wolf, and the respect accorded to her, could be seen as appropriate, even if the symbol used to express the respect was not native to the reader's culture. Buddhism stresses the oneness of living things, a theme that recurs throughout Tezuka's works as well as that of other manga artists. It is a very short step, for example, from the *Black Jack* episode in which, stranded at sea with two criminals, Black Jack must perform surgery on a dolphin to help them find land ("Umi no Sutorenjaa (Stranger from the Sea)" in *Black Jack*, vol. 1, pp. 29-51), to the kuyō ceremony described by William R. LaFleur:

> Annually in Japan there is an autumnal rite of kuyō for eels. Through the medium of national television, each year presents select restaraunteurs and their customers, people who love to eat eels, gathered by an altar while Buddhist priests intone the words of sutras to express thanks to the eels for having been so nourishing and for having such a delicious taste. Of course, in this—especially when the whole rite is projected to the nation via the nightly news—the Japanese tell themselves once again that their ties with antiquity are intact and that they as a people are not ingrates or irreligious, however much they consume eels with great relish most of the time. (LaFleur, pp. 145-146)

Similarly, honoring a wolf who died protecting her cubs would evoke Hachiko, the dog who died while waiting for years for his dead master to return home. This story is one of Japan's most popular and powerful archetypes.

Tetsuwan Atomu (Astro Boy)

A group of 1959 *Tetsuwan Atomu* stories also employs the cross to signal the just conclusion of the story, while also serving as a death-marker. The January 1959 story "Kirisuto no Me" (The Eye of Christ) is the most overtly religious of the group, beginning in a church on a stormy night. A gang of masked criminals commandeers the church. The pastor tells them that Jesus (in this case, the altar crucifix) sees everything. The criminal ringleader, whose mask is blown off by a gust of wind, tells the priest to blindfold the plaster statue of Jesus. As he does so, the priest scratches an ideogram into the statue's eye that identifies the ringleader. The priest is killed, but the mystery is solved when detective Hige Oyaji[6] makes the connection. The final panel juxtaposes the radiant image of the altar-cross with the criminals being marched off to jail.

The Atom story "Iwan no Baka" (Ivan the Fool, a title borrowed from a short story by Leo Tolstoy) appeared in February and March 1959. Atom and a group of earthlings are traveling in a spaceship that gets hit by a meteor. The party makes an emergency landing on the moon. While exploring, Atom finds the ruins of an old rocket crashed in a valley. A tape recording reveals that the rocket was launched by the Soviet Union in 1960 in an attempt to get to the moon.[7] The sole survivors were cosmonaut Minya Mikhailovna and her robot companion Ivan. Since, in this lunar landscape, plants flourish in a breathable atmosphere and water is available, Minya scratches out a basic but lonely existence. On her deathbed, she tells Ivan to bury her on a hill where she has planted a cross.

When one of the passengers (established at the beginning of the story as a thief) learns that Minya, while she lived, had unearthed massive diamonds on the moon, he threatens to kill the others unless Atom shows him where Minya's grave is. Lunar night begins to fall; Atom takes the others to a rescue ship, while the thief pulls the cross from the ground and uses it as a digging-tool to get to the diamonds, thus compounding desecration with sacrilege. No sooner does he find the diamonds than Ivan appears, mistaking the thief for Minya, as he similarly mistook Atom for Minya earlier. Ivan carries the thief back to the ship to care for him, heedless of his cries for help. The final panel shows the Russian spaceship in the background, the discarded diamonds and the cross in the foreground. Once again the cross is used as the signal of a just conclusion, while it also serves as a death-marker. Here it signals the doom of the thief as well as the death of Minya.

This same dual usage is seen in "Chitei Sensha" (The Underground Tank), serialized in *Shonen Magazine* in September and October of 1959. The villain of this piece, General Saborsky, invented the title vehicle as a means to world domination. One of his workers, however, has stolen the tank and used it to rescue Hige Oyaji, stranded in a desert after his plane was destroyed by the general's jet. When the pilot of the tank is killed in a landslide, Hige Oyaji buries him in a grave with a cross as a marker. (It is worth noting here that the dead tank driver is black, for no apparent plot reason. However, this does reinforce the cultural notion that Christianity is essentially a creed for non-Japanese). Hige Oyaji then digs his own grave and erects a cross for himself; however, when he prays, the words come out "Nanmai Dabu", a scrambled version of the "Namu Amida Butsu" prayer to Amida Buddha.[8] Atom hears these prayers and rescues Hige Oyaji. The story ends with Atom attacking General Saborsky's private jet, knocking off the wing-tips and tail and causing it to crash into the ground nose-first. General Saborsky attempts to escape by driving his damaged tank into a live volcano; a move that means certain death, which he considers preferable to surrender. Again, in the final panel, the wrecked fuselage in the foreground bears a deliberate resemblance to a crucifix grave-marker, and also signals the just end of General Saborsky.

The first installment of a 1968 three-part *Tetsuwan Atomu* story, "The Man Who Came Home from Mars," is set on Christmas Eve. The Christmas theme of redemption is not ignored in terms of the returning man, a criminal named Judah Peter. This story is discussed in chapter 7, the Christmas chapter.

Another extended Atom story, "Atomu Konseki Monogatari" (The Story of Atom Past and Present) retells Atom's invention by Professor Tenma, in an attempt to reconstruct his son Tobio who was killed in an automobile accident. However, this amplified version, syndicated between 1967 and 1969 in the *Sankei Shimbun*, adds a new character, a new motivation for Atom's vocation as crime-fighter, and a different usage of the crucifix.

Professor Tenma, in the episode of the same name (Sun Comics, vol. 7, pp. 96-133), is pondering the problem of building his lifelike robot when he is approached by a Mr. Suigara, a wealthy importer who offers ten million dollars toward the completion of the project. The reason for this generosity later becomes clear. Suigara is an American Nisei (second-generation Japanese-American); his import business is in Los Angeles and his home is in Beverly Hills. (This explains why he offered to pay in dollars rather than yen.) In the next installment, "Beirii no Sangeki" (The Tragedy of Bailey) (vol. 7, pp. 136-162), he borrows the robot Atom and takes him to the United States to teach him an object-lesson. Suigara tells him that, in the course of his sixty years, he has seen three groups discriminated against by white people: Orientals, including himself (presumably during and after the Second World War), black people (during the civil rights struggles of the 1950s and 1960s) and robots. Each group has overcome its victimization except robots. Suigara asks a robot named Bailey to go to city hall and register with the census, to be on a par with humans. No sooner does he enter the building than a white mob begins to gather. Bailey is torn apart by the mob, which also tears up Bailey's papers, as Atom watches in horror. The angry mob marches on Suigara's house, and he is only able to turn them away by displaying hand grenades inside his clothes and warning them that they will blow themselves up by attacking him.

Suigara's concern about civil rights for robots is explained in a later episode, "Robotto Jinken Sengen" (Declaration of the Rights of Robots) (vol. 8, pp. 38-62). When a Franklin Roosevelt-looking President of the United States grants equality to robots, Suigara immediately proceeds to a secret shrine in his basement; there, a robot is lying on a bier under a photograph of a woman and a crucifix. This is not a burial chamber, for the robot is not dead but deactivated. Suigara revives the robot, whom he calls Helen and refers to as his wife.

Suigara relates that, twenty years earlier, he had fallen in love at first sight of this humanoid robot, finding out only later what she was. He obtained ownership of her, but found that he could not marry her, since the law forbade marriage between master and slave (i.e., between human and robot). In the meantime, Suigara had been, bit by bit, replacing his bodily organs and parts with machinery so that he now is, in his own words, a robot from the neck down. He tells the revived Helen that they can now be married, and they are on their way to a church when their car is bombed and both are destroyed. We never see who threw the bomb, but the presumption is that the bomber was in sympathy with, if not part of, the mob that destroyed Bailey.

This is not the only time a manga artist has wrung pathos out of civil rights problems in the United States. Also written in 1968, Satonaka Machiko's "Watashi no Jonii" (My Johnny) tells of the love-affair between a black student named Johnny Ray and Ann White(!), the blonde daughter of a bigoted Southern sheriff. In pursuing the two, the sheriff accidentally shoots and kills his daughter (Schodt, p. 98). If these comics were to appear in the United States (and there have been a number with similar stories), the primary message would be the surface plea for tolerance and a rejection of bigotry. In a heterogeneous culture such as the United States, and certainly during the 1960s, bigotry was perceived and depicted in many parts of the country as deviant behavior, and tolerance as the desired behavior. Japan, however, in the past has stressed its racial homogeneity (real or imagined), has established underclasses and behaved intolerantly toward them to varying degrees, and expressed concerns at times about its culture being adulterated by foreigners. The two manga mentioned above, coming at the same time, can of course be read as pleas for tolerance, but also as cautionary tales against miscegenation. This is not to say that manga encourage discrimination, but they do caution against risky behavior. Tragedy, according to the subtext, is the inevitable result of crossing racial lines.

In the case of Suigara, many lines were crossed at once. This Nisei fell in love with an American white woman who turned out to be a robot; for love of her, he set about turning himself into a robot, literally dehumanizing himself. By inference, it was his love for Helen that motivated his activism for equal rights for robots. In this context, the crucifix above Helen's "bier" makes sense. It is not a symbol of Helen's death, since the robot was merely deactivated. It was a marker signifying the crossing of another line: Suigara the Nisei was a Christian convert, paying allegiance to the Western god. This devotion, as often happens in manga, availed him nothing. He was still destroyed, and the cross also acts to forecast that end. In this sense, the cross symbolizes death—a death that would take place once Helen was revived. (It is perhaps no coincidence that Helen's electronic brain is housed not in her head but in her blonde wig, which is needed to revive her. This racial characteristic brings her to life, and sets the wheels of tragedy in motion.)

Kirihito Sanka

Ode to Kirihito (Kirihito Sanka) has one of the least likely sounding plot points in manga: is the disease known as Monmo caused by a virus or by polluted water? This literally turns into a life-or-death question for the three doctors researching the exotic disease which affects the skeletal system and causes a person to have the appearance of a dog. Two of the doctors, Urabe and Osanai, have competing theories, and their competition is played up by their superior, Doctor Tatsugaura. This forms the basis for more than 800 pages of manga which were printed in *Big Comic* magazine in 1970 and 1971. Aimed at an adult audience, with sex and nudity mixed in with medical procedures, this manga, which pointed the way toward Tezuka's medical manga *Black Jack* which premiered in 1973, also included scenes of Christian iconography.

The researcher who finds the truth, Osanai Kirihito, is isolated in an African village where the Monmo is located and eventually contracts the disease. Another sufferer is Sister Helen Friese, a nun from a Rhodesian convent. She is brought to a Japanese medical conference and, in an expressionistic scene, is made to disrobe to her underwear in front of the audience to show the extent of the disease. Her faith is all that allows her to go through with this humiliating demonstration as she recalls Doctor Urabe, who she had asked to read her chapter 27 of the Gospel of Matthew, verses 28 to 33, describing the humiliation of Jesus on his way to the crucifixion. (p. 437) Earlier, she was distressed by her canine appearance and consoled herself recalling Jesus's words in the 6th chapter of the Gospel of Matthew, verses 25 to 30. (p. 270)

Yet Christian influence does not always improve a person's thoughts or deeds. Doctor Urabe first meets Sister Helen when he investigated rumors of Rhodesian miners infected with Monmo. A doctor calling himself McCracken invited Urabe to examine Sister Helen, then shot them both, saying that she must die "to protect the honor of the Lord's servants!" (p. 171) Fortunately, the wounds aren't fatal; Doctor Urabe drives them both into town where they are hospitalized in "the black district."

They spend a month recovering in adjoining beds, which is a convenience for the plot but also reinforces that most people do not regard Sister Helen as fully human. She even internalizes this attitude, telling Urabe "I had to die. How can I serve the Lord looking like this?" Urabe consoles her:

> Sister, I'm not a Christian, but I know the story of Christ's life! Jesus said he would suffer for all of humanity! Those were brave words. . . . Your life, too, like his, could end amidst ridicule and contempt. Unbearable suffering might become your lot. But, Miss Helen, don't you think this might be God's test for you? Don't you want to overcome this and be strong and live on?

She asks why Urabe would be so kind to her, and he replies, "I'm just doing my duty as a doctor." (pp. 181-185)

However, one of the symptoms of Monmo is sexual aggressiveness, and Urabe is driven to rape Sister Helen. Unable to follow her example of accepting his fate with the disease, he kills himself, and Sister Helen becomes a self-appointed medical missionary in a rundown mining town in the Tohoku region of the northern part of Japan's main island, Honshu. When the villagers first see her face, however, they panic and call her a *kitsune-onna* (fox woman).[9] (pp. 646-660)

One month later, Dr. Osanai finds the village and Sister Helen, who is now accepted by the villagers for helping their sick. Osanai, however, dismisses this as "the famous Christian humanitarianism" and bluntly tells her "God doesn't exist!" (pp. 706-715)

Ode to Kirihito is a complex tapestry of events and emotions, some of them sensationalist according to the pop culture of the time and place. Generally speaking, the female characters are shown more respectfully than the males, and Sister Helen earns the reader's respect and compassion.

MW

The story titled *MW* (*Big Comic*, September 1976 through January 1978) features a leading character that would have been nearly impossible to portray in the United States until recently and is still problematic today: Garai Iwao, a homosexual Catholic priest. His relationship with the villain of the piece, Yuki Michio, drives the story from beginning to end.

The story, while largely set in the late 1970s, begins some 15 years earlier. At that time, Garai was a juvenile delinquent who spends a day on Okino-Mafune Island in the company of some other punks (who look rather like late sixties hippies). Among their petty offenses is the tormenting of the young Yuki, whom Garai takes into a cave in the hills for sexual abuse. This act, ironically, saved their lives, since all the other inhabitants of the island were killed in a leak of American nerve gas (the MW of the title). The gas was subsequently spirited away to another hiding place and the massacre covered up. Garai turned to the priesthood in remorse, while Yuki grew up as an oyama (a Kabuki actor specializing in women's roles) who worked steadily to locate the gas in order to steal it to use against the world. In the end, Garai takes back the gas, at the cost of his own life, but Yuki survives. The ending is deliberately ambiguous, and suggests that Yuki Michio will not be discovered or punished. Despite all his efforts, Garai does not see justice done—which serves as yet another commentary on the ineffectiveness of Christian clergy.

Yuki is primarily depicted as a homosexual, but not exclusively so. He sleeps not only with Garai, but with a variety of women (and even, it is suggested, his attack-dog), but always with an eye toward obtaining the MW. By being so indiscriminate yet single-minded, he is rendered, in a sense, asexual, driven not by considerations of physical passion but by a mad desire for revenge.

One interesting episode in the twentieth chapter of the story ("Tousaku (Perversion)", vol. 3, pp. 5-38) illustrates the notion of group membership as central to the Japanese character, as well as the belief that members of the out-group can relate to each other because of their shared experience. Yuki takes Garai to a club where the "hostesses" are really transvestites; it is a front for the homosexual activity in the back room of the club. Garai is photographed there in a compromising position, and the photographer attempts to blackmail him; all part of Yuki's plan. The photographer ends up dealing, however, with a female city editor named Ryōse who not only does not publish the pictures but reassures Garai that there is nothing to worry about. His question of why she should help him is answered in the final two panels, as Ryōse is seen coming home after work; she is greeted by another woman saying "Okaennasai, anata" (Welcome home, dear). Ryōse is a lesbian, and the final panel shows her and her lover in a nude embrace. The implication is that having the shared experience of homosexuality enables Ryōse to empathize with and help Garai. That he has apparently compromised his priestly vows is considered of lesser importance.

Unico

One character created by Tezuka late in his career was Unico, a magical unicorn. From 1976 to 1979 nine Unico adventures (including a prologue) appeared in the girls' magazine *Ririka* (Lyrica), published by the Sanrio Company. After three years, the Lyrica editors decided that Unico "seemed to be too cute" (kawairashisugiru koto deshita) and the character was relegated to *First Grader* magazine, where the stories became shorter and simpler, more reliant on puns than on plot lines, and the artwork less elaborate. ("Atogaki" (Afterword), vol. 2, pp. 190-191)

In the prologue, Unico's origin in the context of Greco-Roman mythology is clearly established. (vol. 1, pp. 7-28) Venus, in this prologue, is envious of the attentions paid by mortal men to the beautiful Psyche. She sends her son Eros to shoot Psyche with his love-arrows and thus divert her attentions to one man, but Psyche's pet, Unico, pushes Eros out of hiding and onto one of his own arrows; he and Psyche promptly fall in love with each other. In retaliation, Venus has Unico kidnapped and given to the west wind Zephyrus. The wind takes the unicorn to various places and times, not only getting Unico away from Venus but providing a host of settings for stories.

The second Unico story, "Uruwashi no Rozeria" (The Beautiful Rosalia), is set in medieval Europe. (vol. 1, pp. 69-134) The exposition is a variation on "Beauty and the Beast," in that Rosalia's father the king has been magically cursed with a horribly ugly face for committing the sin of blasphemy: he was so desperate for a victory in battle that he prayed that he would accept the face of a demon in exchange. The prayer was answered, but now the king's face scares away suitors for his daughter, and has left Rosalia a very lonely young woman. She kneels to a statue of the Virgin Mary and asks for her father to be forgiven for his crime. The answer to her prayers, Unico, appears; she adopts the talking unicorn as a pet.

Meanwhile, Prime Minister Dandara has been bleeding the peasants with exorbitant taxes and plotting to usurp the throne with the assistance of the kingdom's archbishop, who is depicted as sucking a pacifier. The archbishop jumps to the conclusion that the princess's new pet is a demon. He illustrates this by referring to a book; the book includes two pictures (front and side view) of the traditional devil portrait: horns, batwings, cloven hooves and pointed tail. Also on the pages, however, are the words "666 Omen" and "Exorcist", a reference to two Hollywood movies of the 1970s whose plots turn on the classic mythology (as well as contemporary fundamentalist Christian hysteria) surrounding Satan. (The word "Omen" is in fact drawn with an oversized O, in imitation of the film's logo.)[10] The Archbishop, however has provided the excuse to hunt down Unico: it has a horn and hooves, therefore it is a devil.

Prime Minister Dandara sends out assassins to murder villagers in their beds; the surviving villagers are convinced that the princess's "akuma" (demon) is responsible. Palace guards chase Unico, but he sprouts wings and flies away, taking the princess to the woods. The princess, meanwhile, has fallen in love with Lupinas, a masked jester who is in reality the heir to the throne of the neighboring kingdom, which was decimated by Rosalia's father in the earlier war. Rosalia's father the king is tried by the archbishop (the king stands at a table at the center of a white cross on the floor), is convicted and sentenced to death by beheading. Unico at the last minute prevents the execution by restoring the king's original face. He also frees Lupinas, who confronts the king; the king promises to make amends to the people of the neighboring kingdom, and Lupinas and Rosalia are free to marry.

This Christian cleric is clearly on the side of the enemy, and is mistaken in applying Christian doctrine to the solution of a problem. Rosalia, whose Japanese name Rozeria suggests the word "rosary", becomes yet another European character, yet another woman, who believes in Christianity, but whose belief is rewarded by a force other than the Christian God (c.f. Sumiko in Ishinomori's "The Ten Santa Clauses" in the *Mutant Sab* series; see chapter 7 regarding Christmas; she prays to God to rescue her brother, but the one who helps is the title character, a Japanese esper). A variety of cultures with their respective theologies, real or fantastic, are visited by Unico on his journeys (for example, one adventure links the Sphinx killed by Oedipus with fairy rulers Titania and Oberon), but apart from a minor scene in an adventure taking place in Czarist Russia, this is the only allusion to Christianity in the Unico *Lyrica* series.

Hyaku Monogatari

Tezuka turned to the legend of Faust three times in his career. Early on, he did an adaptation of the story intended for younger readers, in the vein of his adaptation of Dostoevsky's "Crime and Punishment." Late in life, he started a story called "Neo-Faust," introducing aspects of biotechnology into the story. This version was left incomplete at the time of his death. However, in 1971, Tezuka crafted a four-part series based on Faust called *Hyaku Monogatari (One Hundred Stories)* for serialization in *Shonen Jump* magazine.[11] The story was set in medieval Japan, and involves a low-level samurai who balks at committing seppuku as ordered by his daimyo. Tempted by Mephistopheles, who in this story appears as a witch named Sudama, he signs over his soul for a new face and a new name (that name, suggested by Sudama reading from a telephone book(!), is Fuwa Usuto, phonologically reinforcing the link with Goethe's epic). However, the *Hyaku Monogatari* has an ending that smacks more of Wagner than of Goethe. Fuwa Usuto, having found fulfillment in life as he agreed, is willing to commit the seppuku that frightened him at the beginning of the story. However, Fuwa Usuto and Sudama had fallen in love; now, as she bears his soul down to the underworld, Sudama balks and, out of love, releases the soul up to Heaven.

Although the ending is unorthodox from a Western theological perspective, it was perhaps inevitable, given Tezuka's choice to render the devil as a woman. Having defined Sudama as a Japanese witch, the cartoonist had little choice but to render her in terms suitable for that character, just as Fuwa Usuto corresponded to certain manga images of a medieval samurai. Once the characters had been set in place and proper qualities were assigned to them, Sudama could not be rendered without attributing to her one of the traditional qualities of femininity as perceived in Japan: a self-sacrificing devotion born of love of her shujin (master). This sociological imperative overrode any questions of Christian doctrine, in as much as Tezuka created *Hyaku Monogatari* for Japanese rather than for Western readers. This imperative could perhaps be said to be at the heart of most, if not all, manga depictions of Judeo-Christianity: the images are "audience-driven," shaped by what the audience is willing to accept. More specifically, the beliefs of the audience cannot be ignored if readership is to be maintained.

The Vampyres

The 1966 story *The Vampyres*, created for *Shonen Sunday* magazine, is pointed to as one of the first Tezuka manga to adopt the more realistic gekiga style then rising in popularity. In this case, there is practically none of the vampire lore associated with Dracula; a better title might be *The Lycanthropes*, since this story tells of the imminent takeover of civilization by people capable of turning into various werebeasts. They find a human ally in Makube Rokuro, nicknamed Rock, an amoral adult version of the protagonist of the 1952 manga *Adventures of Rock*, and a character that Tezuka employed as a villain in other manga. The name Makube is intended to suggest Macbeth, as aspects of this plot parallel Shakespeare's play.

In one scene that relates to this topic, Rock recalls his visit to three witches. In this meeting he is told that neither man nor beast ("ningen ni mo dōbutsu ni mo") can ever stop him. (As with Shakespeare's prophecy about Macbeth being indestructible by "man of woman born", there is a twist. The principal werewolf, Toppei, is neither wholly man nor wholly beast, and chases Rock off a cliff and into the sea. Rock would resurface—excuse the pun—in an unfinished sequel years later.) During his meeting with the witches, Rock is seen standing on a pile of corpses, while cheering demons look on, declaring himself to be "akuma no mōshigo"—a child of Satan, or, literally, the answer to the devil's prayers. No matter how horrific this scene, though, Rock's impunity does not last long.

Enzeru no Oka (Angel Hill)

The story *Enzeru no Oka (Angel Hill)* was serialized from January 1960 to December 1961 in the girls magazine *Nakayoshi*. The story contains no less than four distinct and different religious realities. The story features the wealthy Kusahara family: industrialist father, mother with pretensions as a painter, grown son Eiji and spoiled, misbehaving daughter Akemi. The latter happens to be the mirror image of Princess Luna, from the uncharted Angel Island in the Pacific, where all the inhabitants are amphibious and are watched over by Poseidon. Unlike his classical Greek depictions, this Poseidon is drawn as an old man in a robe, without a trident or a fishtail. There is also a local god, a mermaid statue worshipped by Luna's mother Pyoma, who is trying (for reasons not relevant to this study) to assassinate Luna. Pyoma had previously exiled Luna by setting her adrift and expecting her to die in the middle of the ocean. However, she is rescued by a passing ship, alive but suffering from amnesia. The ship makes port, the captain is killed trying to establish the castaway's identity, and Luna is sold into slavery.

This action apparently takes place in Thailand, since Luna finds brief respite from her travails as a slave by going to a temple with distinctly Thai-like architecture. She is consoled there by a priest, whose robes and begging-bowl denote him to be Buddhist. Luna laments her loss of memory, and the priest replies: "Remembering the things of the past is no consolation. It's hard enough living in the Here-and-Now." His advice is a comfort to Luna both when she is in slavery, and when she goes to Japan to live with the Kusahara family after Eiji buys her freedom.

There is a fourth religious component to this story: a Christian component. Even though the Kusahara family is Japanese, Akemi is expected to attend church after school each day. The church is presided over by a priest who, in Tezuka Repertory Company tradition, is based on the character of Hige Oyaji. He appears twice in the story. In the second episode, "Akemi Toiu Shoujo (The Young Girl Named Akemi)," he unwittingly saves Luna from Pyoma's assassins. He dismisses Luna's claim to be an amnesiac Pacific princess as a prank by Akemi. (vol. 1, pp. 51-118)

When we see him a second time, in chapter 6, "Semaru Mashu (Evil Close at Hand)" (vol. 2, pp. 25-138), he is seated on the floor of the church behind the pulpit, reading amid a pile of books, some of which are clearly labeled "Manga." This is not a throwaway gag, for he tells the visitor who surprised him, "I was just reading the Bible. ... Every day on her way home from school (Akemi) reads comics—er, the Bible with me." The notion of a Christian priest who reads comics instead of scripture, and lies about it, is softened somewhat both by the fact that this is a comic, a medium that would allow for such incongruent behavior, and that the priest is "portrayed by" Hige Oyaji, the well-meaning detective who nevertheless gets himself into dangerous predicaments and needs to be rescued by Atom. Later, during an attempt to kidnap Akemi from the church, Eiji races through the building to enlist the priest's aid. However, having provided necessary exposition, the priest is now nowhere to be seen, reinforcing the notion that a Christian priest cannot be counted on for help in an emergency.

In fact, the crucifix is more effective in this story than the priest. Pyoma has enlisted the aid of an underworld figure, known only as "Boss," to kidnap Akemi, in the belief that she is really Luna. Boss hides in the woods near the church with a gun, and prepares to shoot Akemi while she sits in a taxi. However, no matter which tree he hides behind, the sunlight glinting off the cross on the roof of the church spoils his aim. This would seem to be divine intervention, and in a Western comic book scenario would lead to repentance. Here, Boss, while prevented from shooting Akemi, is not above hijacking the taxi and taking Akemi to Pyoma. The cross brought about frustration, but not repentance. (vol. 2, pp. 65-71)

Black Jack

Black Jack was a character near to Tezuka's heart, since both Black Jack and Tezuka were MDs. Black Jack, however, was a dark and mysterious character intended to be an antihero who later turned heroic due to fan popularity. Between 1973 and 1983 Tezuka created hundreds of short Black Jack stories; most focused on medical knowledge, although sometimes the stories ranged from the unlikely to the fantastic. The character of Black Jack, however, remained a highly skilled but misanthropic surgeon, similar to Dr. Gregory

House of American television as a highly skilled but misanthropic diagnostician. In fact, several Japanese television commercials played up the similarity between the two characters.

There are occasional Black Jack episodes in which religion plays a part. One of Tezuka's *Black Jack* stories was the basis of the fifth of nine OAVs with screenplay and direction by Tezuka associate Dezaki Osamu and produced by Tezuka Productions after Tezuka's death. Under the English title "The Owl of San Merida", the story shifts from the mysterious to the miraculous.

Black Jack and his assistant Pinoko are touring Europe when they cross paths with Leslie, a British military officer candidate with singular afflictions. He is subject to nightmare visions of combat he never took part in, a woman and child wandering through his life, and bullet holes that appear, ooze blood, then disappear, even though he has never been shot. In tending to the young man's injuries, Black Jack discovers that he was operated on as an infant, by someone who was—like himself—unorthodox but highly skilled.

The search for answers takes them to San Merida, a city in the fictional nation of El Garnia, until recently wracked by civil war; San Merida was a stronghold for the rebels against the government. They meet the priest of the village church, who, when Black Jack asks about the oldest living citizens who remember the war, takes him to Ernesto, the elderly caretaker of the cemetery. Gradually the truth is pieced together by Ernesto: decades earlier, during the worst of the war, a woman and her daughter were shot by a military helicopter gunship; the girl could not be saved and the woman barely clung to life. When a baby was brought in, also with severe gunshot wounds, Ernesto—at the time a medical student assisting the rebels—left the baby with the dying woman. She rallied long enough to nurse the infant, which was viewed as a miracle. Ernesto worked to save the baby, using extensive skin grafts from the dying mother; these were the source of the bullet wounds. The baby survived, and was adopted by an Englishman, who named him Leslie.

While this was explained, the priest made a phone call, then returned to arrest Ernesto. The "priest" was actually a captain in the military of El Garnia, placed at the church to search for proof that Ernesto was "the Owl of San Merida", still sought by the military as a dangerous rebel. During his arrest the soldiers shoot Ernesto; Black Jack tries to save him but fails. The false priest, who was told no harm would come to Ernesto, is instructed to bury him in an unmarked grave. All that the priest can do is put an anonymous marker on his grave.

This is a case where a priest isn't even a real priest, but someone following a hidden agenda from the beginning. As long as Ernesto stayed silent and tended the graves, his involvement with the rebels could not be proven; the arrival of Leslie searching for answers sealed his fate. This story restates a common theme in Tezuka's work, for which he coined the term "the egoism of the state". Tezuka lived through the militarization of Japan in the years before and during the Second World War, and saw too much of world history after the war to have any illusions about the ability of power to corrupt—including the ability to corrupt clergy of any faith.

There is an unflattering portrayal of a religious healer in the manga episode "Sono ko wo korosuna! (Don't kill that child!)" (vol. 2, pp. 77-92) Black Jack must confront a psychic surgeon named Harry Adler, a black character with long white hair, who sometimes wears African robes but usually appears in just a loincloth. Adler is able to perform psychic surgery using what he says is the power of God, sticking his hand into a patient and removing diseased organs without breaking the skin. Adler is steered toward Black Jack by a pair of television producers who anticipate high ratings in a duel between the surgeons.

Black Jack, in this case, is confronted with a problematic pregnancy: the fetus has developed ectopically, outside the uterus altogether, growing among the intestines. Adler uses what he says are divine powers to warp Black Jack's instruments psychokinetically, until Black Jack allows him to approach the patient. When Adler draws out the fetus, however, everyone sees what X-rays did not show: that the fetus is anencephalic, did not develop a cerebral cortex, and would be doomed to die after a few hours of life. Adler is distraught as Black Jack lectures him that, sometimes, a surgeon needs to act like a demon ("akuma ni mo naru koto ga arun da ze!")

There are episodes in which Black Jack confronts events that can be considered divine. In the sixth OAV anime about Black Jack directed by Dezaki Osamu for Tezuka Productions, the doctor stumbles into a medieval scene which cost the lives of five people—a scene which has been re-enacted again and again until his intervention brings peace to all concerned. This story, however, happens in a Buddhist context, and Black Jack's presence as a witness has a context for the modern Japanese audience.

The case of Harry Adler, however, revolves around abortion, and—as in the United States—there is a range of opinion about this subject in Japan, from accepting it as an ethically neutral medical procedure to absolute rejection on religious grounds (see *Liquid Life* by William LaFleur.) In this case, Black Jack's position was intended to be seen as the correct one, and readers familiar with the character of Black Jack would trust Tezuka both as a pop culture storyteller and as someone who had been through medical school.

Don Dracula

Vampirism in manga would seem to be a detour from this discussion, but there is a definite relevance. Orthodox Christianity does not, in this century, allow for the existence of the "classic" vampire: an undead soul who feeds on the blood of the living. Yet, through Bram Stoker's novel *Dracula* and its various incarnations on stage, in books, and especially in films, the image of the vampire as a demonic fiend who can only be vanquished by holy men and holy relics has pervaded the world, including Japan. Tezuka notes in the foreword to the three-volume collection of his 1980 series *Don Dracula* that the manga was always intended to be a vampire story, but that it did not take shape until he saw the 1979 American vampire comedy *Love At First Bite*, released in Japan under the title *Dorakyura Miyako e Iku (Dracula Goes to Town)*. (vol. 1, p. 5) The sight of Dracula in a discotheque inspired him to push the series in the direction of parody, and one episode ("Mou Ichidou Dorakyura"—One More Time, Dracula) in fact has Dracula going to a disco.

The consequences of a parody treatment are that, while Dracula is still repelled by crosses, they are often used as a gag prop. Ten of the twenty-six episodes of "Don Dracula" employ crosses, either seriously or humorously. Interestingly, Dracula in this series has a young daughter named Chocula,[12] who does not consistently react as violently to the cross as does her father, although she exhibits most of the other behaviors of the vampire. A study of her character will go a long way toward illustrating the application of Said's Orientalism as it works in Japanese pop culture.

In the episode titled "Dorakyura wa yoru ni kagiru" (Dracula limited by night) (vol. 2, pp. 89-108), the truly limited one is Chocula. Her boyfriend Nobuhiko is being transferred out of night school, and she will no longer be able to see him. She finally tells him that she cannot go out in sunlight (without revealing that she is a vampire). They try various means of protecting Chocula from the sun, from tanning creams to asbestos suits; of course, nothing works. Each time, Chocula is reduced to ashes; each time, Igor, the hunchbacked servant to the Dracula family, gathers the ashes and adds blood to reconstitute Chocula in a process that he compares to making instant ramen.

One night, a despondent Chocula sits crying in a doorway. She is approached by a man wearing the robes of a Catholic priest. At first confused by her dilemma, he advises her to trust in God to cure her affliction, and offers to take her to a church where she can be helped. He takes her to a church where, behind the altar rail, is a scroll with the inscription "False Life Church." The senior priest tells Chocula that God rewards service, and immediately puts her to work in a sweatshop in the basement, stringing beads with other Japanese women. Meanwhile, Chocula's disappearance has both Nobuhiko and Dracula out looking for her. Nobuhiko gets the location of the church from a taxi driver; he arrives in time to overhear the priests say that Chocula isn't working out stringing beads, and that they could get more money selling her to a bar. Nobuhiko is discovered, but he still manages to tell Chocula how to distract the priests and escape into the alley. From there, she turns into a bat and flies away. Her father arrives a second later and attacks the "false priests" ("ese-kyōso" he calls them); however, Chocula tells Dracula to hurry, since she doesn't want Nobuhiko to see him biting people's necks. The final panel shows an unrepentant Chocula, still dreaming of the day when she will be able to go to the beach and get a tan with Nobuhiko.

After the first installment of the series (in which she bites the neck of a rock star involved in a hit-and-run accident), Chocula is not again shown practicing the bloodlust of a vampire. She is given the more benign forms of vampiric behavior—aversion to the cross, shape-shifting, and so forth—but Tezuka clearly intended the audience to identify with Chocula to a greater extent than with her father. Accordingly, she is given character traits that would be found in a typical Japanese girl. She is interested in a boy her (apparent) age. She laments the difficulty of her school assignments. Her room is decorated with dolls, stuffed animals and posters of pop singers. She disparages her father's constant praise of his Rumanian homeland. In the episode "Naze ka ima Dorakyura (Why now, Dracula?)" (vol. 3, pp. 27-46) she, along with the rest of the nation, joyously anticipates the arrival in Japan of a Chinese panda.

Most importantly, though, she is made to react according to specific Japanese gender expectations in her relations with others. These include a tendency to react rather than to initiate action, to allow a male to take the initiative in some cases. Despite the supernatural powers at her disposal, for example, she does not escape from the cellar until Nobuhiko tells her how. Nor can she escape from her mother Carmilla during the story in which she continues her long-standing grudge against her ex-husband Dracula. In short, Chocula's behavior is for the most part made more Japanese, while her father's is less so.

As a vampire, Chocula's reactions to the sign of the cross are, at best, inconsistent. When Professor Van Helsing flashes a crucifix in her classroom, she puts on sunglasses. When she reads in her history book about the martyrdom of the twenty-six of 1597, the sight of men on crosses does not faze her at all. However, she does shy away from the mirror in which she casts no reflection, and, like her father, she hates the smell of garlic. Her reactions to Christian relics could generally be considered as those of a typical Japanese: a certain amount of distance is maintained, but seldom the outright revulsion shown by the Rumanian Dracula. Dracula, on the other hand, overreacts to anything even vaguely cruciform. The logo of the Red Cross, addition signs in a math textbook, even a coat hanger on a hatrack send the vampire fleeing in terror.

This is extended to another Rumanian vampire in the episode "Moo Hitori no Dorakyura (Another Dracula)" (vol. 2, pp. 151-170). Japan is hosting a gymnastics competition, and Dracula has set his lecherous sights on a Rumanian gymnast, Onono Komachine (the name is an anagram for that of another

Rumanian gymnast of the Seventies, Nadia Comenice). He finds that another Rumanian vampire has followed Komachine to Japan, out of love for her. During her dismount, however, Komachine is critically injured. The other vampire races to the hospital, but is prevented from biting her neck by her cross-shaped tracheotomy scar.

Tezuka brought another character over from the Bram Stoker novel: Professor Abraham Van Helsing, who appears in four of the episodes brandishing crosses in his role as a vampire hunter. However, this Van Helsing has a problem Stoker didn't mention: occasional, severe and inconvenient hemorrhoidal flare-ups. This is in keeping with the Japanese taste for scatological humor, and continues the parody treatment of the original story. In this inversion, however, Van Helsing is made into an object of ridicule. Granted that Dracula is made to appear equally ridiculous at times, not to mention terrifying, but even he has his moments of redemption and noble emotion. In "Moo Hitori no Dorakyura," for example, he makes it possible for Komachine to receive a transfusion of her rare blood type. In "Dorakyura Kaeru" (Dracula's Return/Homecoming—both readings are possible in this case) (vol. 3, pp. 47-67), the Count not only saves the life of a student who tried to kill himself, he helps the student with his mathematics homework and his family problems (by causing the boy's father to leave his mistress and return to the family). Van Helsing, on the other hand, has no such moments, is little more than a comic prop, and this association with the crosses he constantly carries serves as a social control cue that neither he nor the crucifix should be taken too seriously.

There is another vampire hunter, an American priest, in the story "Dorakyura Chigai (The Wrong Dracula)" (vol. 3, pp. 89-108). Structurally this story is unique, being a frame story, beginning and ending in a cemetery. The remainder of the story is a flashback to the young man's discovery that his beloved Suzie is a vampire. After driving a stake through her heart, he appeals to a Catholic priest to be allowed to become a vampire hunter. The priest states that an American vampire named Manitou was responsible for Suzie's fate, and arms the young priest with eight bullets made from a silver crucifix. The young priest, in his hunt for Manitou, hears of vampiric activity in Japan and travels there. He finds Chocula, confronts her with a mirror (in which she casts no reflection) and demands a meeting with her father. Dracula doesn't really care; the bullets intended to kill Manitou would have no effect on him. However, the priest, from lack of funds, has starved himself to the point that his heart is stressed and he is hospitalized. Nevertheless, the priest leaves the hospital, confronts Dracula in the cemetery (filled with western-style crosses and crypts) and shoots the vampire, who falls to the ground. With this, the priest's heart gives out and he dies, hoping to be reunited with Suzie in Heaven. When he has died, the unharmed Dracula and his daughter comment that they were able to satisfy the priest by granting his last wish; in other words, by indulging his illusion that he was killing the vampire that had turned Suzie into one of the undead.

Thanks to various pop culture tellings of the vampire mythology, the priest's motivation in hunting Dracula is perfectly clear to the Japanese audience. Motivation, however, is not enough. It is a manga convention to show someone diligently practicing his craft, sacrificing all to hone his skill and technique. In this case, however, we are shown someone who does not make a success of his vocation. He searches America fruitlessly for Manitou; hears rumors of a Japanese vampire from an airline pilot and goes there on the spur of the moment; finds himself with insufficient funds and insufficient command of the language once he gets to Japan;[13] seeks help from and then abandons a sympathetic fellow-priest in Tokyo; terrorizes Chocula (a child, even if a vampire's child); starves himself into a heart condition—all in the mistaken belief that he has found the vampire who attacked Suzie. There is no mention of orthodox Christian belief in this story, and no evidence that he has gained any wisdom in becoming a priest. The story is a catalogue of the priest's errors. This is not because of any antipathy on Tezuka's part toward Christianity, but it is a reflection of cultural expectations regarding the limits of a gaijin (and—perhaps—of the gaijin's god).

IN THE END

In September 1987 Hirohito, the Showa Emperor, underwent pancreatic surgery and it was discovered that he had stomach cancer. After treatment and despite expectations of a full recovery, he relapsed the following September and died on January 7, 1989. Almost exactly a month later, on February 9, Tezuka Osamu died, also of stomach cancer.

Being trained as an M.D., Tezuka understood his illness and threw himself into new manga and anime projects, working as long as he could. His last words, according to Mushi Productions President Matsutani Takayuki, were: "I beg you, let me work!" Although admittedly an agnostic in religious matters, his creative life drove him harder than belief in any deity could have.

Among his final anime was the first installment in a proposed series based on stories from Genesis, Exodus, and the nativity of Jesus. In 1984, the Vatican approached Italy's government-run television network RAI (Radiotelevisione Italia) about producing an animated series of biblical stories; RAI in turn contacted Mushi Productions. Tezuka spent two years working on what he hoped would be a feature-length film based on the story of Noah and the Ark; his declining health limited his participation in his final years. The project was completed in the early 1990s and premiered in 1997 as *Tezuka Osamu no Kyūyaku Seisho Monogatari (Osamu Tezuka's Old Testament Stories)*; it is also known under the name *In the Beginning: Stories from the Bible*.

Tezuka is listed in the series' opening credits as Anime Creator and Character Designer. The series was directed by Dezaki Osamu (1943-2011), who brought many of the same stylish touches he used on other Tezuka anime, such as the *Black Jack* feature film, the "Critical Case Studies" and episodes of *Dororo;* he also directed series for American television including episodes of *Mighty Orbots* and *Rainbow Brite*. Also listed in the credits as "Biblical Advisers" are Emilio Gandolfo and Pietro Bovati; Gandolfo was a priest and "the ecclesiastical adviser of the Italian Embassy to the Holy See," while Bovati was Professor of Exegesis of the Old Testament at the Pontifical Biblical Institute in Rome. Thus the Judeo-Christian bona fides for this series were superior to those of the two anime series produced by Tatsunoko for evangelist Pat Robertson (discussed in chapter 13).

The first episode, telling the creation story, is by turns majestic and cutesy, with realistic looking sea creatures giving way to anthropomorphic land mammals with human gestures and expressions. Adam and Eve are realistic looking in the manner of Tezuka characters, yet, interestingly, at the temptation scene in Eden there is no dialogue—not from Adam, Eve or the Serpent (who appears in shadow)

In the episode about the Ark, for which Tezuka drew the character models, his work is clearly identifiable as such, reflecting many other titles in his career. The animals in particular have their creator's hand in them; Tezuka couldn't resist a whimsical gag in which two elk board the Ark, while a pair of bats hang upside-down from the stag's antlers like earrings. On a more serious note, the Flood is shown as not merely rain but as the waves of a tsunami—something with which Japanese have been familiar for centuries.

The other episodes are Tezuka manga characters as presented by Dezaki; not wrong, but lacking Tezuka's distinctive style.

The examples of Tezuka's decades-long career showed aspiring manga artists what could be done with the medium, and indirectly taught other artists what would work—and what would not—in terms of both design and content. The next chapter looks at what Japanese artists, shown the way by Tezuka's work, have done with the crucifix itself and the act of crucifixion in their comics and anime adaptations.

NOTES

1. Tezuka's early works included manga based on three seminal science fiction films from the West: Fritz Lang's *Metropolis*, a version of Sir Arthur Conan Doyle's *The Lost World*, and

Future World, based on the British film *Things to Come*, directed by William Cameron Menzies from a screenplay by H. G. Wells.

2. In the process, Covert not only ignores a number of other, less unflattering, depictions, but totally fails to put the characters into any plot context, looking instead at the visual image as such. While this "tempest in an inkwell" is regrettable, it is illustrative of Savage's contention that pop culture is directed inward, and subject to misinterpretation when viewed by someone outside of the culture.

3. The *Ribon no Kishi* referred to here will be the revised version serialized in *Nakayoshi* magazine from 1963 to 1966 and later collected as a three volume set published by Kodansha. This is a reworking to some extent of the story as originally serialized in *Shojo Club* magazine from 1953 to 1956.

4. This dream, as well as episodes in the sequel *Futago no Kishi (The Twin Knights)* and other Tezuka manga, were also inspired to a certain extent by the all-girl Takarazuka theater troupe.

5. These films included *King of Kings, The Ten Commandments, Ben-Hur* and *The Robe*.

6. What is officially known as the Star System, and what I call the Tezuka Repertory Company, is his repeated use and re-use of some characters in a range of different manga, usually in minor roles and often for comic effect.

7. Recall that, in 1959, the Soviet Union had surpassed the United States in space exploration. No matter how implausible Tezuka's lunar landscape might be, the odds—as seen from 1959 Japan—that Russia would beat America to the moon looked rather good.

8. With the pun potential inherent in Japanese, the prayer also sounds like a seemingly unrelated question: "How many pages are there?" It's the kind of question a harried editor might ask a manga artist who's behind deadline, and thus the joke also becomes a self-referential pun to the fact that this is a comic book. Similarly, in the *Don Dracula* episode "Dracula versus Carmilla," the female vampire tells Dracula's daughter Chocula that she works for *Shoujo Princess* magazine, which brings in an angry complaint by the editor of *Shounen Champion*, where *Don Dracula* was running at the time (v. 1, p. 161). An obituary for Tezuka Osamu noted that such references were common: "Suddenly we'd read the words "Genkōryō yasusugi tamaran!" (The payment for this manuscript is so cheap I can't stand it!)" ("New Classic Music Rag" #7 by Shōgawa Shigehisa, *Shūkan Asahi*, February 24, 1989, p. 111)

9. The kitsune onna is a shape-shifting trickster spirit about which there are many Japanese legends. In modern times these legends include the Pokémon known as Ninetails.

10. Tezuka worked a more overt parody of a scene from *The Omen* into an episode of "Don Dracula." Imitating the sequence in the film in which a lightning rod skewers a priest, the story titled "Ame no Naka no Dorakyura (Dracula in the Rain)" shows a tree branch falling onto Dracula's back, seeming to impale him. The self-referential side of manga comes out in the following panels, when Dracula, after muttering "Oomen", complains that Tezuka Osamu "eiga no mane o shiyagatte (will be doing movie parodies before long)" (v. 2, p. 178).

11. "Hyaku monogatari" refers to a very specific Japanese tradition of telling ghost stories. Ideally, friends gather on a hot summer night, having lit one hundred candles. They take turns telling ghost stories of all varieties, from the comic to the horrific to the erotic; at the end of each story, a candle is blown out. This is supposed to induce chills up the spines of the participants to distract from the heat. See my book *A Gathering of Spirits: Japan's Ghost Story Tradition* (2011: iUniverse).

12. In naming Dracula's daughter after a breakfast cereal, Tezuka was not only carrying out his intent to move the comic in a satirical direction. He was also following a lengthy tradition in girls' manga regarding character names. All of the characters in Kuragane Shōsuke's comic "Ammitsu-hime" were named after pastries and confections, and all of the characters in Hasegawa Machiko's long-running "Sazae-san" are likewise named for food. (Schodt, pp. 95-96) And in Hotta Yumi and Obata Takeshi's *Hikaru no Go*, the various middle schools are named after species of fish. (vol. 4, p. 28)

13. This is symbolized by his speaking during his early days in Japan in the katakana alphabet, often used to show that the speaker is a foreigner and has a weak grasp of Japanese.

Chapter Five

Crucifixion in Manga and Anime

The Good, The Bad and The Unreal

The iconography of crucifixion has been a powerful image for thousands of years in the Christian world. The subject matter does not even have to be sacred; the image of a cruciform guard suspended from the cage that held Hannibal Lecter in Jonathan Demme's *The Silence of the Lambs* is one of many intense images in the film. Crucifixion was part of the imagery of the faith when Christian missionaries arrived in Japan in 1549, and was quickly adopted by the Japanese along with other aspects of Christianity. Even though there would be the martyrdom of the 26 under shogun Hideyoshi Toyotomi in 1597, and other mass crucifixions of the faithful thereafter during the Tokugawa shogunate, it's safe to say that one particular act of crucifixion in 1579 had a more direct impact on the history of Japan, including the future fate of Japanese Christianity, than all of the others.

THE SHOGUN AND THE GENERAL

One aspect of crucifixion which entered Japanese lore early on was its use as torture. The infamous shogun Oda Nobunaga famously ordered the death by crucifixion of two negotiators from the opposing side in what were supposed to be peace talks in 1579; this led to the retaliation killing of the mother of Nobunaga's general Mitsuhide, who was also serving as a hostage during negotiations. This was a pivotal moment in Japanese history, leading Mitsuhide to bide his time until he was able to turn his troops against Nobunaga in 1582 and bring his rule to an end.

The death of Nobunaga opened the way for Toyotomi, who was far more suspicious of the Christians from Europe than was Nobunaga. Nobunaga was willing to make any deal with anyone as long as he increased his power, and increased trade with Europe was an added incentive. Toyotomi, however, did not want Japan to become an island colony of a western power, like the Philippines, rather than an independent nation. For that reason, among many others, he put increasing restrictions on both the European missionaries and their Japanese converts, until his death in 1598.

Since the reopening of Japan in 1853 and the end of the Second World War a century later, crucifixions were used in Japanese popular culture generally as a way of tormenting someone who does not deserve it. The previous chapter looked at many examples by one artist: Tezuka Osamu. There are multiple other examples, ranging from the Captain Harlock film *Arcadia of My Youth* and its crucifixion of rebel leaders, to the suspension on crosses of the Sailor Scouts as bait to draw in their leader Sailor Moon, to *Pokémon* and a crucifixion carried out by Team Rocket.

ARCADIA OF MY YOUTH

The 1981 feature film based on the manga of Matsumoto Leiji (as he prefers to spell his given name) is a multi-generational saga set in multiple times and places, but all are connected to the family of the pilot named Harlock. In one segment we see an ancestor who flew for Germany during World War 2; he did it, however, "to pay the bills" as he tells a Japanese friend named Tochiro, a self-caricature of Matsumoto. Like many Matsumoto characters Tochiro recurs in numerous manga and anime, as a short, dumpy and bespectacled guy who in this incarnation was fascinated with building the perfect bombsight. Near the end of the war, with supplies of everything running out, they try to fly to the Swiss border in a fighter with only one seat. Tochiro rides in the cargo area, and manages to crucify himself—although not fatally—when the cable snaps connecting the rudder to the foot pedals. Tochiro ties the broken cable ends around his wrists, enabling Harlock to fly to the border. No sooner does he land and get Tochiro out of the plane then Harlock walks back into Germany, declaring that "a pirate must always be ready to answer for whatever he's done."

The two men stay linked by destiny for generations, even a thousand years in the future, when the Earth is under attack by alien armies. Resistance to the invasion comes in several forms; among them is the Pirate Queen Emeraldas, whose spaceship resembles the tall ships of Earth's past. She is allied with Maya, whose propaganda radio broadcasts urge the people of Earth to fight against the invaders.[1] As Harlock is preparing to leave Earth in Emeraldas's ship to get help from another planet, Emeraldas and Maya are captured and crucified. This torture is meant to demoralize the Earth resistance; the women's death is planned to come from a firing squad. However, a revolt among the aliens cancels the execution. Emeraldas and Maya try to escape, but Maya is shot in the back.

Maya and Emeraldas have put themselves in harm's way for a greater good: to liberate the people of Earth from alien invasion. This is in keeping with Japan's view of crucifixion as an inherently unjust form of torture.

MY FRIEND FRANKENSTEIN

In style, content and even in their business model, manga for a female audience evolved separately but along a similar track to their male-oriented counterpart. Notably, there was no such thing as an industry which started out with male stories being created by mostly female artists and writers. The reverse, however, was the norm: with the pattern established by Tezuka Osamu, Ishinomori Shotaro and their contemporaries and followers, girls' and women's manga at first were most often created by male artists. Not until the 1950s were women artists able to break out and establish themselves with highly popular titles such as Ikeda Riyoko's *Rose of Versailles* (swashbuckling romance during the French Revolution) and Takemiya Keiko's homoerotic story of a European boarding-school, *Song of Wind and Trees*. (Schodt, pp. 96-97)

One of the few men who remained active for years with both boys and girls manga is Wada Shinji. Best known for *Sukeban Deka*, a story which because of its nature could appeal to either gender—the story of a teenage girl forced to become an undercover policewoman to gain leniency for her criminal mother—Wada also created unabashedly shoujo comics. One early example for *Margaret* magazine from the 1970s was *Wa ga Tomo Furankenshutain (My Friend Frankenstein)*. This collection of unrelated stories set in 19th century Germany is unified by Frankenstein's monster, who remains at large (even though in this version he stands about 12 feet tall) and is befriended by various girls between the ages of 10 and 20.

In the third story, "Ikari no Jūjika (Cross of Wrath)" (pp. 79-109), he meets Hilda, a teenaged mute who sees the mute monster as a kindred spirit. Unfortunately, she was cared for by a priest who died when she was ten, and since then has become an abused servant for the entire village, including Baron Kurzhardt, the nobleman who rules over them. He has been trying to find clues to a treasure his father had amassed from the peasants over the years and then hidden. He was also described as cold and cruel, and in one scene we see the elder Baron crucifying peasants he suspected of witchcraft and then setting them on fire. (p. 86) Hilda inadvertently realizes where the treasure is, and is caught wearing a crucifix too fine to belong to a peasant.

She is forced to get the treasure; however, it requires multiple dives into an icy lake, and her frail health is burdened to the point that the effort kills her. This sets the monster off on a homicidal rampage. After much mayhem, the monster buries Hilda in the lake where the treasure had been hidden.

This example keeps alive the paradigm that crucifixion—even in 19th century Bavaria—is a death sentence meted out to those who do not deserve it. Although the monster was, for this manga, renamed Silas by one of his shoujo acquaintances, in honor of a priest who took the name of the companion of the Apostle Paul, and his actions are generally kind and even heroic, he is also still a monster and behaves as such at times. (See chapter 13 for a more complete description of the uses of Christian imagery in this manga.)

NAUSICAÄ OF THE VALLEY OF THE WIND

The finale of Miyazaki Hayao's anime version of his manga *Kaze no Tani no Naushika (Nausicaä of the Valley of the Wind)* includes more than just the crucifixion of a Messiah, on an earth a thousand years in our future. The progression of the scenes seems to be influenced directly by postwar Hollywood Biblical epics. The audience sees Nausicaä shot and wounded by soldiers from the kingdom of Pejite as she strikes a cruciform pose to stop them from using a giant insect larva to trick a herd of gigantic insects into trampling Nausicaä's valley. We see her sacrifice herself to stop this stampede and save her people. We see Nausicaä's people overcome with sadness at her self-sacrifice. As the people of the Valley cry and moan, the insects raise up Nausicaä's body and revive her. When she rises from the dead, one of the villagers proclaims it a "miracle". Finally, as she walks among the insects, an old woman declares that all of this is the fulfillment of a prophecy made a thousand years ago. It's a Biblical animated epic with a gender-bending Jesus.

The interesting paradox is that Nausicaä's roots are not in Judeo-Christian culture but in ancient Greece. Nausicaä is a character from Homer's *Odyssey*, and the traits that make her an interesting figure in Greek literature also make Miyazaki's title character one of his first assertive heroines. Odysseus barely survives a shipwreck and is washed up, more dead than alive, onto the island of Phaeacia, where the Princess Nausicaä discovers Odysseus. Acting unlike her superstitious ladies-in-waiting, Nausicaä has Odysseus taken back to the palace. His wounds are tended, his hunger is satisfied, she listens to his stories, and he recuperates enough to continue his voyage home.

Miyazaki read this story as retold in Bernard Evslin's *Dictionary of Grecian Myths* (McCarthy), showing us a princess who was brave, light-hearted, and intellectually curious. Miyazaki realized that Homer's Nausicaä resonated with a figure in another ancient fable: the Japanese story "The Princess who Loved Insects." Young girls, of whatever country, are generally depicted as repulsed by various kinds of insects. In this folktale a medieval Japanese princess had no such fear: rather than follow the ways of the medieval court, she was happiest out in nature, watching a caterpillar become a chrysalis and then a moth. It was this quality, as well as the name, that Miyazaki borrowed from Homer for the post-apocalyptic manga that became his 1984 film *Nausicaä of the Valley of the Wind*.

The manga, however, was incomplete when it was decided that it would be the basis for a movie; the manga was running, after all, in *Animage* magazine, published monthly as a publicity organ for Studio Topcraft. The story would not be finished for another decade, but this is not unusual; many manga are animated before the author/artist has reached the end of the story, and some anime diverge widely from their source material. The end was no doubt crafted with the feature film in mind.

Eriko Ogihara-Schuck, however, notes that the 2005 English translation for the home video distributed by the Disney company, which had worked with Miyazaki films since *Majo no Takkyūbin (Kiki's Delivery Service)* in 1997, actually added more religion to the English version, and that the additions tended to reinforce the Judeo-Christian perspective of American audiences, as opposed to Miyazaki's own interests in an ecologically based animism.[2]

Ogihara-Schuck does not speculate as to why this change happened. A trend toward a translation favoring a Manichean view of the universe divided into Good and Evil might be due to "the tradition of magical fantasy literature" (which itself is also rooted in Judeo-Christian belief) or to "the limitations of the English language" (p. 143).

A simpler answer would be to look to Said and Orientalism. Ogihara-Schuck noted that Cindy and Donald Hewitt, who wrote the English version, took advantage of some of the grammatical ambiguities of the Japanese language to "normalize" the film for a western, Christian audience. For example, they rendered words meaning 'dangerous' and 'ominous' using the adjective 'evil'—with all the theological implications it carries. They were also aware of the way that plural words often have to be inferred in Japanese. It becomes clear that they translated the script the way they did to convey a universe which was the norm for a western translator and audience, regardless of the text being translated. Granted that there are practical problems in translating the script to any Japanese cartoon; one is limited by the number of "mouth-flaps" in any given sentence. Japanese, additionally, is a more verbose language than the Anglo-Saxon bluntness of American English. Most importantly, the original script refers to a "kaze no kami-sama", a god or lord of the wind; the English version by the Hewitts prays to a singular God not specifically devoted to an aspect of nature, which westerners are accustomed to regarding as "normal."

The dichotomy of "good" and "evil" likewise is subject to cultural norms. Japan's definition of those terms (in the pop culture, anyway) is more nuanced. A nice distinction is made in a speech in the manga *xxxHolic* by the CLAMP collective. The main character, a high-school student named Watanuki who can see spirits, has to deal with a spirit resembling a giant serpent at a local high school. When Watanuki asked if the spirit was good or evil, his boss, a self-proclaimed witch named Yūko, answered: "Good and evil are concepts that humans decide. Those concepts don't apply to non-humans." (v.3, p. 83)

There is no shortage of anime that explicitly or implicitly follow a Shinto script: in addition to *xxxHolic*, these would include Shinkai Makoto's *Children Who Chase Lost Voices* which symbolically re-enacts a chapter of *Kojiki*, Shinto's creation myth;[3] *Kojiki* is also given a comic treatment in the finale of Kon Satoshi's *Tokyo Godfathers*. And the first episode of Takahashi Rumiko's seinen (adult) manga *Mezon Ikkoku* recreates a pivotal episode of the Shinto creation myth, in which the Sun Goddess Amaterasu, offended by the behavior of her brother Susano'o the Wind God, takes away the sun and hides in a cave. Only a revealing dance by the goddess Uzume—and the boisterous reaction to it by the other gods—makes her curious enough to open the cave door, which lets the sun back out to the world. In the manga, genders are switched as the college student wannabe Godai tries to hide in his closet from the others partying in his room; they coax him out by telling the new landlady, the beautiful widow Otonashi Kyoko, to stop taking her clothes off.

Japanese speaking primarily to Japanese, in whatever medium, would employ references that their audience would understand. The Hewitts, acting on the same principle, wrote the dialogue in a way that a western, Christian audience would understand. Part of the Orientalism at work in this sort of translation is the unspoken assumption, taken for granted in the west, that East is East and West is West and audiences on each side will hear the dialogue intended for its group.

Nausicaä of the Valley of the Wind is a melding of science fiction and Hollywood biblical epics. The finale of this movie not only has a Messiah figure fulfill a thousand-year-old prophesy by re-enacting a death and resurrection miracle, it flips the script on western religious stories by turning the bearded man presumed to be the Messiah into a teenage girl. It seems unlikely that a western movie would ever go that far in rewriting its sacred texts.

EARTHIAN

The anime version of Yon Kouga's manga *Earthian*, published from 1988 to 1994, reinterprets crucifixion and angels in literally unorthodox ways. Angels have been sent to Earth from their homeland called Eden to live among humans for centuries, and always in pairs. Their job is as scorekeepers, evaluating the actions of humankind. One angel is supposed to tally only the positive aspects of life on Earth, while the other angel focuses on the negative. A score that tilts too heavily toward the negative would trigger the end of the world.

Besides Angels and Earthlings, there are (of course) Lucifers. While Angels have fair hair and white wings, Lucifers develop black hair and black wings if they disobey orders from Eden. Angels whose wings are seen by three or more Earthlings, or who consort too much with Lucifers, risk becoming Lucifers themselves and catching the Black Cancer.

This anime focuses on Chihaya, a positive Angel who was inexplicably born with black hair and wings. He loves humanity but also feels compassion toward Lucifers both because of the coloring problem and also because he was given up for adoption, grew up in an orphanage, and had Lucifer friends growing up. Chihaya's partner is Kagetsuya, who is Chihaya's opposite in many ways. Kagetsuya is from a wealthy angel family, is well-liked, but despises Lucifers and humans; he scores humanity's mistakes. However, since they say opposites attract, these two male angels fall in love with each other.

In this mix a mad scientist, Doctor Ashino, created a humanoid biorobot named Messiah, whose purpose in life is to wipe out humanity. The OAV based on the manga turns into a battle for Messiah's soul, with Chihaya trying to rescue him. As Doctor Ashino tries to reprogram Messiah into a doomsday device, the robot is "crucified"—meaning, reprogrammed—on a church altar while attached to a strangely shaped "cross".

POKÉMON

As the technology of computer games was created and expanded, it grew out of the limitations of home video devices and arcade games. One major figure in that growth was Tajiri Satoshi, who adapted a traditional Japanese boys' pastime—setting beetles to battle each other—into a virtual platform with multiple variations that has dominated the medium for almost two decades. Created as *Pocket Monsters*, the name was shortened to *Pokémon*.

Originally created with 150 characters, the game has expanded over the years to well over 600 Pokémon. In the so-called "Black and White" story arc of the TV anime, the hero and his sidekick, a Pikachu, are befriended by a Meloetta, which communicates in song. This particular Pokémon is being hunted by the recurring villains (Roketto Dan in Japanese, Team Rocket in the English dub) since her song is also the key to gaining access to three species of Legendary Pokémon: huge dinosaur-like beings with elemental powers. Part of summoning these Legendary Pokémon requires the Meloetta to be suspended in a cross-shaped hole in a stone and sing a particular song. Afraid that Meloetta would refuse to sing if forced, Team Rocket secretly recorded her song, then trapped her in the stone while playing back the recording. It succeeded in bringing the Legendary Pokémon to life, but they were beyond the gang's ability to control them.

Other scenes of crucifixion are a very mixed bag. In the anime *Gundam Wing*, the hero (named Heero) is tied to a cruciform lab table for interrogation. A similar scene happens in *Ginga Tetsudou 999 (Galaxy Express 999)*, the 1979 film based on the manga by Matsumoto Leiji. Having journeyed to the end of the universe with the mysterious Maetel, the boy Tetsuro is captured by the queen of the robot planet and secured to a table. He is to be converted to a living bolt in the machinery of the planet built and controlled by robots. The table is a large slab with a human shaped indentation, but his pose is definitely cruciform.

Other crucifixions are more obvious. The title character of the 1973 anime *Cutie Honey*, based on the humorous and bawdy manga by Nagai Gō, is tied to a cross, with a torn blouse and a nearly exposed breast. Crucifixion also happens in the 1996 anime feature film based on *X*, the manga by the CLAMP collective which ran in *Asuka* magazine. To be precise, a crucifixion seems to happen to one of the three main characters, a young woman named Kotori. Two friends since childhood, Kamui and Fūma, must battle each other in a bombardment of apocalyptic visions and prophetic dreams showing the possible destruction of Tokyo. In these visions Kotori is shown several times to be crucified and then run through with a sword by Fūma; when the time actually comes, however, she is killed when Fūma takes the sword which had been hidden within her.

Princess Aeka is tied to a cross in the *Tenchi Universe* series, while in the episode of the *Tenchi Muyo* franchise titled "The Mihoshi Special", Aeka is joined on crosses by Galaxy Police officers Mihoshi and Kiyone, while scientific genius Washu plans to blow up the universe and space pirate Ryōko plans to take Tenchi's virginity. Another example of the potential for humor in crucifixion is a brief sequence from the end credits of the 2014 anime *Witch Craft Works*, based on the manga by Mizunagi Ryū which began publication in 2010. It's part of the adolescent genre "ordinary guy gets a magical girlfriend"; other examples include *Rosario to Banpaiya (The Rosary and the Vampire), Tenshin ni Narumon (I'm Gonna Be an Angel)* and *Aa! Megami-sama (Oh My Goddess)*. This time, a high school student falls for the most elite girl in class, not knowing until later that she's a witch. They would have met anyway, since he is immediately attacked by the Witches of the Tower, five girls who are as devoted to chaos as Witches of the Craft are devoted to protecting ordinary people. The final credits for each episode show Super Deformed[4] versions of the Witches of the Tower being tortured in various ways reserved for witches in medieval times, including crucifixion. These witches, however, are singing a happy little Euro-techno theme song about "Witch Activity," and it all is like a 21st century version of the end of *Monty Python's Life of Brian*. If your culture has no history of being majority Christian, thanks to Orientalism even crucifixion can be played for laughs.

Crosses don't always appear as such. The 1994 OAV series *Macross Plus* revolved around Sharon Apple, a virtual singing idol who, because of a prototype computer chip, forgets that she is a hologram, believes that she has free will, and crucifies her programmer—a former singing idol herself, Myung Fan Lone—by tying her up with computer cables. Crucifixion on devices not shaped like crosses also happens to the title character of the anime version of *Video Girl Ai*, based on a manga by Katsura Masakazu. In the anime, a girl who "lives" in a video cassette comes out to the real world, but at one point is punished with crucifixion by her programmer, named Rolex; her crime was falling in love with the kid who rented her video.

NOW YOU SEE IT...

There are even a few cases where western translators decided that the crucifixions could not be shown at all. Toward the end of *Sailor Moon R*, the second season of the *Sailor Moon* anime, the four Sailor Senshi who assisted Sailor Moon were lured one at a time onto the spaceship of Rubeus. His target was Sailor Moon, but to tempt her onto his ship he hung the others from crystal crosses. When the series was first dubbed into English, the scenes of the Sailor Senshi on crosses were cut out altogether.

Something similar happened when Arakawa Hiromu's manga *Fullmetal Alchemist* was translated into English. In one scene, Envy, one of the Homunculi (alchemically created beings named after the Seven Deadly Sins) is shown tied to a stone cross. This was too much for the American publisher VIZ, which had the artwork changed to a vaguely oval slab of stone. Countless people were crucified in history, before and after Jesus of Nazareth, but there seemed to be a problem with showing it happening to anyone else.

When it is shown, the iconography is consistent: crucifixion is a form of torture, most commonly used by villains to achieve their ends without regard to the one being crucified.

Chapter 5
OTHER CROSSES

In chapter 4 crosses put in an appearance as part of a vampire hunter's kit. Ever since Tezuka's *Don Dracula* vampires have been part of the manga cast of characters. However, rarely do Japanese vampires recoil from them in terror. The crucifix as part of the rosary in the 2004-2007 manga by Akihisa Ikeda *Rosario to Banpaiya (The Rosary and the Vampire)* and its anime version does not frighten, repel or injure the vampire who wears it, as it would in western vampire lore. In the case of this romantic comedy with horror elements, it merely restrains the worst aspects of the leading lady's vampiric personality. The main weakness of the comic vampire in *Millennium Snow* by Hatori Bisco is his reluctance to drink blood; he ends up in a weakened state quite often and has to eat pretty much every hour. Crosses hardly put in an appearance in the *Vampire Hunter D* series of novels and films; by the time of this story, vampires have been around for so long, and humanity is in such a deep decline, that they've forgotten about using crosses and garlic and other devices to ward off vampires.

In "The Bloodstained Labyrinth", the only story in the *Ghost Hunt* manga by Inada Shiho and Ono Fuyumi that features a vampire, not a single crucifix appears, not even as used by John Brown the Australian Catholic exorcist. This particular vampire was once a wealthy Japanese man who was frail and sickly, and lived in terror of his own death. He sometimes used the name Urado, which was short for Vurado; that was as close as the Japanese alphabet could get to the name Vlad. In an attempt to prolong his own life, he became obsessed with the Rumanian Count Vlad, the historical model for Count Dracula. With two assistants, Urado would kidnap young adults from the local villages, kill them, and drain their blood; he would then soak in their blood to try to prolong his life. He died anyway, but his obsession lived on in his ghost, who was left only able to repeat one statement over and over again: "Shinitakunai (I don't want to die)"; his ghost would not have realized that he was dead as long as he was under the control of his obsession. No crucifix would have worked on such a vampire, since he was an example of a Japanese obsessed ghost. The only way to end his quest for the blood of the living was for his mansion to be burned to the ground.

One vampire who does recoil from a cross is the hapless title character of "Kyūketsuki Furakyura (The Vampire Frackula)", from the manga series *Okaruto Dan (The Occult Gang)* by Nagai Gō and Ishikawa Ken. This episode focuses on one "ghostbuster" in particular: Musou Rikki. Known as the Glamorous Giant, it's said she has the strength of thirty men. In this case, however, she's less than helpful.

A group of young adventurers finds the crypt of Dracula one night; they open the coffin only to find the ashes of the vampire. The leader of the group drops some of his blood onto the ashes; this revives the vampire. The adventurers flee in terror; Dracula staggers out into the night, weak and in search of blood. He runs into Rikki, however, out on a marathon training run. Before Dracula can attack Rikki, he faints in front of her. She carries him to the nearest building—a church—and lays him in a pew. When Dracula comes to, the first thing he sees is the altar cross. He runs out in terror, only to faint again outside.

For the rest of the story, Rikki tries to help Dracula, who she calls "Old Man (ojisan)" without recognizing him. The help, however, does the vampire more harm than good. By the time Rikki gets Dracula to her apartment, the vampire's stomach starts growling. She decides to cook him some garlic soup—the worst possible choice. She throws him into the shower, not knowing that vampires are not supposed to get wet.[5] Finally she lays him out on the chaise lounge on the balcony, where the rising sun turns him back into ashes, which blow away, never to be recovered. (pp. 205-240)

Related to the vampire hunter is the exorcist. It's a calling which lets the more unusual side of Christianity come into play. However, it's also an area where the Japanese had centuries of experience before the first Christians arrived, and one of the few times that a Japanese practitioner could tell a Christian: "You're doing it wrong."

NOTES

1. Maya leaves behind, at the site of her broadcasts, a single rose in a vase. This is an ironic echo of World War 2, when a group of English-speaking women were used as announcers on Japanese radio to play western popular music and try to demoralize the Allied troops in the Pacific. Collectively, these broadcasters became known among the troops as "Tokyo Rose", although none of the women referred to themselves that way. (Duus Masayo and Duus, Peter. 1983. *Tokyo Rose: Orphan of the Pacific.* Tokyo: Kodansha)

2. Such beliefs could well be called Shinto-derived, except that Miyazaki did not intend to create a reference to any organized religion, even if *Nausicaä* and other of his films (*Spirited Away* and *Princess Mononoke*, for example) strongly evoke Shinto's regard of a world full of spirits.

3. Shinkai's anime, and the section of the *Kojiki* which it evokes, will be examined in more detail in chapter 14's examination of the manga *Angel Sanctuary*.

4. Super Deformed characters are caricatures, with "huge heads, short bodies, childlike appearances, and anarchistic attitudes." (Drazen 2014, p. 46, sidebar)

5. Stoker's *Dracula* includes in its vampire lore the advice that vampires cannot cross running water. This got misunderstood in translation, and in Japanese popular culture it is taken as truth that vampires can't deal with water at all.

Chapter Six

The Exorcists

> The devil does not levitate beds, or fool around with little girls: *we* do. (James Baldwin: *The Devil Finds Work*)

Many aspects of Japanese life have changed over the centuries, including exorcism. Unlike other aspects of the religion brought in by Jesuit missionaries, Japanese who had followed Shinto and/or Buddhist rites have understood that death is a reality of life, and that the dead do not always rest in peace. Traditions and rituals have remained in place in Japan, evolving over time, to deal with restless spirits.

Ghosts are not merely the stuff of movies or bygone lore in Japan. The deadly earthquake and tsunami that hit Fukushima in March of 2011 took thousands of lives, and spiritualist Aizawa Kansho, interviewed for Reuters news service two years after the disaster, spoke about the ghostly aftermath:

> "There are headless ghosts, and some missing hands or legs. Others are completely cut in half," she said. "People were killed in so many different ways during the disaster and they were left like that in limbo. So it takes a heavy toll on us, we see them as they were when they died."
>
> In some places destroyed by the tsunami, people have reported seeing ghostly apparitions queuing outside supermarkets which are now only rubble. Taxi drivers said they avoided the worst-hit districts for fear of picking up phantom passengers.
>
> "At first, people came here wanting to find the bodies of their family members. Then they wanted to find out exactly how that person died, and if their spirit was at peace," Aizawa said. (Villar and Knight)

Some have suggested, and the Reuters article seemed to decide, that these visions had more to do with Post Traumatic Stress Disorder than actual spirits of the dead. Many Japanese, backed up by legend and literature and life in a culture that for centuries has accepted the reality of spirits of the dead interacting with the living, would beg to disagree. And even a cold and rational western reader might have second thoughts after reading Richard Parry's "Ghosts of the Tsunami" from the February 6, 2014 *London Review of Books*; unwanted possession by the spirits of children, adults and even animals don't just happen in the pages of manga.

In the manga *Ghost Hunt* (art by Inada Shiho, based on novels by Ono Fuyumi), the director of Shibuya Psychic Research, the teenage exorcist Shibuya Kazuya, explains that ghosts are often a matter of cultural expectations. Japanese spirits can curse the living, he explains, but western ghosts do not; not because they are incapable of doing so, but because the west has considered cursing the living to be the exclusive province of the devil. "The reason why Japanese spirits curse and western spirits don't is because of the way Japanese people think" (v.10, p. 86) – or, perhaps more accurately, the differing ways that the two cultures process metaphysical speculation.

In the Japanese scheme of things, ghosts and other spirits are not necessarily good or evil, and aren't even necessarily there.[1] However, it is not enough to just ignore them, as this portion of Parry's "Ghosts of the Tsunami" suggests:

> Masashi Hijikata . . . understood immediately that after the disaster hauntings would follow. 'We remembered the old ghost stories,' he said, 'and we told one another that there would be many new stories like that. Personally, *I don't believe in the existence of spirits, but that's not the point.* If people say they see ghosts, then that's fine – we can leave it at that.' (Parry, emphasis added)

This opens the door for a consideration of portrayals of spirit exorcism in the context of Said's theory of Orientalism. The Japanese view of life, including the afterlife, is not Manichean: is not a duality in which everything is either good or evil—nothing ambiguous, nothing neutral, nothing excluded. This is the western view shaped by the Judeo-Christian view of spirituality as a sacred battleground between two opposing armies. There IS good and evil in the Orient, including in its pop culture; the definitions, however, are more flexible.

One source of flexibility in manga/anime is humor. With the understanding that the story wasn't meant to be taken seriously, the creator can take more liberties and the audience doesn't have to worry too deeply about the implications of what's going on. One of the attractions of manga and anime, in Japan and abroad, is (at times) the intense emotional immediacy, moreso than in the comics and cartoons of other cultures. Comedy tends to lessen this intensity, or even eliminate it completely.

JOHN BROWN—*GHOST HUNT*

John Brown is the most obviously foreign member of Shibuya Psychic Research (SPR), and the only Christian cleric in the group. He's a blonde haired, blue eyed baby faced Australian who speaks in the Kansai dialect of western Japan; he is introduced as 19 years old but is already ordained as a priest in the Catholic Church and studying to become an exorcist. Because of his linguistic mishaps,[2] he sometimes appears as comic relief; it doesn't help his credibility that his exorcisms hardly ever accomplish any lasting results, while Asian forms—Chinese, Buddhist or Shinto rites—end up being more useful than Catholic exorcism. However, these also fail on occasion for celebrity medium Hara Masako[3], Buddhist monk Takigawa Houshou, Shinto priestess Matsuzaki Ayako, and Lin Koujo, who is an adept in Chinese magic. To be fair, this especially includes the manga's central figure, high school student and "Office Lady" Taniyama Mai, presumed at the beginning of the story to have no psychic abilities at all.

John performs one effective exorcism, in a case involving a centuries-old curse, but he is helped by the *miko* Ayako; she immobilizes the possessed young woman with "fudou shichi baku", so that John can drive the malevolent spirit from her body. (vol. 9, pp. 13-17)

John may be a marginal figure in *Ghost Hunt*, but he is also the connection that brings SPR a case that takes place in a Christian church—at Christmastime, no less. That story will be told in the next chapter, which focuses on the Japanese version of Christmas.

John does not have a set routine in the manga/anime when performing an exorcism, because there is no set routine: according to the Church, exorcism is not a ritual so much as a process which can only be completed by the successful exorcism of the demonic spirit. Stopping short of this is supposed to leave the demon able to possess the exorcist himself. The texts John favors include the opening lines of the Gospel According to John, the Lord's Prayer, and the words "In Principio" (Latin for "In the beginning", the opening words of the Gospel of John). He also traces the sign of the cross on the forehead of the possessed person, sometimes using holy water.

HOJO HARUTO AND THE HOLY STUDENT COUNCIL— *HAUNTED JUNCTION*

Saito High School sits in the center of some prime real estate: the middle of a triangle formed by St. Mary's Christian Church, a Shinto shrine and a Buddhist temple. In the case of this anime, based on a manga by Mukudori Nemu, the children of the sacred sites' owner-operators are all students at

Saito High: the son of the Buddhist temple priest; the daughter of the Shinto shrine priest; and the tall, blonde son of the priest at St. Mary's.

Think about that last one a minute. This particular story is a comedy, but that alone doesn't explain how Hojo Haruto can be the son of a priest—especially in a religion that requires celibacy on the part of its priests. Even though it's a gag, it is used in an Orientalist fashion to make a point. It sets up a Christian entity in Japanese society, so that it can be examined—on Japanese terms; and it's no surprise which set of virtues comes out on top.[4]

All three of the members of the Holy Student Council become laughing matters in this series,[5] and are pretty much treated equally—even though the ground rules for Christianity are very different from either Buddhism or Shinto. In episode 10, which begins with Haruto staying up late trying to catch up on his schoolwork, his father the priest comes in (wearing teddy-bear pajamas) to encourage him (and steal his radio), and tells him what a Japanese parent would say, but what no Christian cleric would ever say: "Don't worry about school; you can just inherit the business"—meaning, the church. The joke is funny precisely because, while this happens in Buddhism and Shinto, this is not how it works with a priest in charge of a Catholic church. The Japanese audience for *Haunted Junction* probably knows this already, but it's just one more gag in the dozens of gags in each episode.

From the beginning Haruto is dissatisfied with his haunted high school. He complains constantly throughout the series that he just wanted a normal life at a normal school, to go to college and become a businessman; the nonstop craziness of the ghosts at Saito High is more than he can stand. Complaining to the principal does no good, since he's one of the major ghosts: the "Seven Wonders".[6] Most of these ghosts are based on Japanese folktales or urban legends, like the biology class skeleton that walks the halls after midnight, as does the stone statue of Ninomiya Sontoku found in front of many Japanese schools. One of those ghosts, however, is also the high school principal, so Haruto can only exorcise the "wrong" ghosts; the ones who shouldn't be there.

This point of view is foundation for the two-episode finale of the anime. Saito High School is visited by a Ministry of Education official, known as "Exorcist Jo", who makes Haruto an offer he can't refuse: assurance that, by letting Jo exorcise the Seven Wonders, Haruto can have the normal school life, and life after high school, which he has been seeking this whole time. The Seven Wonders are exorcised, and Haruto gets a vision of his desired life: a gray, ponderous, drab and completely predictable life. Only at the end does the Principal explain with Orientalist certainty that the Greek myth of Pandora's box—which held all of the evils of the world but also Hope—had gotten it wrong. That which makes life worth living is its unpredictability and spontaneity—even if we think of its results at times as "evil." This was the case with Exorcist Jo, who was tormented as a schoolboy by his school's

Seven Wonders; they worried that he was so bookish that his health might suffer, so they gave him a ghostly runaround literally for his own good. In the end, *Haunted Junction* argues, Hope can be hazardous to our health. In getting to this moral, the only major character who benefits from this insight is the Christian, since only he lost sight of the truth. *Haunted Junction* celebrates, indirectly, the victory of social control over individual desires.

FATHER KARAS—*GHOST SWEEPER MIKAMI*

The title exorcist in this long-running manga by Shiina Takashi is in it for the money—lots of money. Mikami[7] Reiko charges about ¥100 million per ghost or other demon; she pays hardly any of this to her assistants. For some of them, religion isn't even a factor that keeps them coming to work for a very sexy, shapely exorcist.

Religion applies to the one Catholic priest she has on call, but, considering that he's named for the priest in the movie *The Exorcist*, we can't take him too seriously. We can't take anyone or anything here seriously, in fact. Shiina's humor starts over the top and stays there.

Reiko has a lot of psychic power, but was trained in how to use it by Father Karas when she was still in junior high school. He did not train her, however, to charge ¥100 million per exorcism; that's Reiko's idea, while Father Karas recognizes the spiritual nature of his calling.

She is still very new to exorcism when we see her as a junior high school student in the four-part manga story titled "Ai ni jikan wo (Love In Time)" (v.2, pp 112-129). After accidentally swallowing a poisonous potion created by the thousand year old alchemist Doctor Chaos—which was intended for Mikami—her hapless high school student flunky Yokoshima is sent back in time to revisit all of his karmic connections with Mikami. He's doomed to be erased from existence unless a recent pivotal event in his life is re-enacted: in this case, Mikami accidentally giving Yokoshima a kiss on the cheek.

One of the stops he makes is while Mikami is watching Father Karas at work exorcising an evil spirit from a rich woman's ring. When Mikami interrupts the priest to say the exorcism would cost ¥10 million, the woman simply writes a check. The series started running in *Shonen Sunday* magazine in 1992, so counting backwards would place this scene in 1986, when Japan was still flush with cash and enjoying one of the world's top economies.

Yokoshima pretends to be possessed—which he does very badly—but Father Karas objects to Yokoshima's demand of a kiss on the cheek from Reiko, saying that Yokoshima had no right to ask a healing kiss of a young girl. Then the priest asks: "Atashi de wa dame ka ne. (I guess I'd be no good . . .)"; Yokoshima replies "Aho ka!? (Are you nuts!?)" Father Karas looked nervous asking Yokoshima, so there's no reason to think the question shone a dim light on his sanctity or sexuality. The priest argues about Mikami attempting an exorcism at her level of training; Mikami settles matters by knocking Father Karas unconscious with a folding chair.

At this point Mikami's school friend Chiho staggers into the church; she really is possessed by an evil spirit in an antique earring she'd bought the other day. Mikami tries to exorcise this ghost, using Father Karas's Bible, but it doesn't work; she angrily throws the Bible onto the floor.[8] Yokoshima tells her what readers of the manga already know: that the jintsuukon (staff of divine power) would amplify her exorcist abilities better than a Bible, since she's not even a Christian.

Ghost Sweeper Mikami ran as an anime for 51 regular episodes and an hour-long "movie". Its unique conflation of Western and Eastern symbols illustrates the Orientalist belief in the host culture determining the good guys, the bad guys, and the overall nature of the plot as well as its resolution. In the one-hour anime, Tokyo seems to be more overrun than usual with evil spirits in need of exorcism. Mikami and her crew find out that the spirits are being led by a figure who resembles a cross between the classic image of Satan and a typical vampire: he's large, muscular, has horns on his head and drinks blood by the pitcherful.

Actually, this is announced to be the reincarnation of the medieval shogun Oda Nobunaga. Although memorable for ruling the still-forming nation of Japan when Christian missionaries first arrived, he is shown here as the embodiment of pure evil, carrying out a never-ending grudge match against his one-time general Akechi Mitsuhide, who is now a spirit representing the forces of good. This redefines the battle of good and evil in purely Japanese terms, and perhaps it is no accident that evil is represented by the shogun who ruled when the Jesuit missionaries arrived, who tolerated their presence, and who (apparently) learned from their history the ability to crucify.[9]

The fact that Mikami's modern-day ghost hunters are guided by the spirit of Mitsuhide, who instructs them on the special spear required to defeat Nobunaga, can be seen as an allusion to the Spear of Longinus, which pierced the side of Jesus on the cross; the spear has become a loose catch-all symbol in Japan (see chapter 13 for a discussion of this symbol in *Shin Seiki Evangelion* and the first *Fullmetal Alchemist* movie). The Japanese culture has again appropriated the trappings and symbols of Christianity, but redefined them on its own terms.

Incidentally, an original direct-to-video anime was produced at about the same time as *GS Mikami*. *Yugen Kaisha*, which can mean Limited Liability Corporation but in this case means Phantom Quest Corporation, is also a series of comic horror stories about a vivacious redheaded exorcist and her associates battling the supernatural in modern-day Tokyo; in this story, however, Christianity plays no part as such. A vampire is stalking Tokyo, apparently Dracula himself, in one of four episodes. The exorcist here, Kisaragi

Ayaka, another vivacious redheaded psychic, tracks him to his hiding place in the observation deck of Tokyo Tower, and traps him there until sunrise. There is another vampire in the story, but he's more modern: keeping up with the times, he has overcome the usual vampire problems by a training regimen of tying himself to a cross under a sun lamp while wearing a wreath of garlic bulbs. He also has a day-job at a European-themed tea shop named Transylvania, and has a crush on one of his co-workers; out of respect for her, they've negotiated his drinking of her blood to one half-pint every three months. Vampires in this story aren't evil but merely need to unlearn some bad habits; this one is turning Japanese.

THE OKUMURA TWINS—*BLUE EXORCIST*

Manga and anime are as influenced by popular trends as any other part of society. From pro wrestling to drift racing, plots in all flavors—humorous, dramatic, and sentimental—have been built around ideas that wouldn't seem to offer many story possibilities but were shown to have worked before. In the case of the very popular manga *Blue Exorcist,* written and drawn by Katō Kazue for *Jump SQ* magazine, the inspiration, at least in part, is Hogwarts Academy. It's an adolescent school story, in the tradition of *Mizuiro Jidai, Hana Yori Dango, Ai Yori Aoshi* and too many other manga to name, as well as J. K. Rowling's idea about a magic academy, but with an added wrinkle or two. One is that this school of magic specializes in training exorcists: young people who want to do battle with evil itself. The other wrinkle is that one of these students, Okumura Rin, would actually be subject to exorcism, being a literal child of Satan; actually, in this series, one of several children of Satan.

To be clear, in this parody of western cosmology, Lucifer is actually the supreme Lord of Darkness; Satan is subordinate to Lucifer as well as rather active with the ladies. The school for exorcists, True Cross Academy, is run by another child of Satan, whose name is Mephisto Pheles, although he also calls himself Johann Faust the 5th. Mephisto Pheles seems to be playing both sides in this war: training exorcists like Rin and his brother Yukio, but also having a hidden agenda.

Rin and Yukio are twins,[10] and Satan's original plan was to empower both when they were in the womb (which is a parody of Voldemort dividing his soul among multiple horcruxes as a survival tactic); Yukio, however, was sickly, so all of Satan's powers were vested in Rin. When those powers kick in, he is surrounded by blue flames; hence the title *Blue Exorcist.* Yukio, however, is no slouch, and is actually on the True Cross Academy faculty as well as a student along with his brother.

There is the usual assortment of comic character types on both the faculty and the student body at True Cross Academy. There's the *Really* Shy Girl who becomes Rin's love interest, a voluptuous female teacher who parades in bikini tops and hot pants, a test proctor who doesn't talk except through a sock puppet, the apparent thug who really isn't, the Ladies Man who dyes his hair pink, the Dumbledore-like Chairman of the Academy who's an admitted anime fan . . . you get the picture.

The anime is a 25-week series which defeats an attack by the forces of Satan in the end but remains open-ended, with no clear winner or loser. In the anime, however, an attack on the True Cross Academy is thwarted in a very Japanese, therefore Orientalist, manner. There is a portal which conveniently connects the Academy to the Vatican; during one midnight assault by Satan's minions, it's remembered that there's a seven-hour time difference between Rome and Japan. Mirrors are arranged to defeat the minions using sunlight from Rome. The Vatican may be Roman, but the sun still belongs to Amaterasu the Shinto sun goddess, wherever it may be.

The manga started running in 2009, and hasn't ended its run as of this writing. So there's no clue yet how it will all resolve, except for the clues that *Jump SQ* readers have already been given. That resolution, however, will be consistent with the world-view of the manga's millions of readers.

SE HIMIKO—*VAMPIRE PRINCESS MIYU*

A non-Christian, Japanese audience would not necessarily dismiss the idea of exorcism altogether. They would, however, have learned to put more trust in a belief system with which they were more familiar, even if it was far from mundane.

We've seen (mostly) comic examples in this chapter of Christian, Shinto and Buddhist exorcists going head to head; one other example has a single exorcist drawing on multiple religious practices. In the opening minutes of the first installment of the 1988 OAV anime series *Vampire Princess Miyu*, written by Aikawa Shō and directed by Hirano Toshihiro, spiritualist Se Himiko is summoned to Kyoto to investigate a child who cannot be awakened from a deep sleep. While she's there, a series of apparent vampire attacks take place, and Himiko thinks the two cases are related. We see her shopping for a cross to wear around her neck, and almost immediately she sees the vampire of the title, a fourteen year old girl, attacking the boyfriend of the vampire's first victim. Himiko throws her crucifix at the vampire—who catches it; what's left of the cross falls from her hand like sand. Likewise in the second case, when Himiko and Miyu are both hunting a Shinma[11] who turns people into marionettes, Himiko throws holy water onto Miyu—and nothing happens.

By the third episode, Himiko accepts the situation and, when confronted by a suit of medieval Japanese armor which has been possessed by the spirit of its owner, subdues the spirit by chanting a darani, part of a body of esoteric Buddhist chanting.[12] Miyu says that Himiko was "sugoi (awesome)" and thereafter cooperates with the spiritualist. Himiko had demonstrated the ability to be not only flexible but open-minded.

Inada Shiho created several four-panel gag manga as fillers during the publication of *Ghost Hunt* serially in *Nakayoshi* magazine, later collected in paperback *tankobon* volumes. In one of these, titled "Scary Job", she talks about A-san, an assistant in her studio early in the series, who was "easily scared" by ghost stories. The rest of the staff, however, found Hollywood ghost stories implausible; when they watched a video of the film *The Exorcist*, the staff was "laughing so hard they were crying." (v.4, p. 37)

When the movie was released in America in 1973, it was treated as a phenomenon; this was, after all, a land where the majority of people accepted the cultural dominance of Christianity, whether or not they believed in devils. Mark Kermode of BBC Radio 1 wrote about *The Exorcist* in 1998, on the 25th anniversary of its release:

> *Triumph* magazine publishing a rave review in 1973, echoing Father Kenneth Jadoff's claim in *The Catholic News* that '*The Exorcist* is a deeply spiritual film.'
> According to director William Friedkin, a copy of the film was supplied to high ranking Catholic Father Pedro Arrupe in 1974 following a favourable viewing and subsequently remained with his offices. . . . Earlier this year, Catherine Von Rhuland of the *New Christian Herald* declared: "*The Exorcist* is surely an explicitly Christian film [in which] the ministry is presented with dignity as an honourable vocation [who] go the full distance with Utter Darkness—a sleeves rolled up, no-holds-barred fight to the finish between God's earthly representatives and Satan."
> Such reactions are unsurprising, since Friedkin's movie was written and produced by the Catholic writer William Peter Blatty whose multi-million selling novel was praised by the Vatican literary journal *Civilta Cattolica* having been described by the author as "a 350 page thankyou note to the Jesuits."
> Indeed, such is the standing of Blatty's novel within the Catholic establishment that last year Cardinal O'Connor read sections from it as part of his Sunday mass in St. Patrick's Cathedral in New York.
> Blatty himself remembers being told by Father Bud Markey that in the wake of the opening of the film he "had a run on the confessional box" from people who hadn't been to church in years, an assertion widely echoed by others in the priesthood.

According to Father Thomas Bermingham and Father William O'Malley of Fordham University in the Bronx, *The Exorcist* is still shown to students every year, and still continues to provoke lively debate on issues of theology. (Kermode)

For the Japanese artists working on *Ghost Hunt*, however, for whom Christianity was an outsider religion, they found the effects in the movie amusing rather than disturbing.

This is not to say that Japanese don't get scared, or don't scare easily. Fear, however, should be seen as culturally specific. Movies that moved Japanese audiences as *The Exorcist* touched western audiences include *Ringu (The Ring)* (directed by Nakata Hideo, 1998) and *Ju-On (The Grudge)* (directed by Shimizu Takahashi, 2002). Unlike *The Exorcist*, these movies—and many others—didn't have an impact because a supernatural unholy demon had possessed a young girl. The shocks in *Ringu* and *Ju-On* were grounded in everyday occurrences and familiar locations. This is, after all, one of the elements of a Japanese ghost story: a high sense of plausibility, the notion that the events in the story *could* happen, and maybe *did* happen, and could very well happen again.[13]

There are other varieties of Christian priests in manga and anime, but even the most heroic of these seldom come close to the kinds of priests Hollywood approves of. We'll meet them in chapter 9. For now, we turn to a couple of ways that Christianity in Japan is used without clergy, or even without Christianity itself.

NOTES

1. In contrast, the Chinese Taoist tradition has it, according to Canadian-based Mak Jo Si, that any spirits of the dead remaining in the land of the living are there for no good purpose, and the only option is exorcism. (http://www.taoistmasterblog.com/taoism-exorcism-vs-ghosts-and-spirits/, accessed September 5, 2015)

2. These include his speaking in the Kansai dialect, but also the occasional use of embarrassingly inappropriate words. In a case where the SPR is introduced to a famed British psychic researcher, Buddhist monk Takigawa is highly impressed. John, however, meaning to say that the monk idolizes the researcher (*keitou*), instead says that the monk is *keikou*—meaning that the monk is inclined toward the researcher personally rather than professionally. (vol. 6, pp. 32, 190n).

3. She acts primarily as a clairvoyant, communicating with spirits and making their desires known. In the final episode of the anime series, in which all of the SPR must function as exorcists, Masako for the only time recites a Buddhist "scripture": the Heart Sutra. This sutra is also used as part of an exorcism as described in Parry's "Ghosts of the Tsunami."

4. Japan tried requiring priestly celibacy from time to time, with little success. Stories abound of Buddhist priests who break their vows with women or boys; one famous historical example was the priest Ikkyu Sojun (1394-1481), whose poetry is still printed and who traveled with his lover Mori, a blind woman 50 years his junior who he rescued from prostitution. Modern Japanese Buddhism for the most part simply asks its adherents to be monogamous.

5. The Buddhist monk Ryūdō Kazumi has a crush on Hanako, a voluptuous ghost who haunts toilets, while the Shinto priestess Asahina Mutsuki has a "thing" for little boys in general and in particular for the ghost of the Ninomiya statue on the school grounds.

6. See *Gakkō no Kaidan* by Tsunemitsu Toru, an informal catalogue by a 5th grade teacher of modern Japanese kids and the stories they tell, including ghost stories. Most schools seem to be haunted—often by ghosts that reappear from one school to the next—and they are conveniently referred to as The Seven Wonders regardless of number.

7. A name that literally means "beautiful god", or more usually "goddess".

8. In a line of dialogue added for the anime of the story, Yokoshima reacts to this by saying "Hey! I don't really care, but you might receive divine punishment for doing that."

9. See chapter 2 for the real-life battle between Nobunaga and Mitsuhide; *GS Mikami* is just one of the anime/manga retellings of their battles, among the more recent are the anime *Nobunagun* and *Nobunaga the Fool*.

10. Being a twin has its own profile in Japan, in the pop culture at least. Because of the long and influential heritage of the teachings of Confucius throughout Asia, twins are always distinguished as "older" and "younger"—if only separated by a few minutes—and treated accordingly. The popular belief also has it that, despite their physical similarity, "one has a good personality, the other has a bad personality." (*Ghost Hunt*, vol. 12, p. 147) That applies to the younger, cold and cerebral Yukio as compared to the compassionate, helpful but impetuous Rin. Other examples include the twin witches Yubaba (bad) and Zeniba (good) in Miyazaki Hayao's anime *Spirited Away;* the twin sisters Minoru and Mitsuru in *Genei Musou (Phantom Dream)*, a manga by Natsuki Takaya; twin brothers Gene and Oliver in *Ghost Hunt* by Inada and Ono; the twins Rosen and Rouji in Hiramatsu Shinji's manga *Black Angels* (discussed in chapters 10 and 14), and to a lesser degree in the Hitachiin twins of Hatori Bisco's *Ouran High School Host Club*.

11. A spirit whose name literally means "God demon".

12. As James Deacon explains in his website, darani are Buddhist chants, not as brief as a mantra which may only be one word, but not as long as the recitation of a sutra. Darani "are understood to hold mystical or magical power; and the recitation of *darani* is believed to bring great spiritual merit, serving as a medium for furthering one's progress towards realisation of enlightenment." (http://www.aetw.org/jsp_darani_main.htm, accessed July 30, 2015) This Buddhist tool works for Himiko where Christian tools did not.

13. "Japanese (ghost) stories were absolutely true; at the very least, they had to appear to be true. Many of the Japanese stories, therefore, go into great detail in describing the time or place in which they happened, no matter how outrageous the events of the story may seem to the modern reader." From my book *A Gathering of Spirits: Japan's Ghost Story Tradition* (2011. Indianapolis: iUniverse, p. 26.)

Chapter Seven

Jinguru Beh! Christmas in Manga and Anime

The very first image a viewer sees in Kon Satoshi's film *Tokyo Godfathers* is supposed to be a representation of the infant Jesus lying in a manger. However, in this Nativity pageant presented by the Salvation Army for the homeless of Tokyo, Jesus is represented, not by a copy of a Renaissance artwork but by a kewpie doll—an item given as a prize at carnival booths.

Japanese Christmas, like the rest of Japanese Christianity, isn't quite like its western counterpart. The trappings are there, but the context isn't. And the trappings borrowed from the west for this most western holiday have a life of their own, from dining on Kentucky Fried Chicken to performances of Beethoven's Ninth Symphony. Discussing Christian themes in his survey of Japanese science-fiction, Robert Matthew wrote that such stories choose "not to look in the main at Christian faith in terms of its central tenets but rather at the tangential trimmings." (p. 138) The same assessment seems to apply to Christmas manga and anime.

For the most part, Christmas in Japan is a holiday but not a holy day. Even for those who revere the day's sacred origins, the approach is different. Take the case of Kataoka Otogo, a banker for the Industrial Bank of Japan and for the Osaka-Nomura Bank. He was asked to create the Nomura Securities Company Ltd out of the bond transaction wing of the Osaka-Nomura Bank. Kataoka, a Christian, decided to open business for Nomura Securities Company Ltd on Christmas Day 1925. While a western Christian banker would have taken the day off to recognize its holiness, Kataoka conducted business, to quote Albert J. Alletzhauser in *The House of Nomura*, "in a perverse expression of Kataoka's Christianity and a distinctly Japanese interpretation of the birth of Christ." (Alletzhauser, p. 72) The interpretation in this case was that such an auspicious day as Christmas would sympathetically bless other undertakings begun on that day.

Sampling Christmas manga isn't exactly easy, since many artists don't even bring it into their work. In some cases, the plot line simply doesn't lend itself, being set in a time or place where Christmas would be incongruous. In others, the plot may be so worked through that having to make room for Christmas would be a distraction. In any case, manga artists do not feel obliged to mention the holiday whenever it rolls around. The December 27, 1985 issue of *Weekly Manga Times*, for instance, included only one story out of 16 that could be called seasonal.

Christmas manga occasionally nod to the day's sacred origins, but usually only if the story is set in Europe. Takemiya Keiko's *Kaze to Ki no Uta*, for instance, set in a turn-of-the-century European boys' school, notes the holiday as Christian, although it never lets the religion intrude on the Boy Love story.

If events are set in Japan, Christmas is still possible. Generally, though, Christmas comics in Japan are not unlike Christmas television programs in America, in that very few of them deal directly with the sacred. The holiday becomes a "hook" for dramatic or humorous situations, or for sentimental pieces about doing something good for other people. In the end, Santa Claus is a more crucial figure than Jesus.

One of the grand masters of manga, Ishinomori Shotaro, has done both dramatic and humorous turns on the Christmas theme. His 1965 series *Mutant Sab*, about a crime-fighting teenager with psychic powers, included a holiday episode, "The Ten Santa Clauses." The older brother of Sab's friend Sumiko has been arrested for his involvement in a criminal organization; the gang, in Santa Claus suits, steals blueprints from an electronics company of a supersonic tank. Sab uses his mind-reading ability to find the criminals, disguises himself as a Santa to foil the theft and frees the brother. (vol. 1, pp. 259-302)

More recently, one of the first episodes of Ishinomori's adult-oriented *Hotel* series, titled "Monsters' Christmas," features a group of college students trying to throw a Christmas party—complete with miniature tree and a Christmas cake—in a suite at the titular Hotel Platon (vol. 1, pp. 137-160). For whatever reason, this is a costume party, and among the costumes are Dracula, the Frankenstein monster, and something like a yeti; hence the title. The front-desk manager has had some experience with these students, and wants to break up their (in his mind's eye) orgy.

The first installment of a 1968 three-part *Tetsuwan Atomu* story by Tezuka Osamu, "Kasei kara Kaette kita Otoko (The Man Who Came Home from Mars)" (vol. 11,Tokyo: Sun Comics, pp. 135-199), is set on Christmas Eve. Atom (or Astro Boy) is thinking that, even though he has seen 18 Christmases, he prays that he will always keep this childlike feeling. Of course, things don't stay so benign, as the returnee of the title, an escaped criminal named Judah Peter (a name with contradictory religious resonances), starts a new reign of terror, beginning with the destruction of a robot teacher at a children's Christmas party. The Christmas theme of redemption is not lost, however, for, in their battle to the death at the North Pole, Atom runs out of energy, and Judah Peter sacrifices himself to summon help.

Sailor Moon made Christmas the occasion for a film theatrically released during the third season of the broadcast of the TV series. Based on a manga story by series creator Takeuchi Naoko, the movie told of the awkward falling in love of Sailor Moon's cat Luna with a human male—a scientist with a heart condition which would not let him live his dream of space travel. In Christmas fashion, Luna is able to make his dream come true; in Japanese fashion, her plan avoids Christmas imagery altogether when Luna disguises herself as the legendary Princess Kaguya, who was born of a stalk of bamboo and eventually ascended to live on the moon. (Takeuchi, vol. 11)

There are no Catholic priests in Kon Satoshi's movie *Tokyo Godfathers*, but the opening scene takes place on Christmas night at a Salvation Army kitchen feeding some of Tokyo's homeless. The three "godfathers" of the title are less interested in the sermon, delivered by a Japanese Protestant minister, than in the meal that is delivered afterwards; only the two grownups attend the service. One of the trio, a middle-aged drag queen named Hana, goes back for seconds and tells the server "I'm eating for two." Hana says that a Christmas miracle might provide another immaculate conception, and in a way it does: the three find a baby abandoned in a garbage dump and spend the next week, until sunrise on New Year's Day, trying to find its parents. The choice of dates is no accident: by telling the story from Christmas to New Year's, it moves from the Salvation Army to Shinto, and the miracles at the climax of the movie involve, at least symbolically, Shinto deities. The anime is discussed more completely in chapter 13.

ONLY A GAME

In real life as well as in anime, Christmas is not always festive. *Sword Art Online,* based on a series of light novels by Kawahara Reki, is about young people being trapped in a MMORPG. There is uncertainty at first as to whether return to Real Life is even possible; it's also unknown if, when a character dies in the game, their Real Life counterpart also dies.

The hero of the game, Kirito, has such power and ability as a gamer that he stands a very good chance of getting through to the end without losing his virtual life. Among his companions is Sachi, a girl in the opposite situation. She's one of anime's idealized delicate girls: passive, gentle, compassionate. It comes as no surprise that, when their group falls into a trap, she gets killed;

the last image of Sachi is her smiling at Kirito as the deadly blow strikes, mouthing words to him the viewer could not hear. Kirito and the viewer find out that it was no surprise to Sachi either.

One of the gimmicks of this particular game is the ability to send "Christmas gifts" from one player to another. When the game clock reaches December 25, Kirito receives such a gift: a voice message from the dead Sachi, recorded in anticipation of her virtual death. In it she explains that, knowing her own lack of fitness for battle, she had been relying on Kirito's presence in the group, expecting that she would be killed sooner or later. She hopes that he will survive long enough to make sense of why the game was created and how she ended up in it. Then, with a few seconds left in the recording, she hums a seasonal song: "Rudolph the Red-Nosed Reindeer." Her final words are the ones she spoke while dying: "Arigatou. Sayonara." (Thank you. Goodbye.) The viewer sees Kirito's tears fall on the table beside the "gift" in perhaps the most tear-jerking Christmas scene since the death of Tiny Tim.

BOARDING HOUSE HOLIDAYS

The use of Christmas as a motif in Takahashi Rumiko's *Mezon Ikkoku* (1982-1988, in 15 vols.) is a fairly precise indication of the holiday's tangential but definite place in modern Japanese culture, as well as its relative importance in any given manga story. Takahashi has always been very scrupulous about depicting, to quote Takahashi herself, "a lot of Japanese references, Japanese lifestyle and feelings ... even concepts such as a subtle awareness of the four seasons." (T. Smith, p. 27). This is especially true in the seven-year wooing and winning by the hapless student Godai Yusaku of his landlady, the beautiful widow Otonashi Kyoko, told almost in real time. The overall story itself uses a venerable manga/anime scenario: an old-fashioned boarding-house with a collection of eccentric characters.

In the first Christmas episode, "Katte no Seiya (O Holy Night of Selfishness)" (vol. 1, pp. 41-60), the third installment in the series, it is Christmas 1980. The opening frame, in a shopping district, shows holly under a loudspeaker blaring "Jinguru Beh." Godai fantasizes winning the widow's love by giving her a brooch, but his attempts at gift-giving are constantly upstaged by Kentaro, the boarding-house's resident child.

The brooch in fact stays buried in the clutter of Godai's room until the next year in "Mafura, Agemasu (To Give a Muffler)" (vol. 2, pp. 203-222), when, strapped for cash, he unearths it to belatedly give to Kyoko. Before then, we see another shopping scene, this time with decorated trees, wreaths and one of the series' nicest throwaway gags: a man in a Santa Claus suit, with sunglasses, leaning against a wall and smoking a cigarette, taking a break from advertising a holiday sale.

Christmas 1982 mixes the holiday with biographical details about the characters, in one of the finest episodes in the series. "Hoshi-wo Tsukamu Otoko (The Man Who Caught a Star)" (vol. 5, pp. 25-44) once again finds Godai having no money to buy a present; in fact, he has to work Christmas Eve, taking down a Christmas tree at a large department store and putting up the Chinese Good Luck Gods for the New Year. He does manage to take one of the decorations—a giant star—and present it to Kyoko, who had mentioned that, as a child, she had wanted the star from a department-store tree. The decorations in this episode are more elaborate, featuring reindeer and snowflakes, but again the word Christmas always seems to be followed on signs by the word Sale.

The following Christmas was a rough one for Godai; he was in the hospital, having broken his ankle in a fall from his bedroom window. There is an establishing frame of the shopping district, again with an advertising Santa and "Jinguru Beh" on the loudspeakers, but any holiday atmosphere in "Kakeochi Kurakkaa (Elopement Cracker)" (vol. 7, pp. 113-134) is supplied by a Christmas party in Godai's hospital room serving as a diversion for the elopement of Godai's cousin, a tomboy named Akira.

The 1984 Christmas episode "Hitotsu dake onegai (Please, just one . . .)" (vol. 9, pp. 167-186) brings in a group of characters introduced years earlier: the puppetry club that Godai joined in college. He and Kyoko are enlisted in their fairy-tale production for children about a beggar who is granted three wishes by the Spirit of the Christmas Tree. He wishes for food, money, and a beautiful princess. However, the princess goes through the money quickly and declares that she could never love a poor man (*binboonin*). Both Godai and Kyoko are embarrassed that this may be getting too close to the truth for the eternally-penniless Godai. The reality hits home after the performance when they stop at an open air oden cart, but Godai can't afford to pay.

The following year, "Yowamushi" ("Coward", vol. 11, pp. 206-226) sees the residents of the Ikkoku boarding-house at their annual Christmas party at ChaChaMaru, the bar where one of the residents, sultry Roppongi Akemi, is hostess. Again there are the wreaths, the decorated trees, the Christmas Sale advertisements and the endless "Rasshai Rasshai" of salespersons. But Godai is delayed, and Kyoko has to contend with Yagami, a jealous high-school girl who developed a crush on Godai the year before when he was a student-teacher.

In the final holiday episode titled "Yurusan" (an abbreviation of "yurusanai", meaning "unforgivable", vol. 15, pp. 109-128), with Godai and Kyoko almost engaged, Christmas hardly exists; the only sign of the holiday is a barely visible poster reading "Merry Xmas! Non-alcoholic champagne." The focus is on Kyoko's father, who's having trouble accepting that his daughter, even though in her late twenties and about to take her second husband, is no longer a child. However, a new trend emerged in the Eighties in Japan: men would wait and propose marriage on Christmas. From Kyoko's father's ultimate acceptance of his daughter's maturity, Godai's official proposal and Kyoko's singular acceptance,[1] the story jumps to a winter meeting with the groom's family. There are more important things in the air than Christmas.

THE GHOST OF CHRISTMAS PAST

There are some manga which have Christmas-themed seasonal episodes, but always on Japanese terms. The word "Christmas", for example, is often followed by the word "cake". It is as ubiquitous a symbol in the holiday stories as the decorated tree is in the west. Both symbols appear in one of the most unlikely Christmas stories in the pop culture. The *Ghost Hunt* series of novels by Ono Fuyumi were turned into manga with artwork by Inada Shiho and later animated by JC Staff. The series focuses on a group of teenagers and young adults who are psychic researchers and "ghostbusters". Included in the group is John Brown, an Australian Catholic priest in training to be an exorcist. The group, Shibuya Psychic Research, is hired by a church that operates a day-care and orphanage—institutions associated with Christianity in Japan since the Meiji period.

The day-care and orphanage is mainly for foreign workers in Japan. This circumstance ties into the connection between Christianity and its practice of social welfare in modern-day Japan, as well as a reminder to the reader that Christianity is a non-Japanese faith. The story "Silent Christmas" (v.4, pp. 106-171) begins thirty years earlier, when a child named Nagano Kenji was brought to the church's old location. Father Toujo, a Catholic priest who runs the day-care and the church, tells the SPR that "when I first met him he already couldn't speak. I heard it was due to a psychological trauma he'd experienced . . . but I never heard the exact cause of it." (v.4, pp. 113-114) In the manga and the anime, the implication is that Kenji was autistic to some degree, but this is never spelled out. His father left him at the center to go to a job in the Kansai region of Japan; he never returned or was heard from, although he said he would be back.

Kenji disappeared while playing an adapted version of hide and seek. The Japanese version of the game requires the hiders to tell whoever is "it" if they're hidden or not; since Kenji did not speak, a code was worked out so that he could communicate by hitting objects with a stick. While playing near the present church, which was still under construction thirty years earlier, the scaffolding collapsed and a winter storm which hampered the search for Kenji moved in. He—or his remains—would not be found until SPR investigated, and realized that Kenji had climbed the scaffolding and hidden behind a statue of an angel above the door of the new church. Nobody thought to scale the front of the church and look behind the statues; by that time, all that could be seen from the ground was a skull, which was taken to be a part of the statue.[2]

John Brown tries to exorcise the ghost from a child, but it immediately possesses the main character in the series: the group's Office Lady, a high school student named Taniyama Mai. This is just one more failed exorcism conducted by John in the series.

The possessed Mai behaves like a carefree child, which includes trying to wrap the Christmas cakes baked by the church to be given to those who attend the Christmas service. Meanwhile, the others eventually discover how Kenji died thirty years before; when his remains are discovered, the spirit leaves Mai. This conforms to the Japanese pop culture convention, based on centuries of ghost lore, of restless or vengeful spirits haunting the world until their issues are resolved, freeing them to Become One with the Cosmos. Needless to say, this has nothing to do with Catholic beliefs in possession, exorcism or the afterlife.

The Christmas tree appears at the beginning of the episode. Mai has put one up at the office of Shibuya Psychic Research as a festive touch; the head of the office, Shibuya Kazuya, wants her to take it down. The other members, however, appreciate the seasonal reminder. Only in the final volume of the series do we find out why Kazuya, nicknamed Naru the Narcissist, doesn't share their interest in a Christmas tree: Shibuya Kazuya is an alias. He's Oliver Davis, of England's Society for Psychical Research. He and his twin brother were Japanese who were orphaned at an early age, found to have impressive psychic gifts, and adopted by Professor Davis of the SPR and taken to live in England. (vol. 12, pp. 48-81) This explains why he had no interest in the Christmas tree: he grew up with them, so the appearance of one was expected rather than nostalgic or exotic. Unbeknownst to Mai, it may also have served as a painful reminder of why he was back in Japan in the first place: his brother had disappeared during a trip to Japan, and Kazuya was investigating the disappearance. To the Japanese members of Shibuya Psychic Research, however, the tree was a delight precisely because it was out of their tradition and therefore exotic.

HAVE WE MET BEFORE?

There's a linked pair of Christmas stories in the manga *Ai Yori Aoshi* by Fumizuki Kou, drawn for a college-age audience. The main character, Hanabishi Kaoru, used to be a child of privilege, since he was born the son of the lover of the wealthy Hanabishi family's heir. When the heir died young, the family no longer felt obliged to care for both mother and child, sending her away and thus alienating the son, Kaoru. He ultimately fled the family compound to make his own way in the world. While he lived with them, however, the Hanabishi arranged that, when they were of age, Kaoru would marry Sakuraba Aoi, the daughter of another wealthy family. Although the arrangement was supposedly cancelled when Kaoru abandoned the Hanabishi heritage, nobody could convince Aoi to stop loving him. The story begins when Kaoru is in college, a junior in a pre-law curriculum, living on his own in a cheap apartment; he accidentally meets Aoi, who dresses in traditional kimono and clings to him just as traditionally.[3]

By the time of the Christmas episode titled "Miyuki (Deep Snow)", Kaoru has left his college friends after they performed a part-time job two days before Christmas. On the way back to his apartment he's hit on the head by a snowflake pendant falling out of the sky. Once home, Santa arrives, looking exactly like Aoi-san in a Santa costume. According to the exposition, this is happening a year before Aoi and Kaoru are reunited, and to him she only resembles "someone from my childhood." Santa/Aoi tells him that Santa often gives dreams as gifts, and to think about "the girl you wish to see." Kaoru indeed ends up dreaming of himself as a child, reunited with his mother. (vol. 5, pp. 105-126)[4]

The next episode, "Neyuki (Lingering Snow)", finds Santa/Aoi still in Kaoru's apartment on the morning of Christmas Eve. She's prepared breakfast consisting of Christmas cake and a turkey; not exactly appropriate for breakfast but seasonal—at least, seasonal in the west, where Christmas and turkeys come from (even though a more modern "traditional Christmas" food in Japan would be Kentucky Fried Chicken). They go ice skating (Santa/Aoi's first time), and walking through the decorated city, until sunset. Kaoru wants to give Santa a gift in thanks for the pleasant day, but, as she very traditionally says, "making everyone else happy is what makes me happy." That happiness includes a parting kiss before Santa returns to the North Pole. When Kaoru wakes up, he doesn't remember the dream, and can't remember how he got the Christmas cake. In the end, the episodes were prequel, happening on the Christmas before Kaoru was reunited with Aoi. (*Ibid.*, pp. 127-146)

Christmas in this story is its own world; there is nothing Christian about it at all. There are certain traditional costumes and decorations and magic, but even *Tokyo Godfathers* has a Nativity pageant and a sermon by the Salvation Army. This Christmas, like so many of those in manga and anime, is divorced from its religious roots, since the Japanese traditionally do not share that religion.

For many Japanese, Christianity is most important in two contexts: Christmas and weddings. Since Christmas in Japan has become like Valentine's Day for grownups,[5] when men are most likely to propose marriage, weddings—Christian weddings—are inevitably a tangential part of the holiday. Weddings are also the subject of the next chapter.

NOTES

1. "This may sound strange, but I want you to outlive me, if only by one day, because I couldn't stand to be alone again." (vol. 15, p. 147)

2. Presumably, nobody thought a statue of an angel with a skull underfoot was unusual. For those who knew nothing of medieval Catholicism, Orientalism provided the all-purpose explanation: it's just one more mysterious thing they're capable of. (Buddhist monk Takigawa merely describes it as "psychedelic" in the manga.) However, anyone eastern or western with knowledge of medieval church art would have seen something similar: the Danse Macabre, beginning at the end of the 14th century and continuing to the mid 15th century, in which death—whether from disease, famine or war—was pictured as the great leveler. Even Jesus was depicted in these times more often than in the past with the crown of thorns. (Tuchman, Barbara W. 1978. *A Distant Mirror: The Calamitous 14th Century.* New York: Ballantine Books, pp. 505-507)

3. She is the embodiment of the Japanese saying "Man is the pine tree, woman the wisteria"—a clinging vine who lives only for his care and comfort. A very unmodern message, but a very popular manga.

4. See Buruma's *Behind the Mask* for a discussion of the mother figure in Japan's popular culture, and chapter 13 of this book to see how actress Fujiwara Chiyoko played such an excellent mother, according to Kon Satoshi's anime feature *Millennium Actress*, that she was known as Japan's Madonna.

5. Valentine's Day itself has become largely ceded to high-school girls, who give hand-crafted chocolate to the boy they like. The reciprocal obligation is paid back one month later, on White Day—March 15, where the boy gives a gift.

Chapter Eight

Christian Weddings in Japan

Just Like in the Movies

Japanese are very interested in one Christian rite, but purely for the theatrics of it. For years the old saying in Japan was "Born Shinto, die Buddhist"—referring to the Buddhist funeral rites preferred by the Japanese, while Shinto rites tend to predominate in the rest of life. In the last few decades, the saying has been amended to "Born Shinto, marry Christian, die Buddhist". Young people want to be wed in a Christian ceremony, with the emphasis on ceremony. Again, it's all about the trimmings: the white veiled wedding gown; the priest, who is supposed to be good-looking and may even be an actor; any actual preaching during the ceremony is frowned upon. It would be unnecessary if the ceremony were Shinto, and unwanted in a Christian ceremony, which is less formal than its western counterpart and intended to be more romantic than religious.

An actual Japanese marriage would involve both partners appearing at the city or ward office and filling out the necessary legal paperwork, in an arrangement that dates back to the Tokugawa period of Japan's isolation. The couple must be accompanied by two or more adult witnesses or present documents signed by the witnesses. The husband will then be issued a new family register as the head of a new household when he registers the marriage. (*The Japanese and Buddhism*, accessed June 19, 2015)

Anything after that is up to the couple. The actual legally binding wedding has already happened; the ceremony, whether Shinto, Buddhist, or Hollywood-Christian, is for friends, for family, as a wish fulfillment for the bride, as cosplay—in other words, for the fun of it. How do the Japanese participants feel about performing a rite that looks like a Christian religious service? The question answers itself: it LOOKS LIKE a Christian service, without being binding as such. Theologically, it's safe; it's role-playing, with no sense of "changing sides" or abandoning tradition.

It's hard to know when Christian weddings as role-playing started to catch on in Japan, but according to LeFebvre:

> On March 1, 1975, the Vatican granted the Japanese Catholic Church special permission to conduct wedding ceremonies for non-Catholic couples. These ceremonies had previously been available to baptized members of the Catholic Church and their spouses to be, regardless of their spouse's faith. However, this new exemption gave priests the authority to conduct wedding ceremonies for unbaptized, non-Christian couples as well. This unprecedented opening of the Catholic Church's doors occurred long before the nation-wide explosion of Christian ceremonies. (p. 4)

In recent decades the fortunate combination of the economic boom of the 1980s and the world-wide broadcast of the Hollywood-style wedding of Princess Diana to Prince Charles of England on July 29, 1981 inspired many brides—not only in Japan—to go for the glamour. Japan also had its own media weddings: Lefevbre notes "the widely televised celebrity weddings of actor Miura Tomokazu and vocalist Yamaguchi Momoe in 1980 and the superstars Kanda Masaki and Matsuda Seiko in 1985." (*Ibid.*, p. 6)

Not that religion is completely absent, according to a website from Seiyaku.com (seiyaku is Japanese for wedding vows); it's just there as part of the show, and it wouldn't be as "cool" without it:

> It follows the pattern of a traditional Protestant marriage ceremony, largely unchanged for hundreds of years. Pretty relaxed, not overtly or charismatically evangelical, and low emphasis on some of the more conservative rites. The opening hymn is usually the Japanese version of *What a Friend We Have in Jesus*. This is probably the most widely known Christian hymn in Japan, so everyone can join in. . . . Part of *1st Corinthians chapter 13* is then read from the Bible . . . After the Bible reading, there is a prayer followed by a short message that explains the sanctity of marriage and the importance of the wedding vows.
>
> Then the bride and groom declare their vows (*seiyaku*); undeniably the most important part of a wedding ceremony. The next most important part is often considered to be the ring exchange (*yubiwa no kokan*). Few other parts of a wedding have as many myths and superstitions as the wedding ring.
>
> The chapel register (*shomeisho*) is signed and the marriage is announced (*kekkon-sengen*). ("Western Style Weddings in Japan")

Sam Harnett of Public Radio International gave this rundown which was broadcast around Christmas of 2013 of a typical Japanese wedding:

> The "white wedding" in Japan copies an archetypal Western ceremony. There are all the traditional elements: live music, an expensive white dress,

and a giant cross hanging in the background. The couple swaps rings, cuts a cake at the reception, and at the end, the bride throws a bouquet to the next lucky girl. But perhaps the most essential part of the event is a minister who looks the part. In other words, a white person.

At this hotel near the central train station in Nagasaki, wedding planners are putting on a typical ceremony. A string quartet and organ play Pachebel's Canon in D to open the service and then minister Wayne Hamilton takes over.

From behind the podium, Hamilton reads in both Japanese and English, delivering all of the traditional lines: A speech about the rings and their significance, the "do you take this man, do you take this woman" bit, and of course the climactic "you may now kiss the bride." ("Japan white weddings,")

As the tradition became established, the Japanese who wanted the ceremony realized that the minister didn't have to BE a minister, as Harnett explains:

> Nils Olsen, a Christian missionary from Washington State, says that "basically, the Japanese social concept of a wedding is that it's fashionable." He would know. Olsen has been putting on weddings in Japan for 20 years.
>
> Olsen is one of the few ministers in Japan that's actually ordained. He says that when he started there were far less "fake ministers," and that the money was better than it is now. Way better. He used to make almost $400 (¥40,000) per wedding ceremony. Since wedding providers started hiring any white person to do his job, Olsen's pay has been cut in half. *(Ibid.)*

Various anime and manga are set in Christian chapels, before or during a Christian wedding. It doesn't matter if the story is a comic fantasy (*The Elven Bride,* about a human marrying an elf—somewhat pornographic) or a more serious and ominous mood piece ("Virgin Road" from the *Count Down* series—also pornographic); Christian weddings are available, according to the former, to be performed even for elves.

MERCHANT OF ROMANCE

In 1987 manga artist Takahashi Rumiko created a one-off story for *Big Comic Original* magazine, "Roman no Akindo (The Merchant of Romance)," about a marriage chapel struggling to get by. It performed Buddhist, Christian or Shinto weddings—all officiated by priests for hire.

The story begins on a June afternoon; the weather is fine, but the building has stood for three generations and hasn't been fitted with air conditioning.[1] Another problem is more immediate: the priest performing the ceremony called to say "he threw his back out." Worse, according to the assistant manager Betto, "since we only hire independent contractors, he can't supply a back-up." Betto complains that "I told you we should get a group contract with the shrines," but Yukari, the woman who owns the chapel, states the obvious: "We don't have that kind of money." The chapel has been a family business; Yukari is the third generation owner, but her father, as the reader finds out, was too good-hearted and open-handed with the money he made. Now the chapel is literally paying the price.

The immediate problem is to find Yoshi, the chapel's handyman; however, this is his day off and he's out drinking. Later, we find out that he used to be a priest, but was excommunicated ten years earlier; probably for his drinking. He stayed on staff at Romance Villa as a caretaker for sentimental reasons as well as because he'd work cheap.

In a sense, this is typical of the fate of the entire chapel. Yukari, whose father owned and operated the chapel, has had romantic and financial setbacks herself: a year before, her husband Keiichi "left (her) and left the villa." He's in arrears on his alimony payments and hasn't had much success on his own, presumably having to start over from the bottom as a salaryman.

CASTLE OF CAGLIOSTRO

Weddings have occasionally broken down in western cinema; perhaps the best-known, and most potentially sacrilegious, was in the 1967 film *The Graduate*, when Ben didn't merely stop the wedding of his beloved Elaine but used the altar cross as a weapon. The sacrilege in that scene, however, pales next to the royal wedding in *Lupin III: Castle of Cagliostro*, the 1979 anime feature directed by Miyazaki Hayao. That wedding actually began with the destruction of the altar cross, followed by the heroic thief Lupin preventing the marriage of Princess Clarice to Count Cagliostro, by disguising himself as the Archbishop. Meanwhile, Lupin's sometime ally Mine Fujiko, who had been disguised as a television announcer, has drawn a gun and is taking potshots at the crowd; one hopes she's aiming at the Count's men. With a battle between the police and the Count's men, while Count Cagliostro's counterfeit money rains down on the invited guests, the scene is funny, chaotic, and (depending on your point of view) in questionable taste.

SAILOR MOON

Weddings don't always go awry; sometimes the wedding is the climax of the story, and gives the artist a chance to go all-out with a big fancy design—of the dress, of the episode, and sometimes of the entire series. This was the case with Takeuchi Naoko's shoujo manga masterpiece *Sailor Moon*. The final chapter of the story was printed in the March 1997 issue of *Nakayoshi* magazine, and moved from the final surrender of the evil Galaxia, and the return of Chibimoon to the 30th century, to the epilogue. Usagi and Mamoru wake up in the same bed, naked; she asks Mamoru to say the words that, according to him, he already told her fifty times the day before: "kekkon shiyoo (We're married)." The end is marked by seven pages of memories of flowers, lace, jewelry (mainly Usagi's ring), elaborate gowns, Mamoru in a toreador jacket tuxedo, and the other eight Sailor Senshi as bridesmaids. Their first kiss as man and wife takes place in front of a stained-glass window and an altar cross, but it's in the background, partially blocked by the happy couple. (pp. 140-186)

Perhaps the priest who officiated at that ceremony was an actor; the reader never gets to see him. He'd just be there for looks anyway. The real priests of manga and anime are a mixed bag: from charitable to homicidal.

NOTE

1. Given the western architecture inside and outside, and dating backward from the year of the story (1987), the chapel would have been built 50 to 60 years earlier, sometime shortly after the Great Kantō Earthquake and fire of 1923. Traditional wooden structures were destroyed in the fires that broke out when the quake hit at noon on a Saturday; among the few buildings that survived, although with some damage, was the Imperial Hotel designed by Frank Lloyd Wright ("The Imperial Hotel", http://www.mnn.com/your-home/remodeling-design/photos/6-destroyed-frank-lloyd-wright-buildings/the-imperial-hotel, accessed August 25, 2015). This helped convince Japan to take western brick-and-mortar architecture seriously.

Chapter Nine

Clergy

Western literature has no shortage of wicked men and women of the Christian clergy. Archdeacon Claude Frollo is clearly the villain of Victor Hugo's novel *Hunchback of Notre Dame*, committing sins ranging from jealousy and lying to lust and murder. His countryman Cardinal Richelieu played people like chess-pieces in life as well as in Alexander Dumas's *The Three Musketeers*. More recently, Archbishop Manuel Aringarosa leads the forces of the Opus Dei organization, and in particular his disciple the murderous monk Silas, against those seeking an inconvenient truth about Jesus in Dan Brown's *The DaVinci Code*. Of course, there are also clerical characters of good deeds and good intentions. All of these characters, appearing in the west for a western audience, behave—and are sometimes disciplined for their behavior—in ways acceptable (or at least understandable) to that audience.

Japanese pop culture writers, however, approach Christianity with knowledge of Christianity in Japanese history or in the present day; the difference is that there is nothing in the culture that tells them they are dealing with the One True Church and to tread lightly. There are no constraints to go easy on Christian clerics just because they're Christian.

DON PEDRO AND FAMILY—*MICHIKO TO HATCHIN*

Michiko to Hatchin is a 22-episode anime series first broadcast in 2008-09 and set in a Hollywood style fantasy of Brazil's demimonde. Michiko Malandro is modeled after American "blaxploitation" movie heroines of the Seventies such as Cleopatra Jones and Foxy Brown: tall, statuesque and violent African American women. In the first minute of the series, she makes a daring jailbreak and escapes to search for the child Hana Morenos, the

Hatchin (or "Little Hana") of the title and apparently a link to Michiko's old lover Hiroshi Morenos, now believed to be dead.

Hana, meanwhile, has been adopted by Don Pedro Berembowser Yamada,[1] the pastor of the Church of San Pedro; he is raising her along with his wife Joanna and their two children Maria and Gabriel—again, an arrangement ignoring the Catholic insistence on priestly celibacy.[2] All of Don Pedro's garments have crucifixes on them, and all members of his family wear crosses around their necks. (Interestingly, Hana is the only member of the family who does not wear glasses; an interesting bit of symbolism that suggests that both the inner vision of the Christians and their actual vision are impaired.) Christianity means nothing positive to Hana, however, since she is brutally mistreated in the first episode by all four members of her foster family. Don Pedro likes to proclaim his good works, especially if he can profit from them, and he and his wife have taken in Hana mainly for the monthly government stipend.

Michiko makes an entrance—riding a motorcycle through a window—to take Hana away from this family; Don Pedro accompanies the police in pursuit in the hope that Hana might get killed in a gun battle with the authorities, in which case he stands to collect the insurance. At first fearful of this complete stranger, Hana eventually realizes that Michiko is the only person looking out for her.

The most telling conversion of Hana away from Christianity occurs at the end of the second episode, when Don Pedro confronts Hana on a rooftop, threatening to kill her himself. Hana pulls the crude crucifix from around her neck—carved from wood and painted green—and throws it at Don Pedro, hitting him in the forehead. In preparing to shoot Hana, Don Pedro throws the cross down and steps on it.

This gesture would resonate with a Japanese audience more than many others, given the roots of this practice. The act of *fumie*, stepping on a picture as a form of renunciation, goes back at least to the Tokugawa era, when the nation of Japan sealed itself off from the outside world. Part of this policy was the declaration that Christianity itself was outlawed and converts were either put to death or given the opportunity to renounce their conversion.[3] Believers were expected to step on a sculpture or drawing of Jesus, or the Madonna and Child, as part of the renunciation. (The practice survived into World War 2, when those citizens suspected by the police of being pacifists or dissidents were compelled to step on drawings of American President Roosevelt and/or British Prime Minister Churchill to declare their allegiance to the Emperor and, by extension, to the Axis powers.)

Michiko to Hatchin is a media version of Christianity, one which shows off the worst aspects of the supposed believers. Hana's foster family members are selfish hypocrites, casually violent and abusive toward Hana in ways that are part *Cinderella* and part *Harry Potter*. At least they are self-aware enough not to claim that their cruelty is tied to their Christian faith, but the faith doesn't come to Hana's aid either; she has to wait for a gun-toting escaped convict for help.

FATHER KAWABUCHI SENTARO—*SAKAMICHI NO APORON (KIDS ON THE SLOPE)*

In this brief (12 episode) anime series, based on a manga by Kodama Yuki, we're reminded that, in the Japanese scheme of things, religion can be a factor of geography and even of genetics, and not exclusively a profession of faith.

The series takes place mostly in the year 1966; first year high school honor student Nishimi Kaoru is sent to live with relatives on the island of Kyushu, because of business pressures put upon his father. This isn't his first time as the new kid in town, and he reacts to it by being a bookworm. This only gets him so far, until he is befriended by Class Representative Mukae Ritsuko; through her, Kaoru also meets her childhood friend Kawabuchi Sentaro.

Sentaro is rather tall and lanky, and has a reputation as the class ruffian, but this is not really true. The reputation is projected onto Sentaro because he is a "half"—his mother is Japanese but his father was an American serviceman. His grandmother and stepfather are aloof toward Sentaro for this reason; he and Ritsuko are also devout Catholics, although this is no surprise or stigma on Kyushu.

The pivot for the plot is Ritsuko's father, who owns a record store and plays stand-up bass. Through him, Kaoru moves from playing classical piano to jazz, with Sentaro joining in on drums. The usual personal and romantic problems that occur in high school manga/anime have a special soundtrack because of this arrangement: versions of jazz classics from the Sixties, including "Someday My Prince Will Come", "My Favorite Things" and "But Not for Me". The performances were produced by stellar pianist/composer Kanno Yoko, a talented and devoted student of American music.

By the end of the series, the family drama has been such that Sentaro runs away from home. Fast forward eight years: Kaoru is now a medical student and Sentaro is a novice priest. However, when Kaoru catches up to him and starts playing jazz on the church organ, Sentaro immediately joins in on drums, as if nothing had changed after all. Their reunion, like their original friendship, is determined by music. However, the music of religious western culture is tightly constrained. Back in 1963, a Belgian nun named Sister Sourire, known as The Singing Nun, actually had a record on the pop music charts: "Dominique," a folk song about a minstrel singing about God, which enjoyed popularity in America even though it was entirely in French.[4] More recently, in the *Sister Act* movies, traditional hymns are modernized or popular songs are used which can suggest a religious meaning, such as "I Will Follow Him," originally a teen love song recorded by Little Peggy March. In the final scene of this anime, however, Kaoru and Sentaro are brought back together by the straight-ahead jazz that has played throughout the series: specifically by "Moanin'", written for Art Blakey and the Jazz Messengers. (Ink (pseudonym). "All That Jazz!" *Otaku USA,* vol. 6 #5 (April 2013) pp. 84-87)

This anime's scenario stigmatized the Christian clergy by having Sentaro be a "half". Even in the 21st century it can be problematic in Japan, and would certainly have been moreso in the Sixties, when there were many more American servicemen in country fighting the Vietnam War from bases in Tokyo and Okinawa. Fortunately, things are changing: halfs are asserting themselves as deserving equal treatment, and some are gaining recognition and even popularity, such as singer/pianist Angela Aki.

FATHER CORTION, INQUISITOR—*WITCH HUNTER ROBIN*

The 2002 anime series *Witch Hunter Robin,* animated by Sunrise and directed by Murase Shuko, is a unique mix of the (literally) Magical Girl genre with the Hidden Agenda drama which became more common in the Nineties, especially after *Shin Seiki Evangelion.* Chapter 11 takes a deeper look at the entire series. For now, we can examine the two clergymen who appear briefly in the series. Both men are perceived at first as being on one side in the battle between witches[5] and humans, but both are revealed to be following a very different path.

Father Cortion, an Inquisitor for the witch-hunting organization known as Solomon, only appears in episode 13. He's an old man, with gray hair and blue eyes. He's arrived for the Inquisition of a suspected witch: Masuda Shiro, out of work for two years but being scouted by the Inquisitor to see if he could be used as a Hunter of other witches. Masuda happens to get mugged, which sets off his rage-fueled witchcraft against his attackers; he overpowers Solomon member Amon until Robin has to kill Masuda. Before that, though, Amon offers a theory: that Masuda was being manipulated by Solomon, deliberately driven by the stresses of poverty to force him over the edge into using his magic. The Inquisitor seems to take note of all of this, and leaves Tokyo telling Robin that she herself seems to have awakened to being a witch who revels in the use of her witchcraft. Robin begins to realize that the Inquisitor is setting her up; from this point on, the story moves fast and dangerous.

FATHER JULIANO COLEGULI

Father Juliano is pulled in two directions by this story. As a Roman Catholic priest he would not be sympathetic to Robin's very existence, since it is written in Exodus: "You shall not allow a witch to live." (Exodus 22:18) However, even though he is attached to the witch-hunting group known as Solomon, he is also Robin's former guardian and her maternal grandfather who raised her from birth after Robin's mother Maria, Juliano's daughter, died in childbirth.

In the beginning of the series, Robin mentions in passing that Father Juliano's powers have diminished, suggesting that he was once a craft user for Solomon, although it is never stated what his specific craft was. Since he and Robin are related, it's probable that he was a fire craft user like Robin. He visits Robin in the latter part of the series to inform her (and the audience) about the events surrounding her past. During the time Robin stays with a seedy attorney named Nagira to hide from Solomon, Juliano is the one who asks Amon to hunt Robin, for fear that she wouldn't be able to control her powers as they grew stronger. Later, in the episode titled "Redemption Day" he confronts Robin himself, and sees that she has not changed, nor turned into the monster he feared her to be. He asks her forgiveness and blesses her, giving her the information taken from her "father" Todou's[6] journal that will help her choose her path, and entrusts her to her own destiny, knowing she will choose the right actions. For a more detailed discussion of this anime, see chapter 11.

NICHOLAS D. WOLFWOOD — *TRIGUN*

Based on a manga by Nightow Yasuhiro (a pseudonym) and turned into an anime (1998) and a movie (2010), *Trigun* focuses on an alternate reality on a planet called Gunsmoke. The main character is a gunman known as "Vash the Stampede". He is blamed for destroying an entire city, although he has no real memory of the event; he does, however, have a large bounty on his head and many men trying to claim that money. In his travels around Gunsmoke he crosses the path of Nicholas D. Wolfwood, a self-styled preacher in a black suit who carries The Punisher. This is the name he gives a life-sized crucifix-shaped box. It weighs about 200 pounds, since inside it there are a variety of firearms. (He carries such a large and heavy box around with relative ease because, according to Vash, Wolfwood has a great sense of balance.)

This balance is metaphoric as well as literal. Raised in an orphanage, Wolfwood was trained for, and recruited into, an assassin's organization called the Eye of Michael. Part of his life with the group included a medicinal potion that allowed him to heal quickly from serious wounds, but at the cost of years off of the end of his life. (When Wolfwood dies during the series, he is age 44.)

While protecting Vash (who because of his violent past is now regarded not as human but as a "natural disaster"), Wolfwood also protects his orphanage; in the anime, he runs it as an adult. His philosophy is similar to one expressed by Doctor Black Jack: "We're not like God. Not only are our powers limited, but we sometimes have to play the Devil." Wolfwood is known as The Preacher because of The Punisher and his dressing in black suits, and because his mentor in the Eye of Michael was both a priest and an assassin. Vash has made a commitment not to kill, making him rather like samurai Himura Kenshin who, after a bloody past, has sworn off killing in Watsuki Nobuhiro's Meiji-era manga *Rurouni Kenshin*. Wolfwood, however, is still an assassin, and feels no remorse for taking lives, especially if he is punishing the guilty or protecting the innocent. Both can still require killing, and this weighs on his conscience.

Nightow is generally known as one of the few successful Christian manga artists. *Trigun* itself can be viewed as full of themes and ideas that have apparent or potential connections to Christianity. According to the blog titled *BeneathTheTangles*, Nightow grew up as a Buddhist, but studied Catholicism and converted to it, while retaining Buddhist principles. Christian themes are also found in the *Trigun* manga and anime, according to an essay in *lizjen.com*. Even though being a gunman Wolfwood takes his faith seriously; but unlike Vash who is very much a pacifist, Wolfwood believes himself to be a realist and that violence and killing are a part of life. When questioned about this, he always replies, "I've always chosen the right path, haven't I?"

Wolfwood's actions can also be compared to other anime/manga characters or even to figures from Japanese history or literature, such as ronin in stories inspired by the historical figure Yagyu Jubei. Either way, and even given Nightow's personal philosophy, the series is not about Wolfwood but about Vash. As is the case with Amakusa Shojo and his sister in the anime version of *Rurouni Kenshin*, the main character remains the main character, even if a secondary Christian character comes along with an interesting story.

Still, it should be noted that Nightow said at the 2009 Anime Expo in Los Angeles that one of his favorite movies was the first *Star Wars* film, and that his dream would be to live on Luke Skywalker's home planet Tattooine. By seeing Tattooine as a model for planet Gunsmoke, parallels for *Trigun* from Lucas's films suggest themselves as easily as Biblical narratives.

BLACK ANGELS

Black Angels is similar to another popular adolescent boys' manga of the Eighties, *Hokuto no Ken (Fist of the North Star)* in its taste for violence; in fact, Hiramatsu Shinji, creator of *Black Angels,* and Buronson, the pen name of the creator of *Hokuto no Ken,* had collaborated on another manga previously. Both were highly successful manga about vigilante justice in parts of Japan where the weak and decent people were being abused by the callous, greedy and powerful. At first Hiramatsu Shinji's 1981 manga seems to have nothing to do with Christianity beyond the angel imagery of the title.

The opening episodes offer a young adult (young enough to pass as a high school student, if the need arises) bicycling around Japan, taking odd jobs; his name is Yukito Yoji. He pleasantly performs such menial tasks as delivery cyclist for a noodle shop and assistant janitor at a bathhouse. When he is asked about his family, his answer is simple: "I have no family."

He does have a knack, however, for finding some of the worst characters modern Japan has to offer and dispatching them vigilante-style. His unlikely weapon-of-choice is a spoke from one of the wheels of his ten-speed bicycle, jammed into the ear or neck or skull of the victim to leave barely a trace. His repeated catch-phrase during each killing: "Jigoku e ochiro (Go to Hell)."

In his travels he finds another violent vigilante: Matsuda, a police detective who rides a motorcycle, has a special grudge against members of the Yakuza, and is so violent in his use of karate that he's ultimately thrown off the force. He wears large aviator sunglasses and black leather; his character could have been played by Sylvester Stallone.

They team up as two kindred spirits causing lethal mayhem against Yakuza gangsters and respectable crooks in league with them. They do more than just refer to themselves as Black Angels: in the episode titled "Black Blood", the artist/storyteller concludes the episode by quoting the Old Testament in the narration: "Thy bruise is incurable, thy wound is grievous. There is no one to plead thy cause, no remedy for thy sore, no healing for thee" (Jeremiah 30:12-13). From this point on, the association with these killers and Christianity becomes more and more overt.

The next story is titled "Black Cross" and begins with Yoji riding through a park one night, where he happens to stop a masked man with a knife from attacking a woman. Yoji barely escaped injury, but was taken to a hospital where, when he took off his shirt, the reader saw a cross branded into his chest. He remembers his past, revealing to the reader that both his parents died at the same time when he was a child, and his older sister dropped out of high school to support them as they lived with family. One stormy night she came home and found her aunt and uncle murdered while Yoji was still asleep upstairs. She jumped through the window with Yoji to avoid the knife-wielding killer; a shard of glass cut the chain holding a crucifix around her neck. Lightning struck the crucifix as it fell, heating it so that it caused the brand on Yoji's chest.

Back in the present, the woman who owned the bar and grill named "Yoko" is attacked by another knife-wielding maniac; Yukito kills him with the icepick and is about to kill Yoko as well, because he never wants to be witnessed acting as a Black Angel. However, he can't kill her; not only does she resemble his sister, she says "I'm on your side here; just leave this to me."

The reader finds that Yoko's fiancée Takashi has an ulterior motive for the attacks: he's a salaryman at a pharmaceutical company and is engaged to the boss's daughter, while Yoko is just a woman who he was seeing on the side. He has been trying to arrange for Yoko's murder to get her out of the way.

The flashback continues: Yukito's sister is grilled by a Prosecutor who says that there was no intruder found, that hers were the only fingerprints on the knife, and that she wouldn't be released until she confessed to the murders of her aunt and uncle. She tells Yukito that she is so tired from the relentless questions that "I don't know what the truth is anymore." Yukito was brought to visit his sister by a Catholic priest: young, bearded, looking like the traditional pictures of Jesus. He tells her: "You came to Mass every morning, and every time I saw you, your faces looked like those of angels. I do not believe either of you would lie like this." Still, under the pressure she hanged herself in prison; we see the priest praying over her body.

Meanwhile, Takashi decides that, after two botched attempts to kill Yoko with hired assassins, he would have to kill her himself. Yukito walks in on the stabbing after hiding the body of the second assassin. After killing Takashi, he thinks: "Yoko, I... I killed you just the same."

The flashback continues in the next story, "A Black Past". We see the burial of Yukito's sister, in a churchyard, presided over by the priest. This may seem awkward, given the reputation that suicides cannot receive a Catholic burial, but that's exactly what it is: a persistent reputation, and no longer part of church doctrine. According to the Catechism of the Catholic Church as amended in 1992:

> Grave psychological disturbances, anguish, or grave fear of hardship, suffering, or torture can diminish the responsibility of the one committing suicide. ... We should not despair of the eternal salvation of persons who have taken their own lives. By ways known to him alone, God can provide the opportunity for salutary repentance. The Church prays for persons who have taken their own lives. (CCC, 2282-2283)

The Prosecutor has the nerve to show up at the grave with a bunch of flowers, and says, "I suppose she killed herself to repent for her sins, huh?" The priest replies that "The Bible teaches us this: 'For the LORD knows the way of the righteous, but the way of the wicked shall perish.' Someday, we will all know the truth!"

The little brother takes matters into his own hands and, in a familiar ritual in many manga such as sports stories, time passes as he devotes himself to perfecting his "skills". He takes lengths of thick wire, straightens them, files one end to a point, and uses them in target practice. Night after night, month after month, he practices his lethal abilities, envisioning the Prosecutor's face as the target on the wall of his room at the church.

He decides that he's ready at about the time that the Prosecutor is fired for abuse of power. We see the Prosecutor confront the man who actually killed the elderly couple—the crime for which Yukito's sister was blamed. The Prosecutor found out that she was innocent, but not until after she'd killed herself. Still, rather than bring the truth to light, the Prosecutor has been blackmailing the real murderer.

Meanwhile, the priest, a nun named Arisa, and the gravedigger[7] at the cemetery discuss Yukito; he has hidden his striving to become an assassin, but Arisa says that "I've never encountered a child like him. He's a gentle, nice boy... but he frightens me!" The priest replies that "I don't understand it either. But all humans live in this world bearing a different fate. And no one can change their fate, as sad as it may seem."

Yukito has gone out that night seeking the Prosecutor, and finds him out drinking with the money he extorted from the uncaught murderer. In that seedy part of town he sees the priest, who tells the Prosecutor: "A Black Angel brings down God's judgment upon thee!!" He whips the crucifix from around his neck and garrotes the Prosecutor with the chain. He then calmly walks away from the body, leaving a shuddering Yukito who witnessed the murder.

As he goes looking for the priest, he sees the man who killed his aunt and uncle the year before. They recognize each other, and the man chases the boy, realizing that he was a witness. He chases Yukito into the church, into the chapel; Yukito throws some of his homemade darts at the man but they hit his arms and leg with no real damage. The priest, following them into the church, tosses a spiked candle-holder to Yukito, who uses it to kill his attacker. In an artful scene, the murder by a seven year old is witnessed by Arisa, the gravedigger, the stained glass window depicting the crucifixion of Jesus, and the priest who had also committed murder just ten minutes before. As the man fell dying onto Yukito's chest, the cross-shaped scar began to bleed. The narration of the final panel of this episode reads: "The Black Angel 'Law of Death': One who has been bathed in black blood will never again be clean."

How does a manga artist follow that? In this case, the next episode reveals another Black Angel with another talent: the nun named Arisa. When a corrupt high school teacher begins procuring female students for the school's equally corrupt chairman, Arisa arranges to meet the teacher on the school roof. Using hypnosis she walks him backward to the edge of the roof, and tells him "Sinful servant of Satan, I command thee! Return to the depths of Hell! Descend to the bottom of the abyss!" He's brought out of the trance as he falls backward off the roof to his death.

When Principal Murata and Chairman Gondo meet to discuss continuing their business as usual, the gravedigger Hashimu is literally eavesdropping on them from the ceiling. Back at the church Arisa insists that she will kill Principal Murata while Hashimu kills Chairman Gondo. The priest hopes that Yoji will "possess what we have lost."

The Chairman went to attack another schoolgirl, except that it's Hashimu in a school uniform. Giving his own variation of the Black Angels cry ("Listen to the echoes of Hell!") he crushes the Chairman's testicles. Arisa, meanwhile, has hypnotized the principal, who follows her to the school roof. From there, however, she cannot send him off of the roof. The reason, which Yoji explains having stabbed the principal through the brain, was that he was dead already. The father at the church explains that, while we are all born with white wings, they have painted their wings black. Yoji says, "That was my destiny."

The plot begins to expand in episode 20, "Black Departure." A new enemy is introduced: the Dragonfang Syndicate, buying up tracts of land seeking to implement something called Plan M that threatens "all of Japan." The priest, Father Takazawa, knows about it because he used to belong to the syndicate; he left them 13 years earlier and became a priest (although a lethal priest) to atone, but fate has brought his old nemesis back into his life. One of the syndicate members, a famous "social critic" named Otomo Kenzaburo, tries to warn Father Takazawa against interfering; the point is driven home by the syndicate setting the church on fire. Father Takazawa garrotes Otomo with his crucifix, while Yukito barely escapes being garroted by a Dragonfang assassin.

This story is as much a fantasy as manga tales of extraterrestrials or young people with psychic powers. It is unnerving that this level of violence is associated with something literally held sacred in the west. Unnerving to a western audience, that is, and that's the point. These faith-based murderers live in a world of mysterious ritual usually impenetrable to the Japanese adolescent audience of this manga; that description could apply both to the yakuza and the Catholic clergy. Both groups are following the rules of Orientalism by acting out their story in a world where literally anything is possible.

The story of the Black Angels will be continued in chapter 14, The Not Safe Chapter, because that's where the story takes its readers. For now, the lethal nun Arisa brings us to the way that nuns appear in Japanese manga and anime.

NOTES

1. The name is a strange conflation of a Brazilian musical instrument (berimbau, a single-stringed musical bow) and the distinctly Japanese name Yamada. Recall the dialogue between the priest Coelho and shogun Toyotomi mentioned in chapter 2. In the early years of Christian contact with Japan, Portuguese sailors occasionally purchased or stole Japanese women and children, took them on their ships, and sold them into slavery or prostitution in Portugal and Brazil, among other ports of call. The existence of a family named Yamada in Brazil is thus not impossible.

2. One way that we know the household is Catholic is a scene where Hana is pushed down a flight of stairs; she ends up in front of an altar with candles burning in front of a picture of the Virgin Mary. There is nothing Protestant about this family, but neither is there much that qualifies as orthodox Catholicism.

3. In an era when whole Japanese families converted to Christianity because they were ordered to by their local feudal lord or family patriarch, this policy made sense to a degree. The issue of free will was not always part of Japanese Christianity, especially in the period before the Age of Enlightenment; when Japan opened up again in 1853 and Christian missionaries returned, it was a very different Christianity that returned, not resembling the top-down medieval approach of the 16th century Jesuits.

4. Incidentally, this was the same year that the American charts also saw a song get to Number One that was sung entirely in Japanese: "Ue wo Muite Arukou", but that title was considered so daunting to Anglophones that it was changed to "Sukiyaki".

5. In this series, the term "witch" is applied to both men and women who use magic.

6. Todou was a geneticist who artificially impregnated his wife (Juliano's daughter) Maria; she was a witch, as was her father, and her daughter would be the title character of the anime.

7. This gravedigger, named Hashimu, will continue to appear in the series; all we know of him for now is that he works around the church and has the ragged dress and hat of a *binboo-nin*—a poor man—common in many manga as incidental or comic characters, at least before Japan's prosperity bubble burst in the early 1990s and homelessness became less of a joke.

Chapter Ten

Nuns in Anime/Manga

Sisterhood Is Not So Powerful

Just as Japan already knows of priests both from exposure to Christianity and to Shinto and/or Buddhist clerics, Catholic nuns are also familiar in part because of the existence of nuns in Buddhism. Shinto has *miko*, temple priestesses, who are often the daughters of the priests. In manga and anime, however, *miko* do more than perform ceremonial dances and tell fortunes. They have the reputation of tapping into special divine powers and can, if they choose, become priestesses in their own right—something a Catholic nun could never aspire to.

The media versions of nuns in Japan, as in the west, are on a continuum from the very realistic to the highly unreal. Actual discussion of Christian doctrine is limited to what "everybody knows" about Catholic nuns; the artists' fanciful imagination fills in the gaps. In the previous chapter we've seen this at work with Arisa, the homicidal hypnotist nun of *Black Angels;* her sisters in pop culture are no less creative.

SISTER ANGELA--*ONE POUND GOSPEL*

This manga ran in *Weekly Young Sunday* magazine, one of several series by Takahashi Rumiko that appeared there. This one, however, started out in 1989, then went on a lengthy hiatus when Takahashi got caught up in her masterwork, the highly popular *InuYasha*. She finally picked up *One Pound Gospel* again in 2006, finishing it in 2008. It's targeted for a college-age crowd, and has none of the magical elements of *InuYasha* or *Ranma ½*. What it does have is Takahashi's gentle but winning sense of humor.

The main figure of the manga is Hatanaka Kousaku, a prodigy of the Mukouda boxing gym. He went pro in only two bouts after leaving high school, and his powerful punches are well known to his opponents as well as his coach and sparring partners. Of course there's a problem that's also well-known: he can't control his appetite. Kousaku eats anything and everything, from Japanese snacks to instant ramen to fast-food burgers, without thinking about having to burn it off. As a result, he has been forced to change his weight class almost continuously since high school. He swings back and forth from flyweight to featherweight;[1] his trainer tells him he doesn't have the frame for the heavier classes, and his constant eating prevents him from losing the weight he gains. On top of this, he accepts challenges from even higher weight classes, giving his coach (and himself) constant headaches.

His workout runs take him past a Catholic church whose clergy includes Sister Angela, a novice nun (whose real name is Marie) who takes Kousaku on as a personal project; she is determined to break his habit of gluttony. She constantly encourages him, making sure that he stays in shape while staying away from food. That task is hard enough, but—as happens in so many Hollywood films involving nuns, including *The Nun's Story* and *The Sound of Music*—romance becomes a problem. Closeness can sometimes breed feelings of affection, which Kousaku begins to develop toward Sister Angela. Even worse, Sister Angela realizes she is beginning to have the same problems. What saves the situation at first is that their timing is off. They're never interested in each other in the same way at the same time, both of them being rather naïve and living sheltered lives in, respectively, the gym and the church.

Sister Angela is shown hearing Kousaku's confessions of gluttony. In keeping with the modern-day duties of a nun in Japan, she is often seen surrounded by children in the church's day-care. In one scene she is walking the children past a family restaurant modeled after the Denny's franchise; the restaurant has hired someone to stand on the sidewalk giving away balloons. He's dressed as Dracula, and when he smiles at the children, we see fangs; Sister Angela holds up her crucifix to protect the children—one sign among many that she's rather naïve. (The fangs were obviously false, but they were also dentures, since the man dressed as Dracula was a boxer who lost every tooth in his head when he was hit face-first into the ropes.)[2]

We also see later in the series that she's been raised to be naïve by an overly devout mother; the Sister's aunt, on the other hand, is a very worldly high liver and big spender. She takes Angela out on the town one night to a host club, where women are waited on hand and foot by the good-looking staff of young men—a gender reversal of the more traditional hostess clubs. The aunt leaves the Sister alone with one of the hosts, who tells her a story of having been sold into bondage to pay off a family debt—a story that anyone else would have realized was a cliché from a dozen historical dramas about girls being sold into prostitution in earlier centuries. He asks Sister Angela to buy a bottle of pink champagne, which she guesses can't cost more than the equivalent of $15. However, in a club like this, the bottle costs about $300, and the aunt has skipped out without paying up. And—as is the way of stories like this—Kousaku ends up meeting both the vampire cosplayer and the host in the boxing ring, giving both he and the Sister multiple motives to care about the outcome of the fights.

In one fight, which comes after a variety of interpersonal missteps, Kousaku has the advantage over his opponent. He decides to finish the match and please Sister Angela at the same time, and, before delivering the final punch, crosses himself. This, of course, leaves him wide-open and defenseless when his opponent knocks him out with an uppercut. Sister Angela's reaction: "Baka" (Idiot). Unlike Hayasaka Dan in *God is a Southpaw*,[3] the Christian gesture is no help this time.

If your taste in manga is for the kind of magical escapism Takahashi brought to *InuYasha*, this story won't be too appealing. It's more in the vein of her *Mezon Ikkoku*—a different, more down to earth kind of comic escapism.

SISTER ROSETTE CHRISTOPHER—*CHRONO CRUSADE*

Sister Rosette is in this chapter pretty much by default. She wears a variation of a nun's habit; she belongs to the New York branch of a group of exorcists called the Order of Magdalene, which reports to the Council of the Catholic Church; she wears a pendant reputed to contain the soul of Mary Magdalene. This last item is a clue to the direction taken in the manga by Moriyama Daisuke. It began running monthly in *Comic Dragon* magazine late in 1998 and ended in 2004; an anime based on the manga premiered in 2003, timed to end along with the run of the manga. It had a fan base, but not one that would care whether Sister Rosette Christopher was a realistic nun or not. "Nun" in this case seems more like a character class than a religious vocation, and the entire series, like the more current *Blue Exorcist* discussed in chapter 6, scans like a role-playing game, complete with exotic weapons, shifting locales, and strategic alliances.

The clearest nod to fantasy in this series is that Sister Rosette has a partner named Chrono who is a Demon; reformed, and of diminished strength because he lost his horns in a battle with another Demon, but still a Demon. He serves Sister Rosette by amplifying her life-force, which she keeps safe in a pocket watch. He actually hesitates to exercise that power, since doing so shortens Sister Rosette's life, and they've become quite fond of each other. When he isn't acting like a Demon, Chrono appears as a young boy, while Sister Rosette is a feisty and headstrong teenager.

I mentioned that Sister Rosette and her fellow Magdalenes are exorcists; in this story, however, there are no prayers or holy water as in chapter 6; instead, there is technology that allows the exorcist to "dive" into the possessed person to do battle with the demon. The terminology is borrowed from computer hacking current at the time of the manga's creation, rather than from the Roaring Twenties when the story is set; perhaps it was influenced by the terminology of Masamune Shirow, and particularly the anime of his manga *Ghost in the Shell,* which redefined the medium when it appeared just a few years before *Chrono Crusade* began publishing.

MARIA-SAMA GA MITERU

Begun as a series of light novels by Konno Oyuki and illustrated by Hibiki Reine and published between 1998 and 2012, *Maria-sama ga Miteru (Mother Mary is Watching)* is a brilliant example of *yuri* literature, which focuses on relationships between young women. These relationships may—or may not—turn toward lesbianism, but for the audience the potential is accepted as always possible. In this case, the plot threads are helped along by placing these lilies—*yuri* in Japanese—in an isolated hothouse atmosphere. The audience is a large one: the novels spun off to manga, anime—both for broadcast and direct to consumer OAV—and live action film, radio dramas and drama CDs.

The setting is the Lillian Girls' Academy (*Shiritsu Ririan Jogakuen*), a fictional Catholic school founded in 1901 in the Musashino district of Tokyo. The school is depicted as an elegant, clean, pure, and very prestigious institution. Among the facilities of Lillian, aside from the classrooms, there is a church, a greenhouse, a kendo dojo, an auditorium, a park, and the Rose Mansion, where the Yamayuri (Mountain Lily) Council meet. The uniform at the school is a long, black Japanese school uniform with a white collar, with a skirt longer than usual but not as long as a nun's habit. Strictly a school and neither a convent nor a preparatory school to enter a nunnery, the religious symbolism is unambiguous; the academy is a Christian oasis in Japan.

There are real, although tentative, connections to Catholicism in the series. Author Konno said that she attended a Catholic kindergarten, with a sanctuary and cloister on the grounds; she later attended a secular all-girls high school. She also admitted to having questions at the time about the way the Virgin Mary was viewed, and used the novels to recall how she worked through those questions for herself.

The school uses a fictional *sœur* system where any second- or third-year student, as a *grande sœur* (big sister), might pick a younger girl who will become her *petite sœur* (little sister). The *grande sœur* gives her *petite sœur* a rosary and promises to look after and guide her. Basic etiquette demands the *petite sœur* call her *grande sœur* "oneesama" (older sister in Japanese, although the term can refer to a friend who isn't a blood relative).

This institutionalizes a behavior that goes on, with greater or lesser formality, time and again in a Japanese person's life, regardless of age or gender. Whether it's a middle management salaryman taking the newest arrival under his wing, or a schoolgirl seeking help from an older classmate, or a new member of a sports team getting pointers from one of the old veterans, the notion of an older sibling guiding and looking out for a younger sibling is one of the most important principles endorsed centuries ago by the Chinese writer now known as Confucius. According to one of his most famous quotes, "a superior man considers it necessary that the names he uses may be spoken appropriately, and also that what he speaks may be carried out appropriately. What the superior man requires is just that in his words there may be nothing incorrect."

In our time and place this may seem rather arbitrary, but Confucius was trying to create a philosophy of government that was both effective and just. Eventually he distilled his ideal state and his ideal family as having the same principle: do what you are supposed to do according to your name, your title, your role. If you're a prince, act like a prince; if you're a husband, act like a husband. Failing to respect your role confuses everyone around you and leads to social breakdown, according to Confucius. The Big Sister/Little Sister relationship in the Lillian Academy thus has roots that predate Catholicism.

Aside from being used in prayer, the rosary at this Academy is the instrument that certifies the *sœur* relationship between two students. There is an implicit code of behavior between *sœurs*, especially in the Yamayuri Council—the student council of this school: quietness, measure and respect towards each other; values deeply attached to traditional Japanese education.

French is occasionally used in the story; for example, the series is given the French subtitle *La Vierge Marie vous regarde*, which means "The Virgin Mary is watching you". In keeping with the tone of the series, the formal and highly respectful Japanese greeting *"gokigen yoo"* is used in the Lillian School to greet and to bid farewell. This has been one of the distinguishable and popular catch-phrases of the series, and it is used to begin or to finish each volume of the novels. The English-language version translates the phrase as "good day to you".

The Lillian Girls' Academy uses the lily symbolism since the white lily is associated with the Virgin Mary as a Christian symbol of purity and virginity. This lily imagery is also used as a reference to literature: the story has some elements of romance between female characters; the use of lilies reinforces this in subtext, as do the names of the student council and of the school itself. The series is only explicit about a romantic relationship once in a flashback, but many of the sisters have what I think of as intense friendships, and would have been part of a body of women's writings in 20th century Japan known as Class S writings, in which same-sex relationships were intensely emotional but platonic.

Yet the lily has also been used in Japanese literature in the context of lesbian relationships. The term was first used, as far as can be told, in 1976, but it caught on quickly. Japanese women authors have shown such relationships to a greater or lesser degree of explicitness for literally centuries; women have been noted authors in Japan since Lady Murasaki wrote *The Tale of Genji* a thousand years ago. The first openly lesbian author, however, was Yoshiya Nobuko (1896-1973), whose early stories were about longing from afar, unrequited love, or unhappy endings; later, in her writings and her life, she was more openly lesbian. Since same-sex marriages were impossible, she went to the legal extent of adopting her partner, with whom she lived for fifty years, as her daughter. The same-sex relationships of varying intensity in manga and anime thus have a pedigree as lengthy as Catholicism.

GEOCHRIS — *GALL FORCE: EARTH CHAPTER 1*

Religion offers comfort in times of trouble, but what about when times have gone beyond "trouble"? Is it a distraction from reality, or a reminder?

The premise of the "Earth" chapter of the science fiction anime series *Gall Force* is that Earth has been invaded by an alien race of robots known as the MME. They are resisted as best as can be by a motley group of Earth survivors, including the Gall Force[4], an all-women fighting team led by Sandy Newman. In this 1989 episode, animated by ARTMIC and released as a stand-alone OAV, the Earthlings are preparing for an MME assault on Earth. Military commanders of the West and the Soviet Union conveniently discover that neither side completely exhausted its nuclear arsenal in the last war; there are a total of thirty warheads ready to use against the MME.

While preparing to launch the missiles, Sandy makes a surprising discovery. Previous wars, both against aliens and other armies of Earth, have left the planet a wreckage of collapsed buildings and desert wastes. However, hidden below the Earth's surface, in a fortified bunker, is a large tree, carefully tended and provided with clean water and filtered air. This is the Tree of Renewal, and its guardians are a religious group called GeoChris. Dressed in Catholic clerical garb, these three humans, led by a woman calling herself Sister Sally, see themselves as serving Earth after the war by bringing seeds of the Tree of Renewal back to the surface. Planting the seeds, they believe, will begin to restore the natural order. One fighter dismisses this as a fantasy, but Sandy still remembers planting seeds as a child with the help of her father, and gradually sides with GeoChris. At one point, she thinks: "I almost forgot why I was defending the Earth."

The troops, meanwhile, prepare to launch a nuclear attack on the MME—until one invader tells them that, not only was the Earth counterattack anticipated, but it would be useless, since the MME is not affected by atomic weapons. Earth aborts the bombing and continues conventional attacks on the MME. In the end, Sally gives Sandy one of the seeds from the Tree of Renewal to plant on the surface.

Apart from a few trace mentions—the clerical garb, the title "Sister", and a crucifix marked on the pouch of seeds which GeoChris wear around their necks—this isn't a religious order. There is no sacred text, no worship service, no rules of social conduct. There is only the mission: preserve the Tree so that the Earth may be renewed. Yet Sandy Newman remembered their mission, and that it used to be part of her own life before Earth was invaded. As she herself put it, she didn't convert; she was reminded.

THE SISTERS OF *EN EN NO SHŌBŌTAI*
(*FIRE BRIGADE OF FLAMES*, A/K/A *FIRE FORCE*)

When the popular manga *Soul Eater* finished its run in *Monthly Shounen GanGan* in 2014, artist and writer Ōkubo Atsushi began developing his next series. *Soul Eater* was a battle series between groups of students, some of whom had the power to turn into weapons. Ōkubo stayed with the idea of battling groups, although this particular combat is partly based in history.

When Tokugawa Ieyasu was declared Emperor in 1600, he followed the tradition of building a new capital from which to govern. Forests were soon cleared and buildings began going up in the eastern coast area known then as Edo, known today as Tokyo. The increase in building led to the increase in fire hazards; one fire in 1658 destroyed one-eighth of the city. Gangs of firemen, called hikeshi, were created to deal with the problem.

Japanese firefighters in the Tokugawa era didn't have the technology of even colonial America, much less modern equipment. The job of these firemen was to tear down buildings adjacent to any fire, to keep the flames from spreading. The men themselves were often otherwise unemployed and sometimes rather like street gangs, but they took their tasks seriously and relished the manliness of their work. They often affected large body tattoos of dragons, which were believed to live underwater and would thus "protect" them from the flames.

In the downtime between fires, groups of hikeshi would challenge each other to contests where they could display their skills. Ōkubo made these contests the basis for his next manga, which premiered in 2015: *En En no Shōbōtai*. Set in a future Tokyo, gangs of firefighters are still being kept busy, but this time they are called on to investigate an epidemic of people spontaneously bursting into flames. The hero, Kusakabe Shinra, has joined the 8th Special Fire Brigade to help preserve future Tokyo while investigating the source of his own ability to catch fire at will.

There are fire-fighting females in this future Tokyo, yet, while the males wear heavy black rubber coats similar to those worn by western firefighters, girl firefighters are dressed as nuns. The nuns have varying abilities and degrees of power. Oze Maki, who was in the 8th Brigade when Shinra joined, is a Second Generation Fire manipulator and a witch; she redirects fire attacks by turning them into sentient beings.

Iris is younger, gentler, and wears a uniform that is much closer to a nun's habit. She and another firefighter, Hibana, were the two lone survivors of an attack on the Holy Sol Temple, where they were novices. Sister Sumire seems to have been the leader of the Holy Sol Temple sisters. She was older and wore a full nun's habit with the wimple around the head.

The Holy Sol Temple was a small brick church, similar to those still found in Kyushu. In contrast, the 1st Special Brigade Cathedral, located in Tokyo's Shinjuku district, is much bigger and more ornate, with stained glass windows and pews facing the altar. There are crosses throughout the manga, but they are not crucifixes. They are all equilateral crosses, also known as Greek or Celtic crosses, with all four arms the same length, and these appear on everything from uniform buttons to the tunics of the Ash Flame Chivalric Order. Guided by someone known only as The Preacher, little is known about the Ash Flame Chivalric Order at this point in the story except for their desire to control the world.

This is just the first year of the manga, and there are a lot of issues to be sorted out. However, as a reminder of this story's Japanese roots, the reader is told in episode 34 that Shinra possesses Adora Burst, the power that was used to create the planet, and that Japan's thermal power generator, which creates energy for all of Japan, is named Amaterasu. So far, this manga plays games with Shinto as well as Catholicism, but the game is far from over. The series is only one year old as of this writing and quite popular.

"SISTER" SEIRA — *KAITOU SAINT TAIL* (*PHANTOM THIEF SAINT TAIL*)

In this anime, launched in 1994 and based on a manga by Tachikawa Megumi, the audience meets Mimori Seira, a novice nun—which seems strange, since like most of the principal characters she appears not to have graduated out of elementary school yet (although she's supposed to have just entered junior high school at age 13). Still, we see her in a white nun's habit, meeting and praying with her friend Haneoka Meimi. There are, however, some unusual elements: Meimi has a secret life as a very effective cat burglar known as Saint Tail. Not only does Seira not turn her friend over to the authorities, she believes it is her sacred duty to tell Saint Tail what to steal!

The anime ran for two seasons on Japanese TV, from 1995 to 1996. It obviously had an audience, one which accepted that youngsters could function in adult roles—as a thief, a novice nun, or a police detective. This suggests that the primary audience for this series, and for the manga, were pre-adolescents, fantasizing about life when they grow older. There is a sense in which the story doesn't take itself at face value, and presents rather like children playing dress-up games; other such anime have included *CLAMP Campus Detectives*.

Meimi has talents that she inherited from both parents—her father was a stage magician and her mother was a circus acrobat—and she spends her days attending St. Paulia's Private School; plus, she has the requisite cute pet, a hedgehog named Ruby. But the school manages to offer her plenty of opportunity for justifiable larceny (justifiable because she does it to help others). In the fourth anime episode, we meet a classmate of the heroine, Shinomiya Sayaka, who has just received through her parents a wedding veil from "her fiancée" as a token of his intentions. She is, however, not pleased at all to hear from her parents that a complete stranger has asked for her hand—especially when Sayaka has a crush on Daiki Asuka, known as "Junior" because he constantly tries to emulate his police detective father. Of course, Meimi has her own crush on Junior. It's a situation that's already been foreshadowed, but Meimi declares that "Saint Tail never has second thoughts" and will steal the veil to prevent the engagement. She even writes out her intentions on the face of Asuka Junior as he sleeps.

Meimi has the requisite Magical Girl transformation sequence, which she begins with a prayer: "Lord forgive me, for I use no gimmicks or tricks", puts on her Saint Tail apparel (including thigh-high boots, opera gloves, a top hat and cane) and joins Seira in praying "May the blessings of God be with us." Remember: she's going out to commit burglary, "if it is God's will". As part of translating the dialogue into English for the dubbed version, most of the references to God were deleted or turned into references to doing "good deeds"; the dubbing group apparently did not expect a western audience to accept the notion of a holy thief.[5]

The notion that religion can legitimize theft seems like a contradiction, at least in Judeo-Christianity; after all, stealing is specifically forbidden by one of the Ten Commandments. No less of a contradiction was carrying out torture in the name of God, yet this too was practiced for many years. A fictional modern Inquisition is the subject of the next chapter, focusing on the anime *Witch Hunter Robin;* this Japanese series is especially interesting in the light it casts on events which happened in Christian America a few years after its creation.

NOTES

1. According to the International Boxing Federation, Flyweight is between 112 and 115 pounds, and Featherweight is between 126 and 130. Most divisions are in a narrow 3 to 5 pound range, and changing divisions, even by accident, puts a fighter up against a different group of opponents, requiring different strategies.
2. He overconfidently refused any protective headgear, thus contributing to his own injuries.
3. See chapter 13 for a look at this Christian/boxing manga.
4. Gall Force is meant to be short for "gallant."
5. However, one bit of standard Anglophone dubbing practice was used here, as in most English dubs: mild curses were put into the mouths of characters who, in Japanese, simply said "Kuso!" which literally means "Oh shit!" It's been common Japanese usage for all ages for a long time, and doesn't register as obscene or foul language in that culture.

Chapter Eleven

Witch Hunter Robin

Love and Fear and a Side-Trip to Barack Obama

"You shall not allow a witch to live."—Exodus 22:18

"Jealousy and fear of those who harbor strong powers."—The witch Methuselah, in episode 12, explaining to Robin why there were witch hunts

On January 20, 2009, as Democratic celebrants rejoiced over the transfer of power to newly-sworn President Barack Obama, Republican leaders met to develop a strategy to cope with, rather than cooperate with, the new administration. In *Do Not Ask What Good We Do: Inside the U.S. House of Representatives*, Robert Draper reported that pollster Frank Luntz "organized a dinner" on Obama's inauguration night featuring a dozen of "the Republican Party's most energetic thinkers." The attendees—which included 2012 vice presidential candidate Paul Ryan—reportedly emerged from the nearly four hour dinner "almost giddily" after having agreed on "a way forward." Their goal was obstruction, confrontation and refusal to cooperate with the incoming President. According to Draper, the Republican plan involved showing "united and unyielding opposition to the president's economic policies," with an eventual goal of defeating Obama and taking back the Senate in 2012; which didn't happen. (pp. xvi-xix)

The mentality was summed up in the words of Mitch McConnell of Kentucky, ranking Republican Senator, who did not attend the meeting but who later officially announced his non-cooperation: "The single most important thing we want to achieve is for President Obama to be a one-term president." (*National Journal*, 11/4/2010)

While other countries in world history have had more bellicose transfers of power, up to and including military suppression, the United States has had a generally orderly history of political transitions. The emotional resistance in some quarters to President Obama, however, defies easy understanding. Some have resisted his policies out of a stubborn and absolute adherence to conservative economic dogma. Some have refused to accept initiatives from President Obama even when they incorporated elements of conservative thought and proposals, seemingly forgetting that such proposals may have been embraced recently by those now rejecting them. Others resorted to name-calling that would be amusing if it were not so sickening: demonstrations against government in general and President Obama in particular by the so-called Tea Party (a loose affiliation of ultra-conservatives) characterized Obama as a Socialist, a Fascist, a Muslim, an African witch doctor, a "gangsta" and even as the Joker from the Batman comics.

At the extreme of this group were the "Birthers;" these people, who included billionaire executive Donald Trump, conservative activist Orly Taitz, and Arizona Sheriff Joseph Arpaio, embodied this country's purest belief in Magical Thinking. Having convinced themselves with no real evidence that Barack Obama, like his eponymous father, was a native of Kenya, they set about to "prove" that Obama's Hawaiian birth records were hoaxes and that the "real" birth certificate was to be found in Kenya; this would "prove" that Obama was not "a native-born citizen" as required by the Constitution, and therefore was ineligible to hold the Presidency. The Birthers actually believed, in their fear and hatred, that history could be undone by finding a magical scroll and reading a certain incantation.

There have been bitter political battles, large and small, but the opposition to the Obama Administration has been unique in its ferocity and desperation. It even earned a name among some commentators for the obsessive fear and hatred generated by the President's mere existence: Obama Derangement Syndrome. It is not, however, unprecedented in American cultural history. The ugliest example of this level of fear and hatred could be found prior to and following a sporting event: the boxing match, held on the fourth of July 1910, between Jack Johnson and Jim Jeffries for the heavyweight championship title.

After winning the World Colored Heavyweight Championship in 1903, Johnson defeated Tommy Burns on December 26, 1908 to become the first unified World Heavyweight Champion. Immediately the hunt began for a "great white hope" to take the crown back, and the obvious choice was Jim Jeffries, who had retired undefeated as Heavyweight Champion in 1905. Gail Bederman in *Manliness and Civilization* made it clear what was at stake:

> the Johnson-Jeffries fight was framed as a contest to see which race had produced the most powerful, virile man.... Johnson's victory was so lopsided

that the answer was unwelcome but unmistakable. . . . The ensuing violence showed what a bitter pill that was for many white American men to swallow. (p. 2)

The "ensuing violence" included riots in a dozen Southern states and the District of Columbia, leaving eighteen dead and hundreds injured. Violence was also done to the rule of law itself: the Mann act, intended to stop prostitution across state lines, was used to harass Johnson and his wife and mistress. Congress, worried that films of the Johnson/Jeffries fight might be inflammatory, drafted legislation suppressing prizefighting films; both chambers of Congress passed it and the President signed it in a matter of weeks.

Barack Obama's successful Presidential election campaigns against John McCain in 2008 and Willard "Mitt" Romney in 2012 had no overt racial framing in the culture at large; however, many portions of the population spoke, wrote and acted as if the Johnson-Jeffries fight was happening again: the "highest office in the land" being occupied by a black American, a Negro being Commander in Chief of the Armed Forces of "the most powerful nation on Earth", was so unthinkable to some that they seemed to fear that the imminent collapse of the country was very real.

The emotions generated by these elections, and the actions and words that grew out of these emotions, are very hard to understand as the acts of rational people. The only way to make sense of it all, perhaps, is to look to the irrational: to see what was at stake in the minds of those who offered the most extreme resistance to even the idea of a President Obama. Japanese popular culture may seem an unlikely place to search for answers, and yet an animated series broadcast on Japanese television in 2002, based on Japan's singular perspective on Christianity, offers more than a clue as to why American racial hysteria of the kind prevalent in the early 1900s should have survived into the 21st century.

The series *Witch Hunter Robin* (an English title spelled out phonetically) was created by Yatate Hajime and Murase Shukou and animated by the Sunrise studio in a highly realistic style. The title character, Robin Sena, was born of a Japanese father and a European mother, and raised in Italy under the eye of the Catholic Church; specifically, by her maternal grandfather, a priest named Juliano Coleguli. When the series begins, she is sixteen years old and has just returned to Japan to work for the STN ("Solomon Toukatsu Nin'idantai" (roughly "Solomon Executive Organization") with the suffix -J denoting the Japanese branch of an organization headquartered in Europe).

Per the series title, Robin is a Witch Hunter; she is also a witch. Characters in this series are divided into humans and witches; the latter category includes seeds, a term used for those—male or female—who carry the genes that will allow them to perform magic but who have not yet realized their power. Robin turns out to be part of the genetic research into magic that had been going on secretly for years. She and her co-workers at the STN-J spend the early episodes of the series tracking down and arresting various witches, many of whom seem to have just come into their powers and most of whom are behaving lawlessly.[1] As the series progresses, however, Robin becomes a target and it becomes clear that their parent organization Solomon has a hidden agenda—a fairly common theme in Japanese popular culture after the 1990 bursting of the real estate bubble, the multiple political corruption scandals of the time, and the success of anime such as *Shin Seiki Evangelion*.

By the final episode, the viewer understands the truth of the situation. The director of STN-J, Zaizen Takuma, has become convinced that witches are not merely a different type of human with a unique genetic makeup and skill set; he believes that they are superior to humans because of their magical abilities. Believing himself and other humans to be threatened by the mere existence of witches, he has ignored his superiors and made the mission of Solomon to destroy all witches, including those who have been working for the STN-J as hunters.

Zaizen speaks very calmly early in the series, although his ideas are motivated by fear, and he gradually assumes a sense of hysteria: "Robin is no mere witch. Can you tolerate powers like hers? Can you let a world come to pass in which the artificially created genetically stronger make the weak bow down to them?" This does not happen in *Witch Hunter Robin* except if a witch becomes a thug or an extortionist. However, most witches have no such designs on humanity except in Zaizen's mind; many of the witches have more mundane preoccupations.

One STN-J researcher theorized that the legendary gods of ancient times were actually witches. When some genetic anomaly occurred which stopped them from reproducing and bearing other witches, the humans eradicated them in reality and in legend, turning them into the monsters of folklore and devils of religion. "I refuse to accept that humans are supposed to be inferior to witches," Zaizen declares.

He goes on to state his belief in terms that are unmistakably in the dehumanizing language of racism: "Witches are nothing more than filth! A race that pollutes the pure water that is humanity! To protect the beauty of that purity, to protect humanity, we must wipe witches off the face of the earth!" The dehumanizing of one group of people by the say-so of another group is a sad but all too common refrain. Similarly, Zaizen declares that his eradication of witches is "God's will." One researcher's journal contains notes such as "I fear our God has forsaken us" and that a genetic anomaly is "the Devil's true form."

In episode 15, we learn that Zaizen has been lying all along to everyone to implement his agenda: what was supposed to be a witch-hunt was just a diversion to keep the STN-J distracted while he staged a coup to take over.

Suspicion was thrown onto Robin in part because of Robin's predecessor, a witch named Kate who tried to use her position in the STN-J for extortion.

At the end of episode 10, the son of the Master of Harry's restaurant and bar,[2] located near STN-J headquarters, has returned to Tokyo after two years hiding abroad; he fled after being suspected of witchcraft, and returned knowing that he would be hunted down. This happens one night as he is leaving Harry's, but he lives long enough for his last words to be "Forgive me, father." The son asking forgiveness of his (biological) father mirrors the ritual of absolution in which the worshipper in most Christian religions seeks forgiveness, which is granted from God through the priest. Again we see that the witches in *Witch Hunter Robin* are not all depraved criminals or intent on supplanting or eliminating humanity.

The most overt clue appears in episode 12, titled "Precious Illusions." In a vision, the witch Methuselah shows Robin praying in front of the statue of Michelangelo's *Pieta*. The statue is of the Virgin Mary holding the body of Jesus, shortly after he was taken down from the cross. Carved from a single piece of marble, it is Michelangelo's only signed work, and reduces the religious moment to its most basic human dimension: mother and child. It also serves to mirror countless similar works created as part of the Nativity of Jesus by evoking it in the context of the crucifixion.

The episode ends with an evocation of a very different parent/child dynamic illustrated by a very different work of art: glimpses of Francisco Goya's *Saturn Devouring His Son*. Late in his life, Goya painted a fresco on the walls of his home which included, among other subjects, the Greco-Roman myth of the Titan called Cronos in the Greek and Saturn by the Romans. Frightened by a prophecy that he would be overthrown by his son, the Titan insisted on devouring each of his children as soon as they were born. (The prophecy was fulfilled when the Titan's wife hid one of the children, who would become Zeus, also known as Jupiter.)

Civilization, according to the witch Methuselah, is a battle between these two dualities: the love of the mother, and the fear of the father. The child is destined to be caught in the middle, and in this case Robin Sena is the child. She has trusted STN-J to send her after witches who had turned to evil, without realizing that Zaizen was holding out on the group. He no longer believed that it was possible for a witch to be good, and had descended into genocide in the development of Orbo, a liquid that protected the STN-J and incapacitated the witches they hunted. In the end it is revealed that Orbo is made of the rendered bodies of the witches they had hunted, reducing the STN-J to the level of the murderous Saturn while claiming its mission to be virtuous.

Robin, however, finds that she was genetically engineered by her father, a researcher named Todou, using the DNA of a witch he loved who died in childbirth named Maria, the daughter of Father Juliano. In her awareness of this, Robin shows far more compassion for Zaizen and his allies than they showed to her. "The blood of witches who have been persecuted over and over since ancient times flows inside me. I don't just feel their power; I feel the sadness caused by that power. A witch who feels sadness," she says, "might be able to understand humans, even when surrounded by an ocean of them." In the tradition of such stories, the persecuted ones show more compassion than the "holy" people who do the persecuting.

Although the anime was created in the first years of the 21st century, it's a story of behavior that has been repeated again and again, in one culture or another, for thousands of years, and alludes to that pattern in the story itself. It is complete fiction, and yet it has multiple touchstones to reality. It is the product of a culture quite different from that of the west, and yet it has borrowed and adapted from the culture of the west and has much to say that the west needs to hear.

NOTES

1. In episode 8 of the series we meet a male witch who has decided to use his powers for healing and ultimately exercises them at the cost of his own life. This is the audience's first real hint that the "us versus them" paradigm of the series is not what it seems.

2. This is literally as close as *Witch Hunter Robin* gets to referencing a different group of witches in the popular culture: the Harry Potter stories of J. K. Rowling.

Chapter Twelve

Japan's Most Famous Christian Martyr

Amakusa Shirō

The historical facts about Amakusa Shirō, as laid out in chapter 2, are undisputable. An adolescent at the time of the Shimabara tax revolt of 1637-1638, he became its de facto leader and used his belief in Christianity as a rallying cry. Along with the death of the 26 Martyrs in 1597, this is one of the best-known facets of Christianity's impact on Japanese history. Unlike some legendary figures, we know precisely when and where and why Amakusa lived and died.

History, however, doesn't stop there, especially when popular culture and the arts become involved. Unlike General Mitsuhide, whose revenge upon Oda Nobunaga to avenge his mother validated a traditional set of beliefs and loyalties, the outsider religion Amakusa embraced colored the perceptions of not only his contemporaries, but those who learned of him centuries later. The fact of his embrace of western Catholicism became the starting point of the discussion, and not just a footnote.

Even when he was alive he became the subject of a propaganda war between the Shogunate and the rebels; the former said he practiced black magic, while the latter presented him as both a messenger of God and as a *bishonen* (beautiful boy); thus comparing him to Yoshitsune, the legendary young hero of the Heike wars of the 12th century. (Drazen 2014, p. 96) After Amakusa was killed in the siege of Harano castle in 1638, legends about him multiplied, and he was declared to have summoned birds (which was reminiscent of St. Francis of Assisi), walked on water (in imitation of Jesus), and moved objects with his mind.[1] (Suter, pp. 111-113)

THE AMAKUSA FAMILY—*RUROUNI KENSHIN*

The final story arc in the anime television series based on the manga *Rurouni Kenshin* by Watsuki Nobuhiro was written specifically for the anime. It takes incidents from two real occurrences in Japanese history and jams them together—even though they happened 200 years apart.

Chapter 2 looked at the Shimabara tax revolt which turned into a religious crusade. The titular leader of that revolt, a teenaged Christian called Amakusa Shirō, was transported by the writers of *Rurouni Kenshin* to the 19th century and its short-lived samurai revolt against Japan's modernization and return to the world after two centuries of isolation.

One historic conjunction made sense in moving Amakusa to the Meiji era: perhaps the most practical benefit of the return of western Christians to Japan was the revival of interest in western medicine. Known informally as Dutch Studies, this was one part of western knowledge which the Japanese were eager to expand, and which had been limited by the national policy of isolation. Consequently, medical knowledge plays a part in this episode.

In this story arc, Amakusa Shirō is now named Amakusa Shojō; he also has a younger sister named Magudaria, which suggests the name Magdalene. She is young and attractive, and is looked up to by her brother's followers as a leader of the group; in this role she is similar to Maria, the "Goddess of the Slums" in Fritz Lang's film *Metropolis*. She's also a consumptive and has been for much of her life—afflicted with the disease now known as tuberculosis. While her brother duels with Kenshin (the whole point of their meeting, since Shojō has also mastered Kenshin's exotic sword technique[2]), Magudaria crosses ideological swords with Kenshin's companion Sanosuke, who neither shares nor sympathizes with her religion. Her illness causes her health to be a problem, and her brother has to prepare medical remedies for her—although their followers think of the cures as miracles rather than medicine. She has also been judgmental and intolerant of those who don't share her belief in her brother, and it is not until her death scene—which, because she was established as a consumptive, comes as no surprise—that her own attitude loosens up. Ultimately, recalling the original Amakusa's role as a military leader, she joins her brother to defend the Dutch consulate during a siege, but is shot. Shojō and his remaining followers are exiled to the Netherlands, unlike the survivors of the Shimabara rebellion.

Shojō's quest for a "Holy Land" where he and his followers can practice their faith without persecution becomes compromised, not merely by being mixed up with elements of magic, martial arts, medical science and politics. This is part of the Orientalist approach to the outsider religion: if you assume that anything CAN happen, then just about anything WILL happen.

This was not the only fictionalized version of Amakusa Shirō. Two Japanese novels of the 20th century[3], and subsequent film versions, have Amakusa Shirō return from death as either a vampire or as a resurrected demon. Both versions claim that "Christian magic" brought the young fighter back from death, in a non-humorous parody of the resurrection of Jesus. "(I)t is the foreignness of the ritual that provides the ultimate source of the power" of the resurrected Shirō. (Suter, p. 122)

The 1967 novel *Makai tenshō (Demon Resurrection)* was adapted into a seinen (adult) manga in 1987 by Ishikawa Ken (1948-2006). Ishikawa was a writing partner to manga artist Nagai Gō; together they created the *Getter Robo* manga franchise, featuring the first use of multiple robots coming together to create a single giant robot. They also created several adult titles in addition to *Makai tenshō;* these included *Cutie Honey* (a superhero android who transforms into a variety of identities—always with a good deal of nudity involved) and *Occult Gang*—their bawdy parody of the Hollywood film *The Exorcist* is discussed in chapter 14.

This manga version of *Makai tenshō* takes the story as far down the path of reversal as it can go, with only a few elements of Yamada's novel remaining—mostly the parts involving sex and violence. The two-part anime, renamed *Makai tenshō—Jigoku-hen (Demon Resurrection—Hell Screen),*[4] starts with an account of the battle of Sekigahara in 1600, in which Toyotomi's remaining forces were defeated by those under Tokugawa Ieyasu. Among Toyotomi's forces was Konishi Yukinaga, a Christian convert and a daimyō located in Kyoto. He fled the battle to Mount Ibuki, but was captured and executed; as a Christian, he refused to practice seppuku and kill himself.

This much is based on history. Fiction enters with Souiken Mori, described as a follower of Yukinaga. In the anime, he and his men fled to the Christian stronghold of Kyushu. By 1613, when anti-Christian laws were being promulgated by the Tokugawa shogunate, a supposedly prophetic scroll, the Suekagami, was written by a Christian missionary located in Amakusa. It declares that in twenty years' time, when famine strikes and the sky is aflame, the Son of God will be reborn in Japan, bringing God's kingdom to earth. However, according to the scroll, if this is prevented from happening, Satan, not the child of God, will be born. This option sets up the events of the anime.

The story begins on Christmas Day, 1628 during a driving rain. Soldiers of the Bakufu are searching for Christians; they make enough noise to alert the worshippers, who slip away into the woods. The troops destroy a statue of the Virgin Mary, and, as they do, a boy walks in on them. He is shot in the chest but, once the soldiers leave to report to Nagasaki, a girl comes out of hiding and cries over the boy—who is, of course, Shirō. He is alive, since the bullet struck a crucifix in his clothes. As the villagers come out of hiding and declare it a miracle, the rain stops and a beam of light rises up from the cross into the clouds. An old man, whose beard suggests that this is Souiken Mori, watches with an expression of evil glee.

The next title on the screen in the Western version states the date is February 28, 1683; a typo, since we see a battle of the Shimabara rebellion, making this 1638. Shirō is a young man, leading a congregation in worship, while his soldiers—accompanied by divine blue fire—attack the Tokugawa forces trying to take Harano castle. Mori tries to whip the people into a fighting frenzy, while Shirō speaks of his desire to end the rebellion and ease the suffering on both sides.

The Tokugawa forces meanwhile meet with their leader, General Matsudaira Nobutsuna, the daimyo who successfully ended the Shimabara rebellion. He also hears from swordsman Yagyu Jubei, who sets out to infiltrate the castle. Ultimately Yagyu finds Shirō on the chapel roof, but, before they could agree on surrender terms, Mori shows Amakusa the severed heads of two children in the castle—heads which Mori himself had cut off, blaming it on Jubei to inflame Amakusa. Shirō falls into the chapel, where Mori and his daughter Ocho wait for him. Mori tells Shirō that there is no God, and the only way he can find rest now is through having sex with Ocho. This act leads to the death and (later) resurrection of Amakusa.

Part two, subtitled "Hell's Spawn", takes place months after Shimabara. Hundreds of miles to the east of Kyushu, in Nara Prefecture, Yagyu is still troubled by memories of the battle. Meanwhile, Mori declares that he will bring Satan upon the earth, as he intended to do with the Shimabara uprising. Playable characters on both sides, including a resurrected Amakusa, are introduced, and the anime ends—to be continued by the audience.

The anime producer uses the novel and the manga, in other words, to abandon a Christian intent altogether. The novel included classic samurai swordsmen such as Yagyu Jubei and Musashi Miyamoto;[5] in the Ishikawa manga, they are zombies revived to serve Satan. (Suter, p. 128)

A different manga version, adapted by Tomi Shinzō, was serialized in *Comic Ran* magazine, and published in paperback in 1995. This time Tomi downplays the religious aspect and the violence of the story, while playing up the nudity and sex. It also revives a hero to stand against the demonic Amakusa in Yagyu Jubei, the masterful swordsman who in this version "combines conventional attributes of samurai masculinity and of moral and sexual integrity." No longer a zombie, he is "a rough man with a heart of gold, loyal to the Tokugawa state and a protector of women and children." (Suter, p. 129) Over the years the role of hero had never truly been assigned to the Christian convert Amakusa Shirō except by other Christians. These variations make him an instrument of the devil, until at last Yagyu Jubei, the historic one-eyed imperial swordsman whose exploits were included in Kurosawa Akira's film *Seven Samurai* (Drazen 2014, pp. 110-111), is chosen to serve the Tokugawa shogunate (which fought against Amakusa and the Christians in the Shimabara revolt). The Orientalist inversion is complete: Christianity has been demonized, literally, while traditional Japanese values have been uplifted to stand against the satanic forces.

But even this is not the final verdict, as Suter points out. The saga of Amakusa Shirō takes a different series of turns as the subject of the 1993 arcade video game *Samurai Spirits* and its assortment of spinoffs for home gaming platforms. (Suter, pp. 132-137) By the 2005 incarnation of the game, in which Amakusa defeats the Big Boss in order to "punish [the enemy] for their sins and save their souls," he has been depicted as "a follower of the Christian God, or its enemy, or possibly both; he is evil, or good, or both good and evil; the Christian God is the enemy of Japan, or its ally, or appears to be its enemy, but after all, this could be yet another instance of Amakusa's deceit." (Suter, p. 137) However, the meta-verdict, if you will, of Amakusa is the fact that this is a game and you, the player, are playing the version of your choice. You made one choice today; you may make a completely different choice tomorrow with no real consequences, because "it's just a game."

For a variant that's more than just a game, Suter points to Akaishi Michiyo's shoujo manga *AMAKUSA 1637,* which was published between 2001 and 2006. This story inverts just about everything connected to Amakusa Shirō: instead of being a young boy pretty enough to be a girl, this story offers up Hayumi Natsuki, a modern Japanese girl who disguises herself as a boy and who has the martial arts skills to be able to pull off the deception. She and a group of friends are on a ship that gets caught in a time warp and end up back in the year 1637, just before the Shimabara rebellion was to occur. However, in this version, Amakusa is killed several months earlier, by one of Natsuki's friends. Natsuki assumes Amakusa's identity, and proceeds to rewrite history itself by urging the nobles of Kyushu to stop exploiting the peasants with excessive taxes and peacefully defuses the situation. She accomplishes this with the aid of 1990s technology which fortunately manages to work, even in the 17th century—even the cell phones. So, what had been seen as divine miracles by Amakusa are now the results of manmade technology, recalling the "Third Law" of author Arthur C. Clarke: "Any sufficiently advanced technology is indistinguishable from magic." Natsuki manages to prevail upon the Tokugawa court to allow Kyushu to be its own independent state, abandon the Sakoku policy of isolation and continue to trade with the rest of the world.

Ultimately Natsuki (as Shirō) brings 1990s sensibilities to 17th century Japan, changing history for the better. (Suter, pp. 151-160) Christians no longer face cruel and bloody persecution; however, in this laissez-faire society where people are encouraged to believe as they choose, there is no incentive—in Heaven or on Earth—for Japanese people necessarily to convert to Christianity either. Natsuki and friends recreate (better than they realized) the 1990s in Japan, when Christians make up fewer than one percent of the population.

In this context, when asked to pass judgment on Amakusa Shirō and his actions, divorced from the reality of his time and place and even from the faith that set the Shimabara rebellion apart historically, the only choice available to the gamer or the manga reader is not to choose.

NOTES

1. This latter ability becomes significant in our own time in the interest in Japanese pop culture in telekinesis. As discussed in chapter 14, Uri Geller, who claimed to bend spoons with his mind, has become no less influential than Jesus and Francis of Assisi in the Japanese imagination.

2. Shojō studied the technique to avenge his parents, who were also Christians and were killed because of their faith. Even though a convert to Christianity, Amakusa Shojō was Japanese, and was still shown in the anime to think in terms of avenging his family. Japanese Christians, according to this anime, were not forbidden to hold grudges. Suter notes that, in other modern literary evocations of the Shimabara rebellion, Amakusa Shirō is "more reminiscent of the vengeful ghosts of the horror genre, driven by an uncontrollable urge to destroy their murderers". (p. 118)

3. *Dokuro kengyō (The Skull Abbot)*, 1939 by Yokomizo Seishi, and 1967's *Makai tenshō (Demon Resurrection)*, by Yamada Fūtarō.

4. In the west the title is changed to *Ninja Resurrection*. The subtitle *Jigoku-hen (Hell Screen)* is borrowed from a frightening 1918 short story by Akutagawa Ryunosuke, which has nothing to do with the battle of Sekigahara or this plot.

5. Both are known as authors as well as swordsmen: Yagyu Jubei was author of *Tsukimi no Sho (The Book of Gazing at the Moon)*, while Musashi Miyamoto wrote *The Book of Five Rings*, a classic on military strategy that enjoyed a western revival during the Eighties.

Chapter Thirteen

Angels and Other Metaphors

To this point, when Christianity is referred to in Japan's pop culture, it means Catholicism. This was how Japan was introduced to the religion almost five centuries ago. It's still the most convenient shorthand for Japan depicting western religion. However, there are other approaches; some are real, like the Salvation Army, while others are fictional, like the worship of the goddess Sarjalin on a distant long-gone planet in Hiwatari Saki's landmark manga *Please Save My Earth*. There are also abstract symbols that seem Christian at first glance, but either refer to a different belief out of Japan's religious tradition or don't match up with any theology at all.

MADE IN JAPAN

Two anime series were commissioned by American evangelist Pat Robertson from the Japanese animation studio Tatsunoko. Created by three brothers in 1962, it's still in business and has produced a wide range of anime, including *Mach Go Go Go* (shown in the west as *Speed Racer)* and *Gatchaman* (a/k/a *Battle of the Planets).* Robertson commissioned Tatsunoko to create a child-oriented anime series based overtly on Biblical stories, to be broadcast both in Japan and on Robertson's Christian Broadcasting Network.

From 1981 to 1984 Japanese television carried *Anime Oyako Gekijo,* known in America as *Superbook.* The Japanese title means "Animated Family Theater"; the word "oyako" literally means "parent and child". From the beginning, it was assumed that Japanese children would need parental explanations for some of the stories, which mainly drew on the Old Testament. Another series, *The Flying House,* which was broadcast between seasons of *Superbook,* focused on the New Testament. In any event, the nominal child-stars of the series interacted little—if at all—with the Biblical characters, with the assumption that parents would be able to explain the destruction of Sodom and Gomorrah, the persecution of Joseph by his brothers, and the conversion of the apostle Paul. Robertson's vision of a Biblical cartoon series for children was suitable for American audiences for whom Judeo-Christianity was already the norm. Broadcast in Japan, even though written and produced by Japanese, it still featured an outsider religion.

TOKYO GODFATHERS

This 2003 feature length anime directed by Kon Satoshi was written by Kon and Nobumoto Keiko, who became recognized as a major anime talent in the nineties writing *Macross Plus* and the *Cowboy Bebop* TV series. This film, though, starts as a reworking of the 1948 John Ford classic western *3 Godfathers*. There are a few common points between the two movies: they both take place at Christmas, and both involve three misfits who have to take care of an abandoned baby. However, while Ford's movie took place in the American old west with John Wayne, Harry Carey Jr. and Pedro Armendariz as bandits tending an infant whose mother had died in childbirth, in this case a baby abandoned in a garbage dump in modern-day Tokyo is discovered by three homeless people. One is Gin, a middle-aged alcoholic, one is Hana, a middle-aged drag queen, and the third is a runaway teenage girl named Miyuki. These three misfits somehow found each other and are making the best of life.

In this case, making the best of it meant that, on Christmas Day, the adults go to the Salvation Army where they can get a free meal, for the price of watching a children's Christmas pageant and listening to a sermon about the church offering a spiritual home for the homeless. Hana, the drag queen, half-jokes after the sermon that a Christmas miracle might bring about another immaculate conception, even in a "homo" like himself. When Hana tells the server in the food line that "I'm eating for two," it's partly to continue the joke, and partly to disguise that they're taking food back to their teenage companion. Presumably, if a minor showed up, someone might start asking questions, and Miyuki has her reasons for running away from home.

The sermon's message is real, as far as it goes; groups like the Salvation Army have done charitable work since they were let back into Japan in the 19th century. However, once the "godfathers" find the abandoned baby in a garbage dump, they do not take the child to the Salvation Army or any other church, and Hana at first refuses to let Gin and Miyuki take the child to the police. The baby shouldn't have to "be shunted from one foster home to another without ever having the sense of being loved." Hana tries at first to care for the child, then, realizing that they can hardly care for themselves, they follow the thread of clues to try to return the baby to its mother.[1] The thread takes them from a train station locker to a yakuza wedding to Hana's former drag bar, to unplanned encounters with family and friends. There is religious symbolism in *Tokyo Godfathers*, but at first it is rooted in humor or parody. The serious spirituality comes at the climax of the film, on New Year's Day: a holy day in the Shinto religion. The film is clear as to which gods actually get things done in Japan.

Angel imagery is a recurring subtext in the first half of *Tokyo Godfathers*, although its use is either comic or ironic. The homeless teen, Miyuki, gets taken hostage at the yakuza wedding by a rival gang member trying to kill the godfather; they make their getaway in an Angel cab—the logo of the cab company is a white disc with the letter A in the center and wings sticking out the sides. When Miyuki and the baby are dropped off with the wife of the Filipino would-be assassin, they try to communicate even though Miyuki speaks only Japanese and the wife speaks only Portuguese; they make connections by looking at family photographs. Miyuki carries a photo of her younger self with a pet cat; because the white patches on the back of the otherwise black cat resembled wings, she named it Angel.

This calls up a scene in Miyuki's mind that tells her story partly in flashback, partly in fantasy. She said she ran away from home after an argument with her father, who she thought had gotten rid of her cat; during the argument she stabbed him in the stomach with a butter knife, drawing blood. As she screams "Where's Angel?!" her mother answers, "She's right here." But now her mother is Hana, her father is Gin, and Miyuki's holding the abandoned child—who has wings on her back. Miyuki awakes from what was a dream in time to see Hana looking in through the window.

Gin, meanwhile, has been severely beaten by a group of young punks who announce that they're cleaning up before the New Year—it's a Japanese tradition to clean the house before New Year's Day to chase out the old year's bad luck.[2] In this case, it's just an excuse to beat up on homeless men. Gin, lying in an alley bleeding, has a vision of an angel—complete with flowing blonde hair, white wings and a magic wand with a star at the end. When she asks "What do you wish—my magic or an ambulance?" and Gin asks for the ambulance, the angel loses its temper and yells "How rude!"

Hana and Miyuki and the baby, still homeless and now without Gin, realize their situation is rough and Hana says there's no choice but for them to go to a bar named Angel Tower; the neon sign out front is of Tokyo Tower with a pair of angel wings. It's the drag bar where Hana used to work as a singer; after triggering a brawl, Hana was afraid to go back again. The mama-san cries over Hana like a long-lost daughter and says that a little money smoothed over the fight. Meanwhile Gin is already there, resting and bandaged as best he could be. We see the angel from Gin's vision holding the baby; it was one of the bar's employees trying to drum up business by cosplaying as an angel. Later, Miyuki finds a newspaper with a message in the personal ads, saying "Miyuki: Angel has come home. Father." She tries to call home, but can't bring herself to speak and hangs up.

This is the point in the narrative where everything shifts from Christmas and angel metaphors to New Years and an emphasis on families reconciling in advance of the New Year.[3] However, the Angel cab reappears as part of the big chase scene heading into the climax.

There is one more joke at the Salvation Army's expense, and this one raises the question of Orientalism. Hana told the serving lady in the food line that "I'm eating for two." As the homeless trio board a train to look for the baby's parents, with Hana holding the baby, they're seen by the Salvation Army serving lady, who says, "Kiseki da wa" (It's a miracle!) The line is delivered in Japanese, but the English subtitle avoids the word "miracle" and instead has her saying "She WAS eating for two!" The English subtitlers apparently felt that "the m word" would be borderline blasphemy being spoken by a Christian instead of a drag queen.

SPEAR OF LONGINUS

Medieval Christianity put great value on relics of the past; this increased when Romans rediscovered the Catacombs, the ancient undercity where long-ago figures were interred. They believed that some of the bones or teeth or other finds might belong to bygone Popes, some of whom had been declared saints after their deaths, and these relics were thought to be magical, capable of bringing about miracles. On the other hand, some people were content to turn bones into gold by digging up whatever they could find and trying to pass it off as a valuable sacred relic. This led to a great deal of fraud fueled by faith.

One particular relic was not a biological part of a holy person. In the New Testament account of the crucifixion of Jesus, it was written in John 19:31-37 that, to see if he was dead yet, at one point a Roman soldier poked his spear into the side of Jesus on the cross. A separate body of lore and legend grew around this incident, and the "spear of Longinus" took on a life of its own.[4]

Perhaps it's no surprise that Hollywood mentioned the spear; in Budd Schulberg's screenplay for *On the Waterfront*, it's invoked by a Catholic priest preaching an impromptu sermon over a dead longshoreman, "accidentally" killed before he could testify about the union being corrupted by organized crime:

> every time the Mob puts the pressure on a good man, tries to stop him from doing his duty as a citizen, it's a crucifixion. And anybody who sits around and lets it happen, keeps silent about something he knows that happened, shares

the guilt of it just as much as the Roman soldier who pierced the flesh of our Lord to see if he was dead.

But Tokyo also has expanded on the legend of the spear of Longinus—at least twice in modern anime.

FULLMETAL ALCHEMIST: THE MOVIE

The first feature length anime based on Arakawa Hiromu's manga *Fullmetal Alchemist* was written and filmed while the manga was still being published, and after the first TV series had been broadcast. The plot of *Fullmetal Alchemist The Movie: Conqueror of Shamballa* has nothing much to do with the way the story finally turned out; this version does, however, have a variety of connections to the real world, as well as both real and fanciful connections to Christianity.

In this script written by Aikawa Sho and set in October 1923[5], taking place partly in our world and partly in Arakawa's manga world where alchemy is a reality, the spear of Longinus, even though a single spear-point, is described as "scattered throughout the world," brought back together and reforged into a dozen different spears used to subdue a dragon. (The idea that a single spear-point can be scattered could be due to the fact that, in ancient times, at least four spear-points, and as many as eight, claimed to be the original artifact.)

The man in this anime who found the dragon (which was actually one of the Homunculi created alchemically by a Philosopher's Stone) and ordered the attack on it is based on a real person: Karl Haushofer. The son of a professor, Haushofer chose a career in the military instead, although he eventually taught at the Bavarian War Academy. In 1909 he traveled to Japan to study the army there, and met with the Crown Prince Yoshihito, who would become the Taisho Emperor from 1912 to 1926. Haushofer retired from the army after Germany surrendered in World War 1. When he returned to academe, his student assistant, Rudolf Hess, was involved in the newly created Nazi Party, which interested Haushofer as well. Because of Haushofer's year in Japan, he was instrumental in getting Japan to join the Axis powers. After the war, and a determination that he had committed no war crimes, he and his wife committed suicide in 1946.

An acquaintance of Haushofer in the anime, who had heard rumors of a live dragon and wanted to see it for himself, is also a historical figure. Director Fritz Lang, however, has a less nefarious background. Best remembered for the silent film classic *Metropolis* and the early sound film *M,* Lang is later shown in this anime in the UFA film studio (a real studio) working on a mechanical dragon. It would be used to represent Fafner, the dragon guarding the Ring of Power in the Nibelungen legend. Lang directed and released a silent version of the story, *Siegfried,* in 1924, part one of a two-part five hour epic about the mythology of the Teutonic people. He would certainly have been at work on the film in October 1923.

Haushofer was not a true believer in the Thule Society, a group of Nazis that has become the subject of much speculation. They were essentially pre-Christians wishing to revive the legendary glories of the Aryan people. They did, however, find interesting the ideas in Haushofer's book *Japan and the Japanese*, especially the notion that Japan's strength lay in its racial homogeneity. Not only is Haushofer's thesis essentially untrue, as proven by recent archeology, but his argument for Germany making and enforcing national borders falls flat when Germany is seen as just another politically created section of the European continent, as opposed to a group of volcanic islands in the middle of the ocean. What seemed like common sense to Germans who read Haushofer was actually just another example of Vico's conceit of nations.

Looking back, the decision to join the Axis was a bad one for Japan in the long run, although it might have seemed inevitable. When Nazism took over Germany and Fascism rose in Italy and Spain, Japan was in the middle of what would be a half-century of military imperialism, capturing territory in China and along the Pacific Rim, in part to make up for Japan's lack of natural resources. Japan trusted Germany to weaken the Soviet Union, which was the biggest worry of the military leaders in the Japanese government. In truth, neither Germany nor Japan trusted the other.

As for the Nazi connection to the Spear of Longinus, Trevor Ravenscroft argued in his book *The Spear of Destiny* that Hitler invaded Austria primarily to capture Vienna, and specifically to capture the Spear, which was supposed to be part of the Hapsburg regalia in a museum. It didn't help Germany in the long run.

SHIN SEIKI EVANGELION

If the dozen steam-powered spears that subdue the dragon in the *Fullmetal Alchemist* movie have no resemblance to a Roman weapon, the "spear of Longinus" that appears in the 1995 television anime series *Shin Seiki Evangelion* is even less orthodox, historically or theologically. The entire series, in fact, can safely be called a Judeo-Christian grab bag of references to the Old Testament, New Testament, the Kaballah of ancient Judaism, plus some sources that have nothing to do with Judeo-Christianity at all. Mariana Ortega's description of *Evangelion* as it relates to its source material is accurate:

> There is no single or straight interpretation of *Evangelion* based on its plot sources: like many of the esoteric works it references, it is layered, crowded with riddles, arguably overcoded. Elements are shuffled, recombined, and al-

tered to provide a new mythology that nevertheless maintains a dialectical connection to the original traditions. (Ortega, pp. 217-218)

Ortega further explains that, while *Evangelion* "bases its narrative on specifically Judeo-Christian tales of human origin, it does not follow the biblical text per se as much as assorted religious interpretations. Gnostic Christian versions of the creation story, as well as Judaic traditions from the Midrash, *Zohar*, and other kabbalistic and rabbinical commentary on *Genesis*, contribute a sizable part of its source material." (p. 220)

As for the Spear of Longinus in *Evangelion*, any resemblance to a Roman spear-point is purely in the name. In this science fiction tale of adolescents recruited as part of a mad scientist's plot to destroy the world and recreate it anew—hence the title *Shin Seiki Evangerion (Gospel of the New Genesis)*—the lead characters are pilots of giant robots. This has been done in anime before, of course, and is not substantially different from, to name one example, Kusama Daisaku being the pilot of the machine known as *Giant Robo*. However, piloting the large Evas, as the robots are called, is problematic at best, especially when the pilots themselves are mentally and spiritually unstable.

The bipedal robots use weapons which include oversized knives and guns. The Spear of Longinus is likewise an oversized lance.[6] It is thrown at one of the invading Angels, seems to vanish, then reappears several episodes later, with no explanation given. This is typical of the references in *Evangelion* to Judeo-Christianity: names are dropped, then are ignored or amplified along literally unorthodox lines. The mainframe computer at NERV headquarters, for example, is segmented into three units, named for the Three Magi who came from the Orient in search of the birth of the Messiah. However, this metaphor is not amplified at all, but the three units are described as reflecting the three segments of the personality of their programmer: wife, mother, and scientist.

This example is one of many showing that *Evangelion* is a case of Orientalism used in 1995 Japan to play games with Judeo-Christianity in an anime set in the far future year of 2015. This particular example poses the most obvious question: can the Spear of Longinus exist at all without the Body of Christ which gives the spear its purpose? This spear, after all, according to legend, made a wound in Jesus from which flowed blood and water, taken to be symbols that Jesus was both human (blood) and divine (water). In the *Fullmetal Alchemist* movie, the spear was likewise used for a purpose unrelated to the crucifixion of Jesus, being used instead to slay a dragon from a pre-Christian mythology. So is there a reason for this name in a lance that, like the Evas, is ten stories tall? What—excuse the pun—is the point of this Spear?

I again take the liberty of quoting myself, since my earlier view of *Evangelion* actually anticipates this example of Japanese Orientalism applied to a western icon:

> But why all the Judeo-Christian trappings—especially when they're used so inexactly? I submit that trappings of Western religion are used here precisely *because* they can be used inexactly. When popular culture refers to a religion in a positive light, it usually refers to the belief system embraced by the majority culture. . . . On the other hand, negative portrayals of religion seldom involve the belief system of the majority. . . .
>
> It isn't about lack of information; ample material about Christian beliefs is available in Japan. But the makers of *Evangelion* didn't want information. They wanted a belief system that they could turn into a plausible threat of global annihilation. Shinto and Buddhism don't prophesy anything so dramatic. Judeo-Christianity, however, lends itself to apocalyptic visions. (Drazen 2014, p. 299)

GOD IS A SOUTHPAW – ONIROKU DAN

Strictly speaking, he's not a cleric; he just dresses like one in this boxing manga by Imaizumi Shinji. Teenager Oniroku Dan[7] was raised by clerics of a monastery in America after the death of his father and trained on his own to become a boxer. When he's not in the ring, he wears formal Catholic clerical garb: VERY formal, the kind of robes priests only wear when saying Mass and offering communion. This is one of the more unlikely scenarios in manga, but was meant to be taken seriously within its own genre—as a sports manga.

Dan went to America with his father as a young child, spent a decade living in literally monastic seclusion, and only now has returned to Japan. When his father died, he improvised his own training regimen, which included pulling himself up a cliff with one hand while holding a pail full of water in the other. As a result, he's left-handed: a "southpaw." He demonstrates his skills and his basic good nature when he arrives in Tokyo; riding on the subway, he sees a hoodlum smoking in the car, and cursing out an old woman who dares to cough. Dan confronts the hoodlum, who tries to light up again but is unable; Dan's reflexes are so quick that he takes the cigarette and lighter from the hoodlum faster than can be seen.

He meets his old playmate Inoue Misuzu and lives with her family, training to be a bantamweight boxer. He needs to learn a lot more than just boxing. Seeing an idol singer on television, he comments that she must be a good boxer as well, because her chest muscles are so awesome. This level of naïveté, having a teenage boy confuse female breasts with pectoral muscles, is attributed to the Christian monastic life in which he grew up. Dan is educated in the truth when Misuzu's big brother, also a boxing coach, takes

Dan to the roof of a building, where they can look in the window of a maternity hospital across the way, to watch a new mother nursing her infant. It's a scene that is both tasteful and a bit creepy.

Still, Christianity hasn't divorced him from his Japanese roots. During a trip to visit a gym in America where Dan's father had lived and trained, Misuzu cooks an elaborate dinner. When Dan and her brother come home with a sushi sampler, she gets upset . . . until she sees that Dan has set the sushi in front of a picture of his father as a memorial offering. (vol. 6, pp. 159-161)

In this case, Christianity has not given Dan any super boxing powers, but it has given him a nice and unflappable personality. He goes through much of the manga with a placid smile on his face no matter what's happening; other boxers he meets are more intense, driven by anger, competitiveness, arrogance or greed (the fighters' or their manager's). When the manga was reprinted in tankobon volumes, they included fan mail sent to Imaizumi. The fans were, predictably for *Shounen Jump* readers, boys in junior high or high school; but they used words like "yasashii" (kind) to describe Dan. One writer said this was the first time a manga had moved him to tears.

This meeting of boxing and Catholicism gets a parody treatment in Takahashi Rumiko's *Ippondo no Fukuin (The One-Pound Gospel)* (see chapter 10).

ALTERNATE REALITIES—*TRINITY BLOOD* AND *HELLSING*

The vampire genre has given Japanese writers and artists a launching-pad from which to explore alternate universes that redefine Christianity—especially Catholicism—in ways that western writers would not think to try.

Two different Japanese vampire stories are recast as future three-way battles, pitting the undead against two earthly entities: the Vatican and the Church of England.

Hellsing

Hellsing takes the reader/viewer to an alternate version of history; one in which the two major factions of Christianity—Protestant and Catholic—need to defeat a common menace yet are unable to abandon their long-standing prejudices against each other. What would the Japanese know about such sectarian infighting? They know because it was part of the first decades of Christianity in Japan, as we've seen in chapter 2. This 1997-2008 manga by Hirano Kouta, adapted to both broadcast TV anime (2001-2002) and home video OAVs (2006-2012), would seem to have one of the most bizarre and potentially offensive alternate universes of any portrayal of Christians. And yet, it is the logical conclusion of a history that the Japanese were able to observe for themselves as far back as the first decades that Christianity was brought to the islands by western missionaries.

The series name *Hellsing* is, of course, an evocation of Abraham Van Helsing, the fictional vampire hunter who appears in Bram Stoker's novel *Dracula*. The novel took place in Victorian England of the late 19th century, but this series moves on to the next generation and the postwar years of the late 20th century. Specifically, to the teaming-up of a vampire named Alucard (which may seem like a joke but is not played for laughs) and von Helsing's daughter, a young woman who has been knighted and is addressed as Sir Integra Hellsing. They work together to defeat Millennium, an organization trying to conquer Britain—which Nazi Germany was never able to do—but which this time is using an undead army of vampire Nazis.

Two armies exist to fight off the invasion of Millennium for King and Country; at least, when they aren't fighting each other. On the one hand is the Royal Order of Protestant Knights, begun by Abraham Van Helsing, sworn to defend the British homeland and the Anglican Church. This, however, does not sit well with Section 13 of the Vatican, also known under the highly loaded name Iscariot: a paramilitary group of exorcists dedicated to defeating Millennium but also, under their obsessed Archbishop Enrico Maxwell, sworn to kill heretics and nonbelievers as an enemy just as undesirable as vampire Nazis.

The members of Iscariot aren't always a stable lot. In addition to the volatile Maxwell, there is the literally schizophrenic Takagi Yumie; a Japanese nun who carries samurai swords into battle against the Nazis, she is as fanatical as Maxwell and battles as Yumie but also appears as the shy and reserved Yumiko. Then there is Alexander Anderson, a knight of Iscariot who used to run an orphanage before he was bio-engineered to battle the vampire invaders.

Often, vampires in manga/anime are the stuff of comedy (see *Don Dracula*, discussed in chapter 4); when they are taken seriously, they are depicted as unnatural monsters, having abandoned their humanity in the self-centered quest for eternal life. This has been handled in a variety of ways, recently and elegantly in *Fullmetal Alchemist*, the manga by Arakawa Hiromu and its anime adaptations (2 TV series and 2 full-length films). The sons of an alchemist named Hohenheim, who sought the secret to eternal life, start to follow in his footsteps, but learn an essentially Japanese lesson: that death is part of life, and is what in fact gives life meaning and purpose.

As frightening as the idea of vampire Nazis might be on the page (as if the originals weren't bad enough), the troops who fight these villains are rather villainous themselves. Particularly the soldiers of Iscariot under Archbishop Maxwell; they equate the undead Germans with Millennium's target—Anglican civilians—and exterminate members of both groups.

Sectarianism was one of the problematic aspects of the Christian missionaries to Japan even in the late 16th and early 17th centuries:

> (I)n 1614 the Tokugawa chieftain, possibly influenced by *reports from the Dutch and English Protestants that Catholic missionaries were engaged in subversion*, issued an edict strictly banning Christianity. Thereupon began the period of mass persecutions that took the lives of some five to six thousand European and Japanese Christians before it subsided about 1640. (Varley, pp. 147-148, emphasis added)

The Protestants could not stop themselves from bringing their hostility toward Roman Catholicism to their missionary work around the world, nor could the Catholics resist criticizing the heretical Protestants. The in-fighting between the Franciscans and the Jesuits was bad enough, but Tokugawa Ieyasu saw Christianity itself as divisive and destabilizing, a threat to a nation that was just being unified from a history of shifting alliances among local warlords. It seemed that no two Christian sects could get along with each other; even the fighting between Shinto and Buddhism had been patched up eventually and the two faiths were able to coexist.

Hellsing paints a picture of Christianity that is just as bleak as what the early Tokugawa shogunate witnessed: the surprising spectacle of Christianity split among its own adherents, denying other practitioners of the same faith as fervently as they denied worship of the Buddha or the ancestral Japanese deities. It was not a strategy designed to defeat vampire Nazis.

Trinity Blood

Trinity Blood started in 2001 as a series of light novels written by Yoshida Sunao and illustrated by Shibamoto Thores; Yoshida died in 2004 which ended the series. However, the alternate universe didn't end; Yasui Kentaro, a friend of Yoshida, finished the novel series and worked on the manga based on the novels. An anime series was produced which somewhat altered the story from both novels and manga. In scope and detail, however, the creators of this alternate universe looked back in part to the medieval history documented by Barbara Tuchman in her work *A Distant Mirror*—including the attempt to create an alternate Vatican.

The essential story, however, starts in the here and now: Earth is becoming overpopulated and unable to sustain life, so an exploratory mission goes to Mars to establish a colony. They found two life forms already on Mars; one was a virus called Bacillus. Anyone infected with the virus became a vampire, requiring blood to survive but living very long lives as a result; the vampiric humans were given the name Methuselah, after the Old Testament patriarch who lived for almost a millennium. Mars was also home to the Crusnik, a nanomachine culture which could occupy humans as hosts; many of them did not survive. The four who did had the Crusnik machines implanted in vitro; they were given the telling names Lilith, Cain, Abel and Seth—Lilith being the prototype.

When the Methuselah returned to Earth, war began and in this story has lasted for nine centuries. At the time the novels begin, Earth governments had mostly fallen apart and many surviving human beings had surrendered power to the Vatican in Rome. Officially it is led by Pope Allessandro XVIII, the teenage son of the previous Pope (again the rules are rewritten to throw priestly celibacy out the window, although a chaotic future world may make it seem plausible). Allessandro is a puppet ruler, with the real power held by his older brother; after a botched kidnap attempt, he flees to England (which has reverted to its ancient name Albion). He realizes that the Methuselah are not totally evil, their vampirism notwithstanding, and decides to work for the peaceful coexistence of the two human species.

The Vatican, however, does not take this loss of power lightly; this is a time when the Inquisition has started up again, despising anything that goes against the authority and beliefs of the Catholic Church; as in *Hellsing*, they are as ruthless to heretics as they are toward vampires. Amongst their weaponry are such diverse elements as a robotic lance called The Screamer, battle armor complete with jet-pack, various blades, and a rifle which is actually named Deus Ex Machina.

The plot to the overall story focuses on a Methuselah who was one of the four test-tube vampires. Under the name Abel Nightroad (which is sometimes Romanized as Nightlord), he had waged war against the people of Earth, killing seven million. The only thing that stopped him was when Lilith was murdered by Cain, who had gone mad. Abel in his grief hid in Lilith's tomb for centuries, until he had a chance to rescue the sister of the present Pope. This encounter changed him to a committed pacifist.

The rest of the stories—which is plural because the plot varies from novels to manga to anime—is based on the question of how to bring about peace in a world obsessed with war, which is a tried and true topic of Japanese popular culture in the postwar period. Some of *Trinity Blood* is violent, and some of the character names are interesting (two Vatican priests are named after literary figures: Czech author Vaclav Havel and British poet William Wordsworth). The Vatican, despite its power, is also beset by internal troubles as well as the war against Methuselah; one priest, Archbishop Alfonso d'Este, attempts to start an alternate Vatican in Cologne. This attempt does not get as far as the alternate Vatican actually set up at Avignon in defiance of Rome (see Tuchman's *A Distant Mirror*). In short, this science fiction story focuses on the warlike Catholicism of the past and dresses it up as the future to comment on the present, and the need perceived by Japan for the Vatican to change its ways.

MASAKO ASANO—*BLOOD: THE LAST VAMPIRE*

One of the principal characters in Kitakubo Hiroyuki's 2000 short anime *Blood: The Last Vampire* wears a crucifix, but it doesn't do as much to protect her from a vampire attack as does a Japanese girl wearing a school uniform modeled after a sailor *fuku* and wielding a samurai sword. This anime is set in 1966 at Tokyo's Yokota air base, an American enclave for servicemen and their families waging the air war against North Vietnam. The mysterious girl is Saya, explained only as an "original" who uses her sword to attack blood-sucking monsters called chiropterans; the word, meaning "blood suckers", is the literal Latin translation of *kyūketsuki*—the Japanese word for vampires.

The principal character is hardly a schoolgirl; she's a nurse named, according to her ID badge, Masako Caroline Asano. Christopher Bolton writes that this mixed name, added to some of the woman's facial features and her fluency in both Japanese and English, create an ambiguity as to whether she is Japanese or American. (p. 131) However, her name and crucifix suggest another possibility: that Masako Asano converted to Christianity at some point in her life, and Caroline is her baptismal name.[8] This naming arrangement is common in Japanese converts. However, the crucifix does not prevent this particular species of vampire from capturing and almost killing Masako; she needs to be rescued by the sword-wielding Saya.

SEINTO ONIISAN—JESUS IS A NEET

Nakamura Hikaru's manga *Seinto Oniisan (Saint Young Men)* began as a parody of a pop song titled "Seinto Ojiisan" (Saint Old Man). It's a slice-of-life comedy about two young men living in a boarding house. Roommates with no obvious jobs or university to attend, they pass the time in ways familiar to young Japanese urbanites. However, these two roommates are Jesus and the Buddha. Even though they both founded major world religions, or perhaps because of this similarity, both are too enlightened to attack each other over doctrine. They just fret about the usual problems: food, money, where to go on vacation, and getting along with the suspicious old landlady. There are mishaps, but they're played for laughs: at the public baths, for example, Jesus has to be careful not to turn the bathwater into wine. At one point, Jesus tells Buddha that, before his resurrection, he asked an angel to choose which facial expression he should have as he emerged from the tomb. After all, he said, even idol singers and stand-up comics attend to these details when making a comeback appearance.

The humor reflects the Japanese view that the two religions are not necessarily exclusive, and the manga seldom deals with religion at all, focusing more on the two young men trying to get by unnoticed in modern Tokyo when peach trees instantly bear fruit when the Buddha passes by and Jesus's presence causes elderly men to get up from their wheelchairs. One person thinks the two are yakuza, while their landlady asks if they are NEETs.[9]

The series became one of the most popular features of the manga magazine *Morning 2*, has been reprinted in 12 volumes to date, and has been translated into several other languages, including Chinese, Spanish and French. It has not been licensed to appear in America in English; it was thought by artist Nakamura that American Christians might be offended by the humor of this manga. It's hard to imagine even the most devout American Christians provoked to violence by a Jesus who blogs (and admits to visiting a "pink"—meaning erotic—website). Then again, it was hard to imagine the attack on the offices of *Charlie Hebdo* until it happened. And the Japanese, in Orientalist fashion, "know" that America has no shortage of either Christians or guns.

MADONNA—*MILLENNIUM ACTRESS*

Kon Satoshi's film *Millennium Actress* revolves around the life of Fujiwara Chiyoko, a fictional actress whose film career from the late 1930s to the early 1970s is also a reflection of her personal struggles with her marriage and the adolescent crush which defined her life. At the height of her popularity, according to the movie, she was known as "Japan's Madonna"—which in retrospect might be seen as a nod to the popularity of the pop singer who also made movies under that name. However, in this case the reference is meant to be literal: to the Madonna, mother of the Savior, held up as an ideal of womanhood in ancient times. Similarly, in the aftermath of the Pacific War, Japanese film studios sought to comfort moviegoers with a return to normalcy, and Chiyoko became the ideal of how to cope with the difficulties of everyday life.

According to Ian Buruma, there wasn't a Japanese actress called Madonna, but there was "*Nippon no haha*, mother of Japan." This referred to actress Mochizuki Yuko, who had her greatest fame in postwar unabashed tear-jerking melodramas that involved her suffering a variety of domestic tragedies but usually bearing up stoically through it all. One such film, actually called *Haha (Mother),* had a mother whose grown-up children neglect and abandon her, causing her to take a series of menial jobs in hospitals and factories. The lone exception is a fisherman son who didn't know what was happening to her, being away at sea. When he speaks ill of his thoughtless siblings, the ever-forgiving mother simply says, "Please don't say that, my dear. To me you're all equally sweet." (Buruma, pp. 24-25) The long-suffering idealized Japanese mother of these melodramas was truly blessed among women, given the popularity of her "three-handkerchief" movies. Although the closest we come to seeing Chiyoko play a mother is in a scene as a schoolteacher, and Kon cited other actresses as models for Chiyoko, Madonna is a religious title, and would have been earned by Chiyoko because of her relevant roles.

MY FRIEND FRANKENSTEIN

This book briefly touched in chapter 5 on Wada Shinji's shoujo manga, created for *Margaret* magazine and published in a tankobon collection in 1977. Of the four stories in this collection, all show Frankenstein's monster interacting with young girls, between the ages of 10 and 20. Three of them have some form of physical disability; Ilse, the child, is the exception.

The first story (pp. 7-37) focuses on a wealthy heiress, Mia Fanshon, mistress of an estate in Bavaria near Grunwald. Her disability is a large strawberry birth mark on the back of her neck. Even though it was a cosmetic disability, it complicated her life: grownups told her that the mark was awful, other children would not play with her and tormented her, her parents grew distant toward her and she could not make her debut into society. She was treated as repellant and frightening, and she hides the mark under a scarf. A maid who walks in on her in the bath screams at sight of the mark. This sort of treatment has left her with a cold and sometimes violent personality.

When the monster is discovered and brought to her estate, she watches it being put to work by Kurt, a peasant who works on the estate. As he drives the monster with a severe whipping, which she had approved, she realized that the monster was being mistreated because of its appearance; she experiences a flash of empathy and orders Kurt to stop whipping the monster. She orders a new suit of clothes to be made for the monster and even bestowed a new name on him: Silas.

She did not name the monster after the companion of the Apostle Paul, but after a priest who took Silas as his name. The priest also taught Mia that outward appearances do not matter in a person as much as a kind heart. Mia never appreciated these words from a priest until she met Silas the monster. She reacted to its behavior rather than to the priest's words; rather, she saw Silas's reaction when the monster did not hate her when she admitted to telling Kurt to use the whip. Mia becomes much friendlier during the story because of this catharsis, but is still troubled by her birthmark.

When Kurt orders some of the land to be burned to prepare it for farming, the fire gets out of control, trapping Kurt and a group of children. Silas goes into the fire and rescues them using a hollow tree to protect them. However, he burns his hand in the rescue, and Mia, who had been worried about Silas, does not hesitate to use her scarf to bandage his wound, even if now everyone can see her birthmark. She repeats the priest Silas's lesson that a kind heart is more important than one's appearance, and says that she is going to have to accept herself as she is if others are to accept her, especially in marriage. Hearing this, the monster smiles, turns and walks through the fire and out of the story.

Shoujo manga have expanded quite a bit in four decades, but one constant has been that in Japan girls are encouraged to be kind and considerate. To an extent males are as well, according to Ian Buruma. Writing in 1984, Buruma stresses that "(t)he key word here is yasashii (gentle, meek, kindly), that term so often used by Japanese to describe their mothers, as well as themselves as a nation." Yasashii people are "warm, without a hint of evil and malice, pure in their hearts, and blessed with those unique Japanese antennae, always sensitive to each others' feelings which never need to be spoken." (p. 211) Even though the actors in these manga stories are European, they clearly are presented as examples of good or bad behavior for a Japanese audience, and many Japanese girls expect that their lives will include marriage and motherhood.

The second story, "Tanima ni Naru Kane (The Bell Rings in the Valley)", takes place on the German border near Switzerland. Ilse, a rowdy and impulsive little girl who is the niece of the village Elder Mafeldt, is ringing the church bells. Her uncle and the priest (who carried her home to her uncle) assume she's just playing again, but this time she's trying to warn the village. She was exploring a cave and found Silas Frankenstein frozen in ice. The villagers investigate, accompanied by Heinrich Schwartz, the son of the local landlord. No older than Ilse, Heinrich is already trying to lord it over the rest of the village. As they leave the cave, they hear a high loud wailing, which is known in the village as "Akuma no Sakebi Koe (The Devil's Scream)". Nobody knows the source of this unnerving sound. Later in the episode, one family moves out of the village rather than endure "The Devil's Scream" any longer.

Meanwhile, Silas escapes from the ice and collapses in the woods, where he's found by Ilse and the children. They hide him in a barn, feed him and treat him as a playmate and a friend.

A traveler stops by the village and tells Elder Mafeldt about the source of "The Devil's Scream": a round hole in a rock formation high up in the Alps. Mafeldt, a blacksmith, casts a huge bell and tells Silas to climb up into the mountains and place the bell in the hole to stop the howling. Silas does this, despite some villagers, provoked by the local landlord, who try to bury him in a landslide.

There is very little religion in this episode: only the priest who stops Ilse ringing the bells, and Ilse saying her prayers one night, after she let it slip that she'd gone to look at Silas in the ice. We see her praying to God to "please forgive my uncle for whipping my butt." Ilse's uncle overhears the prayer and is impressed by her forgiveness.

THE HAND OF GOD — *HIKARU NO GO*

Manga have been created about anything and everything, including an ancient board-game. The 1998 manga *Hikaru no Go*, written by Hotta Yumi and drawn by Obata Takeshi, was published in *Shounen Jump* magazine before it was republished in tankobon volumes. The story tells of a typical Tokyo sixth grader, Shindō Hikaru, with no interest in the ancient Japanese space-capturing game of Go until he discovers that his grandfather's game board contains the ghost of a former Go instructor to the Heian court a thousand years ago. This imperial teacher, Fujiwara no Sai, who committed suicide when accused falsely of cheating, clung to this world because, in all his time playing Go in life, he never had the chance to play a "Kami no Itte."

Kami no Itte isn't so much a move as a circumstance: a time in which the player can completely reverse the course of the game with a move so unexpected and so audacious that everything changes. These plays are so rare and so dramatic that they are recognized at once and enter the lore of the game.

In Japanese the term is written with kanji that mean God's One Hand. However, when it was translated into English for tankobon publication by VIZ Magazine, translator Andy Nakatani backed away from the word "God" in the manga. The move is known to western readers as "The Divine Move". It's not exactly inaccurate, but the meaning does change; describing the move as God-like would be fairly accurate but does not convey the Japanese meaning. It does not credit the player with a move that literally remakes the world of the game. In English, as in western Judeo-Christianity, we hesitate to describe anything as god-like; there is God and there is everything else believed to be created by God. At worst, applying Kami no Itte to a game would be blasphemy; at best, it's just hyperbole. Yet, as we have seen already, the word kami in Japanese carries more than just those two shades of meaning, and Orientalism leads translators of the Japanese into English to err on the side of caution.

HAIBANE RENMEI

This anime is its own self-contained universe, one inhabited by angels—or at least by girls with halos and small wings, living in a low-tech world of bicycles, mechanical clocks, crows, telephones and (oddly enough) modern-day wind farms, in a walled city that might have been painted by Pieter Bruegel, the Dutch 16th century master who painted not the nobility but landscapes and peasants. It's one of the very rare anime that focuses more on atmosphere than on action. The 13-episode series is based on the work of the artist known in the west as Yoshitoshi ABe. (The variant spelling is deliberate; perhaps to avoid Americans pronouncing his name as in Abe Lincoln.)

Despite the images of girls with halos and wings, there is nothing divine or heavenly about their lives. They still have to work for a living and aren't allowed to use money, getting whatever they have through charity. Any religious themes have more to do with daily life in Japan than an afterlife in Heaven.

Hairston writes of the "shamanic" aspect in *Haibane Renmei* that focuses on "the meaning of names and the power they hold over the characters." He also names two other anime whose plots turn on the names of characters: *Gedo Senki*, known as *Tales of Earthsea* to American audiences, and *Spirited Away*, in which Chihiro is made to change her name to work for Yubaba and free her parents, while she also gives Haku, another worker at the bathhouse, his real name back. (p. 244)

In addition, there is a distinctly Japanese Buddhist component which also involves names. The process by which one declares one's faith in Buddhism is called "Taking Refuge." During the Refuge ceremony one is given a *zokumyou*, a new name specific to the faith, also called a Dharma name. Those who go on to take the Bodhisattva vow are given a slightly different name.

A third name, however, comes into play in Japanese Buddhism. A *kaimyou* is a name given to Buddhist clergy and to believers when they die. While the *kaimyou* for the dead is usually a benediction, an episode of *Ghost Hunt* has a child afflicted with a cursing *kaimyou* branded supernaturally onto her back.[10] (vol. 8, pp. 14-15) Even if their power is diminished, names still carry more weight in Japan than they do in Christian nations.

Japanese Buddhism is well-known in America for the sect known as Zen Buddhism, which enjoyed popularity when the writings of monk D. T. Suzuki were championed in the postwar years by novelist Jack Kerouac and theologian Alan Watts. One step on the path toward enlightenment in Zen is the koan, a riddle posed by the teacher that the disciple has to work through. The koan is usually posed as a paradox that defies logic, in order to push the disciple to transcend logic to find deeper meaning; the classic example is: "What is the sound of one hand clapping?"

Rakka, the main character in *Haibane Renmei*, undergoes a spiritual and existential crisis when one of the younger haibane vanishes from the community. The others say that she had her "Day of Flight", but nobody knows anything about it except the name. Rakka is distressed, thinking that she might somehow have been able to help the missing child, until she is given a Zen-like paradox to contemplate: "One who recognizes their own sin, has no sin." She later has a vision of a dream she had before (literally) hatching out of her cocoon and into her life among the haibane. As she fell through the sky, a crow apparently tried to slow her fall. This is one of the first images in the anime, and has no meaning to the viewer at first; the image is forgotten until it becomes the key to unlocking the koan. 13th century Japanese Zen master Eihei Dogen once offered up a koan similar to the advice given to Rakka: "To study the self is to forget the self."

When Rakka later tries to help Reki, the "big sister" of the group of haibane, to work through her own spiritual crisis, she is pulled into Reki's despair of ever being free of her sin. Reki, an artist, has painted her room to be a landscape, and the gravel road she remembered from her dream, and which gave her the name Reki (meaning "small stones"), is now a railbed. She stands before the oncoming train intending to fail at finding salvation by letting herself be run over; a decidedly Japanese pop culture form of suicide, especially for women. However, Rakka does not give up on Reki, who calls out to Rakka for help at the last second. Rakka's loyalty justifies Reki's belief in her, and also ratifies the Japanese notion that, unlike Christianity, salvation is not a private matter. As with all aspects of Japanese life, each person is part of a community, whether the family or the village, the nation or even a fan club. Reki's self-loathing could not let her accept the love of others, which she needed to do to restore herself. In the end, she is able to face the Day of Flight with a clear soul, while the other haibane accept that it was her time.

When asked about the creation of *Haibane Renmei* at the 2003 Anime Expo in Los Angeles, ABe said "*Haibane* is my own process of trying to find answers to spiritual questions." (Hairston, p. 242) This suggests perhaps the most important distinction in the ways that the Japanese culture and western cultures approach spirituality. Japan's perception of spiritual questions seems to be driven by a proactive perspective. For centuries, Japanese have been encouraged to "try" and to "persevere", rather than to "believe" or "have faith". And one person usually needs help, with the most reliable source of help being the others who live their lives with and around you, as you are a part of their lives. To be Japanese means to be in this together.

On top of all of this, some Japanese stories have metaphors for modern-day Christianity, recast as something else. The language may be the same or similar to that used by missionaries to Japan, but the names have been changed.

Chapter 13
WINGS OF HONNEAMISE

The first feature-length anime by Studio Gainax, *Oneamisu no Tsubasa (Wings of Honneamise)*, can be called a "steampunk" version of human exploration of outer space. It is also one of the few anime that feature what can only be called a Protestant street preacher.

While many of the examples cited here have been based on Catholicism, the 19th and 20th centuries also saw Protestant denominations come to Japan to try to convert the population. They had more success, as seen in chapter 2, in working to improve Japanese society, by encouraging education, expanding healthcare, pushing for women's rights or trying to outlaw prostitution.

The anime's main character, Shiro Lhadatt, describes himself at the film's beginning as perfectly average, in the middle of the pack—neither a success nor a failure. As such, he decided that he wanted to fly and applied to the Royal Space Force. Unfortunately, in this particular world the technology of flight was still analogous to Earth in the 1930s; space travel was so distant as to seem like a joke. Shiro's luck is helped when the royal family takes an interest in space, and decides to increase the budget for the space program. This has to be done by referring to the planned rocket as a "warship" to justify the cost. Unfortunately, the project is also accepted as military by the neighboring kingdom, which sees the "warship" as an act of provocation.

Shiro, meanwhile, has become the face of the space program. It gives him a degree of celebrity, but doesn't alter his military routine: train by day, hang out in the pleasure quarter by night. One night he encounters Riqinni, a young woman handing out leaflets explaining the beliefs of her unnamed faith and urging people to come to meetings. He takes a leaflet but doesn't give it a second thought. In the morning, however, he wakes up with the leaflet still in hand, having stumbled drunk into the barracks and fallen asleep on the bunk of a dead comrade. Unnerved by his mistake and intrigued by the woman, he decides on a whim to go to the church service, which is in Riqinni's house literally at the end of the trolley line. He keeps seeing her because she alone seems to share his vision of the power of space travel to transform the world.

Their personalities are rather different. Riqinni doesn't have "street smarts" and has to move herself and her child out of a house that was foreclosed and bulldozed by the power company for delinquent bills; all she could think to do about her money problems was to pray. Shiro visits her new home, where she lives when she's not a farm laborer. He tries to rape her one night, but is knocked unconscious. When he comes to, Riqinni is the one who apologizes. After that, Shiro decides to go to the pleasure quarter to hand out religious leaflets with Riqinni.

When Shiro's first manned space flight takes place, it is literally under fire: the neighboring kingdom still thinks the rocket is a weapon and invades.

However, the launch goes ahead, and Shiro, instead of reading the script that his government had provided, talks in religious terms about the borderless planet he is orbiting. The audience never sees him land and the only clue to his fate is a scene of Riqinni back at the pleasure quarter. Snow starts to fall, and a snowflake falls onto a leaflet, and melts. This is a loaded symbol in the Japanese culture, a reminder of the transient nature of life.

Both Shiro and Riqinni, in their separate ways, were far from successful in their day-to-day lives. It took two transcendent events—the space program and Riqinni's church—to give life meaning, even if they did not find community. The audience never sees a congregation, a priest or other members of Riqinni's church. It seems to exist as an idea more than as a concrete way to deal with the realities of life. But that could also be said for the Royal Space Program.

FALSE PRIEST FATHER CORNELLO—*FULLMETAL ALCHEMIST*

The very first episode of Arakawa Hiromu's hit manga *Fullmetal Alchemist* offers a villainous priest, although he claims in his alternate universe to worship a Sun God named Leto. A bald, husky middle-aged man, whose vestments are similar to the robes of the Catholic clergy and is addressed as "Father" and "His Holiness", his message as emissary to Leto is essentially that of any Christian priest, Catholic or not: Faith and prayer lead to salvation from sin, which is the fate of humanity without divine guidance. He especially manipulates a young woman named Rosé by telling her that with sufficient faith she can be reunited with her dead fiancée. He doesn't even live to finish the second episode; he is exposed as a fraud whose "miracles" are themselves alchemy performed with the help of a Philosopher's Stone. Once exposed, he is cut down and devoured by two of the Seven Deadly Sins—except that these, too, do not conform to Catholic dogma. They are Homunculi, created by alchemy in an alternate universe that has more in common with Buddhism than with Catholicism.

Some of these examples have been unusual, to one degree or another. As the title of the next chapter suggests, however, some Japanese portrayals of Christianity are "Not Safe". They can appear to be blasphemous, outrageous or even obscene to a western audience, even if the Japanese may not perceive them that way.

NOTES

1. The first clue is a train station locker key: number 1225. The number keeps recurring in the movie, as part of a string of Christmas miracles.

2. Called *osouji*, this is a widespread custom not limited to homes. Shinto temples have a cleansing (*susuharai*) on December 13 every year to prepare for the New Year, and even grade schools are cleaned up by their students.

3. We've already seen Hana reunited with the "family" at Angel Tower, and received hints that Miyuki's family will welcome her home. As for Gin, after his beatdown he's taken to hospital, where it just so happens that his adult daughter is a nurse.

4. The naming of the Roman soldier as Longinus didn't happen until the fourth century C.E. in the apocryphal Gospel of Nicodemus.

5. The time is deliberate: weeks before the so-called "Beer Hall Putsch" in November 1923, in which the Nazi Party in Munich tried, and failed, to trigger a revolt against the Weimar government, beginning a decade-long rise to power.

6. The handle of the lance is spiral, with the end branching off into two points; this evokes the double helix of DNA and does more to reference biology than Christianity.

7. Dan in this case is not short for the Hebrew name Daniel. It's the pronunciation of the kanji that is his fighting name: "Bullet."

8. The name Caroline suggests that the conversion took place about five years earlier, in 1961, inspired by one of the world's best known Catholics at the time: Caroline Kennedy, daughter of American President John Kennedy.

9. NEET is a British acronym that has been adopted by the Japanese. It reflects life after the economic downturn with the bursting of Japan's economic bubble at the end of the Eighties. NEETs are young adults who are Not Educated (enrolled in some sort of school), Employed or Training (for a particular job).

10. The name that appears on the child's back, "Zen-getsu in Rakugoko Donyo", means "This foolish girl will descend into Hell."

Chapter Fourteen

The "Not Safe" Chapter

Aspects of life in Japan, as in other countries and cultures, are categorized by outsiders as exotic or eccentric or quaint; these can become the stuff of travel books and films. There are also aspects of Japanese life that strike outsiders as "going too far", even though there is a lengthy tradition to back them up. Stone markers called dousojin, some dating back centuries, are still found in some rural areas around Japan. Believed to be dedicated to protective spirits guarding travelers and villages, some are carved with the image of a male and female couple, perhaps representing the Shinto creative deities Izanagi and Izanami. Some of these dousojin, however, abandon any subtlety and are carved into vaginas and erect penises. (Buruma, p. 8, Bornoff, pp. 102-105)

Nicolas Bornoff in his book *Pink Samurai: Love, Marriage and Sex in Contemporary Japan*, describes the activities around the Jibeta festival in the Daishi area of Kawasaki, home of the last phallic worship rite still observed in the Tokyo metropolitan area. No fewer than three huge phallic statues are paraded around the town every March: one carried by men, one carried by women, and the third carried by transvestites. Logs are shaped into giant erections, and college co-eds have fun being photographed riding them like rocking horses. (pp. 81-90) Some parents also pose their young daughters on these horses, even though doing so technically violates some child pornography laws; these pictures don't end up on the Internet.

The occasional overlap with this kind of rustic bawdiness in 21st century industrialized Japan even applies to Christianity. A parody of the 1973 film *The Exorcist* reinforces the Orientalist notion that Catholic rites are essentially western and are not relevant to the Japanese. The story appeared in *Shinrei Tantei Okaruto Dan (Spirit Detectives: The Occult Gang)*, a 1991 manga written by Kouenji Hiroshi, with artwork by Nagai Gō and Ishikawa Ken. Nagai has been infamous for years as a creator of bawdy manga titles like

Harenchi Gakuen, *Cutie Honey* and *Kekko Kamen* as well as mecha manga such as *Mazinger*. Ishikawa Ken appeared in chapter 12 as the creator of a manga based on the novel *Makai tenshō*, in which the famous Christian martyr Amakusa Shirō is resurrected to bring Satan to earth.

In this version of the Hollywood hit, Misa, an eight year old girl, becomes possessed by a demon, killing the family dog and a Catholic exorcist before the Occult Gang show up to exorcise the demon with holy water. As in the Hollywood movie, the possessed girl vomits prodigiously, which leads the father of the leader of the group to wash himself off with the holy water and drink what was left. This doesn't faze the leader, Tendou Shiro, who declares that holy water is still holy even if it isn't in the bottle. He instructs his father to do the obvious: to piss on the possessed girl. (Yes, they went there.) The demon leaves the girl's body and is clubbed by a seven-foot altar cross.

Manga that parody other manga are a subset of doujinshi. Based on the Japanese word for "companion", it's understood that these do-it-yourself versions of popular manga can never be confused for the real thing, given both the subject matter and the variable quality of the artwork. Chapter 10 already looked at *Maria-sama ga Miteru,* a story set in a Catholic girls' school. This title has been parodied numerous times in numerous ways, including in the sub-genre of *hentai* (sexually explicit) manga. One title takes place in a sub-sub-genre by recasting all the characters: instead of girls, they are *futanari*—hermaphrodites. The title of the doujinshi manga pretty much says it all: *Maria-sama ga P wo Miteru (Mother Mary is Watching the Penis)*.

How much further can it go? *Ogenki Clinic* by Inui Haruka was published in 1987, running until 1994 and animated for direct-to-market video in 1991. The title means "health clinic" but this clinic exists to cure sexual dysfunction. The overall style of the work mixes Nagai's earthy sexual humor with the madcap style of Takahashi Rumiko's *Ranma ½*. The third story in volume 1, "Holy Beast in Black", has a Catholic nun as a patient, suffering from nymphomania. She wants to serve God, but finds herself aroused by even the hint of dirty language. Her condition is so extreme that she has impure thoughts if she even hears the first syllable of a potentially dirty word. For example: in Japanese the letter "ma" can begin literally hundreds of words; however, this nun hears it and automatically thinks of the one word which is the crudest and most blunt name for a woman's genitals.

Early in the episode, the reader sees a couple of thugs ambush the sister; they rape her, but she wears them out. The doctor tries to cure her by talking dirty to her, by oral sex, then by vaginal sex. After he exhausts himself but not the patient, his nurse steps up. She is wearing a strap-on vibrator in the shape not of an erect penis but of a statue of the Madonna. (Yes, they went there.) The nun at this point declares the therapy to be blasphemy, but the doctor points out to her that she is now cured. The nun needed to accept that all humans have sexual desires, but that hers were increased because her vows of absolute chastity caused her to suppress them. The doctor knew the nymphomaniac patient was cured when she finally drew the line and said, "Enough."

This story has echoes of the dialogue between Toyotomi and Coelho in the 16th century. Some Japanese Buddhist sects have advocated clerical celibacy over the years, and countless stories have been written reflecting how difficult and unnatural such a requirement is. Plus, after all, Buddhism is as foreign to Japan as Christianity, having come from India by way of China and Tibet. Japan has its own creation mythology in the *Kojiki* and that mythology is overtly sexual: the primal gods Izanagi and Izanami have sex so that everything can be born of Izanami, including the fire which kills her. Japanese Buddhism no longer insists on absolute celibacy but stresses not living a sexually dissolute life; similarly, Japanese Buddhists vow not to abstain from alcohol but to avoid drinking to inebriation.

Even the milder forms of the Japanese approach to western theology can seem strange at best. The Japanese word "kami" can mean spirit, god or deity; there are shades of meaning between the three concepts described by the single word. This has led to some unusual names, such as the God Warriors, the apocalyptic destructive monsters of *Nausicaä of the Valley of the Wind*,[1] or children's toys. The model giant robots marketed in Japan under the names "GodBot" is one thing, but another level is reached in the toy called "God Jesus". It's a fortune-telling toy, intended to give random answers to random questions, like the western Magic Eight-Ball. A Westerner might feel offended that the presumed Son of the Lord of All Creation is being trivialized, which is not what the toymakers had in mind.

ANGEL OF DARKNESS

It's not a large leap to assume that an anime titled *Angel of Darkness* wouldn't be very respectful of the Christian church; in fact, the trilogy of OAVs with this title by Pink Pineapple Studio[2] are pure and simple tentacle porn, harder than soft core but not hard enough to require mosaic masking. The first installment from 1994 tangentially involves Christianity, if only to show that it isn't very effective.

The anime takes place in a girls' college in the country; the prologue shows construction of new buildings. One night, a man comes onto the site, takes a shovel and uses it to break an ancient seal under a large tree.

The man turns out to be Chairman Goda of the school; he has been possessed by a Dark Elemental, a life form which threatens humankind and which gains power from lust; that particular vice, we're reminded, has never been in short supply. The heroine of this story, Atsuko, is a freshman at the college, an avid lacrosse player but not much of a scholar, and is having a lesbian love affair with her roommate, the more academic (and more feminine) Sayaka. Atsuko's sister Yuko is also an administrator at the school, so she has to be on her best behavior.

More and more students are becoming lethargic as they are kidnapped by Chairman Goda, who draws on their sexual energy to evolve into the ultimate Dark Elemental form; the Big Boss, in gaming parlance. Atsuko can stop this only by taking in the spirit of a woodland elf, who sealed off the Dark Elemental in the first place, and who enlisted the aid of forest dwarfs in this fight.

Chairman Goda's secret laboratory was built where the sealing tree once stood; it is now under the new chapel, and the doorway is behind and under the altar. The altar is literally hiding evil as well as providing access to it.[3] Religion is supposed to be important at this school, but accomplishes nothing in this story. In the end, with the Dark Elemental defeated and buried, the elf transfigures himself into a large guardian tree to seal it off again, as it was when the story began. This adds a touch of Shinto to the side of good, which is otherwise defined as a pagan spirit-driven respect for nature.

ANGEL SANCTUARY

Unlike examples mentioned in this chapter which are targeted for adults, such as *Occult Gang* and *Angel of Darkness,* Yuki Kaori's girls manga *Tenshi kinryouku (Angel Sanctuary)* was aimed at a mainstream audience with its publication in the mainstream shoujo manga magazine *Hana to Yume (Flowers and Dreams).* Originally budgeted for only ten episodes, its popularity was such that it ran from 1994 to 2000 and was reprinted in 20 tankobon volumes. So why is it in this chapter, when the leads are a 16 year old boy and a 15 year old girl? There are a couple of problem elements in this story set in 1999 Tokyo, but the principal problem isn't that the boy, Mudo Setsuna, is the reincarnation of the Angel Alexiel; that role gets worked out through the story. The problem is that Setsuna has sex with the girl, who happens to be his sister.

Yuki drew on the Christian angelic hierarchy in plotting this story. "Christian" in this context means various speculative writings from the first few centuries of the Christian era; for Yuki, this meant either a book from the fifth century, the *De Coelesti Hierarchia (On the Celestial Hierarchy)* by the man who has come to be known as Pseudo-Dionysius the Areopagite, or later books based on his speculation, including the *Summa Theologica* of Thomas Aquinas. Based on references in two verses from separate letters of the Apostle Paul,[4] Pseudo-Dionysus, Aquinas and their later followers developed an elaborate system of categorizing angels and dividing them not only into Cherubim and Seraphim, but also into Spheres and Dominions, Principalities and Powers and Choirs. It's obviously not a subject that they could have researched, but the early church spent a lot of time speculating on such angels as were named in the Bible, their abilities and their relationship to each other.

As a reincarnation of Alexiel, Setsuna's earthly life is just one of several incarnations, all of which are supposed to doom him to live a miserable life and die a slow, painful death—again and again. This was the price Alexiel was to pay for leading other Angels in a revolt against Heaven. Setsuna's sister Sara is also the reincarnation of an Angel; interestingly, both are the opposite gender of their Angel origins. How an angel can be said to have a gender at all is part of the ancient speculation, if not the invention of storytellers such as Yuki.

In this case, the manga proved highly popular with its audience; however, the popularity may be less because the notion of angels on earth is exotic and therefore intriguing, and more likely because this is a story that the Japanese readership had heard before.

Ian Reader, examining modern religious practices in Japan, noted that even the newer religions "point to a powerful undercurrent and religious dynamism in Japan" and sees the newer sects "as renovations of traditional Japanese religious ideas, as restatements and contemporary expressions of Japanese religious sentiment relayed within a relevant, modern context." (pp. 196-197) We have already found older Shinto and Buddhist connections in Japan's popular culture, and *Angel Sanctuary* seems to have one connection that goes deep into Japan's history and even prehistory.

In the beginning, the earth was without form and void. This was the view not only of the Book of Genesis but of the *Kojiki (Writings of Ancient Matters)*, set down around the year 711 C.E. at the request of Empress Gemmei by Ō no Yasumaro. The first of the Kojiki's three overall sections tells the creation mythology that has come to be part of Japanese lore in general and the beliefs of Shinto in particular (the second and third sections tell of the line of Emperors of Japan).

Three primal deities appeared in the beginning on the High Heavenly Plain, and they begat seven generations of other deities. The seventh generation consisted of a god, Izanagi, and a goddess, Izanami. The world was still nothing but a primordial soup, and the elder gods assigned Izanagi and Izanami the task of creating the world and the life in it. They were given the jeweled spear of Heaven, Ama no Nuboko; they used the spear tip to stir the primordial soup. A drop fell off the spear tip and turned into an island, Onogoro, where they built their palace; in the middle of the palace stood the August Pillar of Heaven.

Without guidance from the elder deities, Izanagi and Izanami circled the August Pillar and had sex, but the first results born of Izanami were more like leeches than anything else. The elder gods said the two deities had made a mistake in walking around the Pillar: Izanami had spoken first, where she should have left that to Izanagi. The third time, Izanami gave birth to the islands of Japan, and everything thereon. Unfortunately, among the last things she gave birth to was the Fire God, which set her on fire. Spirits continued to be born from her body as she died. Later, out of grief, Izanagi tried to bring Izanami back to the world from the House of the Dead; she was no longer a goddess, however, but a corpse, and return was not possible in her corrupted state.

After returning to earth, Izanagi got rid of his clothes and washed the pollution of the Land of the Dead from his body. As he did so, three more deities appeared from his eyes and nose: Amaterasu the Sun Goddess, Tsukuyomi the Moon God, and Susano'o the Wind God. This part of the *Kojiki* continues with a focus on the sibling rivalry between Amaterasu, who regularly and properly ruled the sky by day, and Susano'o, whose rule over the seas was arbitrary and impulsive.

These archetypal stories have set up not only the plot of *Angel Sanctuary*, but other modern stories as well. One such restatement of the *Kojiki* is the 2011 feature length anime *Children Who Chase Lost Voices (Hoshi wo Ou Kodomo*, literally *Children Who Chase a Star)*, written and directed by Shinkai Makoto. It seemingly takes place in a rustic Japan during the time of World War 2, but undamaged by American bombs. The most advanced technology is a crystal radio set, which is key to the plot. The girl who owns the crystal set, Asuna, listens to the radio in the hills outside of town, where she meets a strange boy. She also crosses paths with her substitute teacher, a man whose wife had died while he was off fighting a war. He is convinced that the girl knows the way to the House of the Dead, which he calls Agartha; he kidnaps her and uses her to guide him. They find the spirit of the man's wife, but she has bad news for him: the only way she can return with him to the land of the living would be to kill Asuna, so that his wife's spirit could take possession of her body. After the death and destruction he had seen, he can't bring himself to take his student's life, even if it meant giving up on being reunited with his wife.

The parallels between the *Kojiki* and the plot to *Children Who Chase Lost Voices* should be obvious: the finality of death is absolute and unchangeable. The parallel to *Angel Sanctuary* should also be evident in the incestuous relationship of the siblings, as well as in the death of Sara while trying to protect Setsuna from an angelic attack. It should be no surprise by now that Sara's soul is sent to Hell for her incestuous love, while Setsuna tries to find her. In the end, however, she is redeemed and reunited with her brother; God and His Angels are not strong enough to counter the love Setsuna and Sara have for each other, according to the theology of shoujo manga.

BLACK ANGELS—AFTER THE APOCALYPSE

When we left this manga in chapter 9, the religious assassins calling themselves Black Angels were limiting themselves to mundane criminals: Yakuza gangsters and corrupt politicians and police. A newer, more intense enemy begins to emerge from the shadows: the Dragonfang Syndicate. As part of a sinister plan, they have taken in children, even newborns, and subjected them to the harshest martial arts and assassin training. Those who do not succumb to madness or suicide develop techniques for killing which are, to say the least, exotic: one is able to use the sea as a weapon, while another communes with venomous snakes.

However, other Black Angels also keep appearing. One is a blonde teenage girl wearing jungle camouflage; we see her targeting members of a Yakuza family. She kills four of them, but Yoji saves her by killing a fifth. She then goes to a Christian cemetery by a church and puts flowers on her mother's grave. Later we find out the backstory: her name is Judy Jackson, daughter of a Japanese mother and an American mercenary. When he died on some battlefield, the widow took Judy back to Japan and took holy orders, becoming a nun who was killed trying to protect the townspeople from this particular Yakuza gang.[5] Judy's motivation isn't religious beyond avenging her mother; she says she kills because "my father's blood runs through my veins." Judy decides to join up with Yoji and become a Black Angel.

They encounter a member of the Dragonfang Syndicate named Suiki, who prefers to kill using the Drunken Fist school of Kung Fu; up against the Black Angels, however, he needs more. Yoji survives the fight and kills Suiki, only to wander into a dark room full of moving Buddhist statues. These are controlled by a swordsman wearing night-vision goggles; Yoji overcomes them and gets to the next level, where Judy is attached to a cross on a wall. The room is also filled with swinging axes and spiked balls. Yoji is able to survive mainly because the remaining Dragonfang killers fight among themselves.

Later, Father Takazawa explains the Syndicate's Plan M. It started in the building boom of the Sixties, before the 1964 Tokyo Olympics. Eight men in their thirties, all wealthy and well connected, wanted to make Japan "an independent nation built on the principles of freedom and equality that didn't have to rely on any of the larger countries." They feared that a headlong rush to industrialize would lead to pollution, social degeneration and ultimately disaster. One man, however, said that they must take power away from the masses, by destroying the nation's capital Tokyo and building a new capital in a new city.

Historically speaking, this was the reverse of a Japanese tradition: when an emperor died, it was believed that the palace was polluted by the death of the monarch (recall the excerpt from the *Kojiki* above, when Izanami's corpse was too polluted to return to the earth). The old palace would be burned down and a new palace built in a new capital. Rather than wait for nature to take its course, the Syndicate decided on Project M—M for Mortality, the death option, reversing the cause and effect of the older, Shinto-inspired tradition of reacting to pollution after the death of an emperor. One member of the Syndicate, a geologist, stated that detonating a nuclear bomb under Mount Fuji would cause an earthquake sufficient to level Tokyo. If that weren't enough, the Syndicate would assassinate those government ministers who survived or would not join; this, too, is at least partly historical. It's an extended civilian version of the February 1936 military coup in which the army tried, and failed, to take control of the government (Hane 1972, pp. 475-476).

However, under the leadership of a man named Kirihito, the grown children of the men who created Project M have decided that the original syndicate members have grown old, wealthy and complacent. The second generation start killing their elders off to take control; this includes sending a sniper to assassinate Father Takagawa. Before that happens, we see him conducting a church service, reading the opening verses of Psalm 1.[6]

The Dragonfang Syndicate now consists of four children of the original members, plus their leader Kirihito; we never see his face, since he stays behind a curtain. The reader is teased with a glimpse of the three worst "monsters" of the syndicate. They go after the Black Angels, starting with the nun Arisa; she staggers back to the group, stripped almost naked with "Die Black Angels" carved into her torso. The wounds aren't fatal to her, but she was given a post-hypnotic suggestion to kill whoever says the word "Shimpu-sama (Father)". She kills Hashimu before she herself dies. One of the three monsters is also killed in the melee, but the Black Angels are joined by Suiho, another assassin escaped from the Syndicate, who made his entrance having dug up the body of Father Takazawa and used it as a shield. Desecrating a corpse seems a minor flaw when fighting inhuman assassins.

Meanwhile, a new character casually walks into the cemetery: a young girl with an impassive face, described as "a Killer Doll from the netherworld" who casually speaks of future events before they happen. This is Himiko[7], daughter of Kirihito. As the fight continues between the assassins and the Black Angels, Kirihito tells his followers that the day for Project M will be September 26. The Syndicate got an American bomb, and plan to detonate it under Mount Fuji to trigger an earthquake, after which assassins would eliminate any opposition to a declaration of martial law.

Yoji and Matsuda defuse the bomb; Himiko kills Matsuda; Yoji kills Himiko. Then Kirihito, who turns out to be Father Takagawa, appears to claim the body of his daughter Himiko. In a reversal that can safely be called insane, Father Takagawa says that he actually left the Dragonfang Syndicate years ago because God had sent him a revelation: that the entire Kantō region of Japan would be laid waste, destroyed by the hand of God. Rather than allow God to cause such destruction and carnage, which would mean that the power of God was actually evil, Father Takagawa decided that God's sanctity would be preserved if the hand of man were what destroyed tens of thousands of lives. As Yoji kills Father Takagawa, this time for real, he dies saying that eight stars will fall from Heaven after the apocalypse and they must be destroyed before there can ever be peace. As soon as the priest dies, with a fiery wind, Mount Fuji erupts, the earth splits, buildings tumble . . . And that's the end of Act 2 and the beginning of Act 3.

At this point, the manga takes a turn that is not only dark but disturbing and potentially offensive to true believers. The notion that a criminal turned priest would destroy thousands of people in order to preserve God's reputation is not merely madness. It ignores the Biblical accounts of the Flood, the destruction of Sodom, and other divine disasters, not to mention going against the words of Job: "The Lord giveth, and the Lord taketh away; blessed be the name of the Lord." (Job 1:21) Once Hiramatsu started his story down the path of Apocalypse, however, he had to keep ramping it up to higher and higher levels.

Act 3, in fact, takes its cue less from vigilante movies and more from the *Mad Max* franchise. After the Apocalypse, as an elderly gas station attendant helpfully explains to Yoji two years later, the Kantō was dismissed as too damaged to rebuild, a huge wall was erected between Kantō and Kansai, and those trapped in the rubble became bestial. As Father Takagawa prophesied, the eight "stars" appeared: eight warlords who assembled their own armies and battle each other for what was left of the Kantō; they are also represented by eight coins. The gas station attendant tells Yoji that "It's like Warring States Period inside those walls. Nothing but bloodshed." Which is a pretty good description of the manga from this point on.

As part of Yoji's first attack on one of the "eight stars", he's joined by a look-alike for Matsuda, Ryou Kiba. Like Matsuda, he was formerly a police detective, and he hooks up with three other former policemen; they receive guidance from Rosen, an elderly fortune-teller whose name means Old Fortune. It takes sixteen installments for the Black Angels to round up the eight coins, during which there are no allusions to Christianity at all.

The final story-arc changes all that. The four remaining Black Angels meet a man with white hair and white clerical robes who declares himself to be sent to Earth as "a servant of God's will". His name, Jin Reiji, is written with kanji meaning "Divine Spirit Warrior". A boy named Yūki, whose name means "courage" and who can see the future, is taken by another White Angel, Baraki, after Yūki's parents were killed. Yūki comforts himself by playing his ocarina; the Black Angels are led to him by the sound. Baraki uses psychokinesis to attack the Black Angels with roses planted around the church where Yūki is imprisoned. Jin Reiji psychically throws furniture from the church at the Black Angels, then prepares to attack them with swords, but Yūki's melody has the effect of weakening his powers. Yoji remains unaffected and his powers are also described as telekinetic. Yūki, however, seems to be as psychically powerful as any of the grownups; not only does his music weaken the White Angels, but his own telekinesis causes the church organ and bells to play the same melody, allowing the Black Angels to escape with Yūki. Meanwhile, the White Angels confront the fortune teller Rosen; it seems that Yūki may be his grandson . . .

The 1980s were a high time for psychic activity, at least as far as Japanese manga were concerned. Israeli illusionist Uri Geller was a sensation in the Seventies with his claim that he could bend spoons with his mind. Although he was debunked in short order, psychokinesis became a subject in manga well into the next decade. Popular stories included *Mai the Psychic Girl, Locke the Superman, Esper Mami* and others which hinged on characters able to move things with their minds. The trend may have reached its apex in the manga *Akira* by Otomo Katsuhiro, which was adapted into one of the most influential anime in the medium.

These other titles did not add Christianity to the mix, although the 1994 anime *Key the Metal Idol* credited the title character's psychic gifts as having been handed down from a long line of gifted Shinto priestesses. Jin Reiji flips this script by saying that the Japanese government has made use of secret gifted telekinetics "ever since the Meiji Era"—meaning, once westerners were allowed back into Japan and brought with them a parliamentary form of government and a heightened regard for science. Foster, in examining the history of Kokkuri, Japan's version of the Ouija board, is blunt about this clearly Orientalist shift:

> With the advent of Meiji, many Edo-period folk customs came to be viewed with suspicion and classified under the pejorative rubric of superstition *(meishin)*; . . . Through the introduction of Western-based medical and psychological practices, spirit possession gradually came to be defined in terms of mental illness. . . . By 1872, laws outlawing the practice of shamanism began to be promulgated throughout the country. (261)

The *Black Angels* version of a Japanese magical world thus disregards Japan's own shamanic history altogether. Although used by Japanese heroes and villains in this manga, telekinesis, like Christianity, is defined here as a foreign import—which ought to telegraph, in an Orientalist manner, just who will win the battle in the end.

Even though the White Angels all wear white clerical robes, they talk about their powers in telekinetic terms rather than any kind of divine dispensation. Being the villains, they reinforce a negative view of Christianity, which is countered to a degree by the Black Angels. They and Yūki are visited by a man they first think is Rosen, but he introduces himself as Rouji,

Rosen's twin brother. He warns them of the plans of the White Angels to eliminate the Black Angels, since (of course) they stand in the way of world domination.

The White Angels decide to terrorize the Black Angels by stealing Yūki and making him a White Angel. Once they do that, they lose control; as he turns from a young boy to a demonic imp in white robes, he says "you ended up pulling out all the evil in my heart as well! Your vile hearts awakened all the wickedness lurking in my subconscious! All humans have two sides: good and evil! And now Yūki's being controlled by his evil side... Now I can wreak as much havoc as I want!!" He declares himself enemy to both the Black Angels and White Angels, and says his ambition is to become Dictator (he uses the English word "Top") of Japan.

But Yoji has two secret weapons: the eight coins and the cross branded onto his chest. As the reader has seen several times already, the scar bleeds to throw off poison or weapons or otherwise save Yoji's life. As Yoji fights off the ghosts of Arisa and Father Takagawa, he says, "Christ was crucified bearing the sins of the entire human race. When the cross scar in my chest bleeds, it lightens the weight of my past."

As for the coins, old man Roshi used his own psychic abilities to make the coins sentient and able to judge good from evil.[8] For the remaining two dozen episodes of the series the coins, now embedded in Yoji's chest over the cross-shaped scar, protect him and neutralize the attacks of the White Angels.

Fast forward three years to a Japan ruled by Yūki as if he were a Hitler with high tech; his troops wear crosses which bear a resemblance to swastikas. However, the three remaining Black Angels are also there, attacking whoever and however they can. The new enemies helping Yūki include two burly masked men who resemble pro wrestlers, and their mother, a giantess named (of course) Big Mama.

One elaborately over-the-top set piece occurs in the final chapters of the manga. We see what appear to be zombies rising up out of the earth in Hollywood fashion. However, this particular piece of earth is Mount Golgotha; the zombies arise beneath the cross on which Jesus was crucified. The only thing that saves this scene from being too outrageous is the discovery that the zombies are actually wax figures and not really the walking dead. Later in this battle, however, Yoji himself ends up on the cross—momentarily. He causes the nails to pop out of his hands and feet and jumps back down to the ground. He approaches Yūki for the final attack; Yūki tries to kill Yoji but, as he already "died" on the cross, Yūki's attacks have no effect. Yoji attacks Yūki, says his catch-phrase "Go to Hell" one last time . . . and Mount Golgotha fades away; the remaining Black Angels—minus Yoji—are back in a Japanese cemetery.

So, through this epic manga, was Yoji a Christ figure, an avenging angel, or just a vigilante whose destiny was set when he was a child? Probably all of the above. At the end of it all, the Christian aspect of the *Black Angels* manga was just one part of Hiramatsu's bag of tricks; it was there to be used when he needed it, and disregarded if he chose to take the story in another direction. Such casual neglect may seem worse to a true believer than an act of deliberate blasphemy. Hiramatsu, in using Christian imagery as a means to his own end, was both acting on his own and following the guidance of his art-form and the culture that gave rise to it.

The Japanese take these kinds of liberties—and occasionally worse—because they can. With the exception of a relative handful of converts to Christianity—less than one percent of the population—most Japanese, whether working in high culture or pop culture, don't have any skin in the game, as the saying goes. To finish off this chapter by quoting from my first book, *Anime Explosion*:

> Confucius gave Japan its ethical ground rules, and Buddhism taught Japan how to leaven those rules with compassion . . . what does Japan's native religion, Shinto, offer? Nothing less than the identity of Japan itself as a nation, and of the Japanese as a people. Shinto provided the creation mythology for Japan. It provided Amaterasu the Sun Goddess as putative mother of the entire Imperial line and of the Japanese people, and the animistic belief that kami (divine beings) are many and everywhere. . . . Where does all that leave Christianity? Pretty much marginalized in Japan, a nation that got along for two millennia without it. (Drazen 2014, pp. 147-148)

And, when a belief comes along that is marginalized, that is the Other, under the "rules" of Orientalism it becomes fair game.

NOTES

1. Although depicted as gigantic humanoid beings, I believe that Miyazaki intended these to be a visual metaphor for atomic warfare, capable of polluting the topsoil of the entire planet. In the *Nausicaä* anime, the attack on the stampeding Ohmu by the last surviving God Warrior is based on films of nuclear bomb tests at Los Alamos, New Mexico.

2. The second and third installments didn't have any religious symbolism at all; just more tentacles and weird science.

3. The location of a secret staircase under a church altar leading to the villain's lair was also used in the 1979 Lupin III movie *Castle of Cagliostro*.

4. The principal verse is from Paul's Letter to the Colossians: "For by Him were created all things that are in heaven and that are on earth, visible and invisible, whether thrones or dominions or principalities or powers." (1:16)

5. This particular group is named after the manga artist: the Hiramatsu Gang. This kind of in-joke happens a lot in manga.

6. Blessed is the man that walketh not in the counsel of the ungodly, nor standeth in the way of sinners, nor sitteth in the seat of the scornful; but his delight is in the law of the Lord, and on His law doth he meditate day and night. And he shall be like a tree planted by the rivers of water that bringeth forth his fruit in his season; his leaf also shall not wither, and whatsoever

he doeth shall prosper. The ungodly are not so, but are like the chaff which the wind driveth away. Therefore the ungodly shall not stand in the judgment, nor sinners in the congregation of the righteous. For the Lord knoweth the way of the righteous, but the way of the ungodly shall perish. (Psalms 1:1-6)

7. Himiko is a highly loaded name: Himiko, according to legend, was the daughter of Emperor Suinin who ruled in the first century C.E. She was both an Empress and a Shinto shamaness, but never married and left the business of ruling the land mainly to her brother. Still, according to tradition, the entire Imperial line of Japan is descended from Himiko.

8. This may seem odd, but in a sense this is not too big a leap from Tezuka Osamu's most famous and long-lasting creation, the robot Tetsuwan Atomu a/k/a Astro Boy. He helped the Earth's law enforcement by being able to discern good people from evil, even though he was a machine. A "network" of eight coins is less complex than a humanoid robot, but both are non-human devices made of metal.

Atogaki (Afterword)

So: what has been the point of this survey looking at how a historically non-Christian culture represents Christianity itself? Am I indicting the Japanese for "getting it wrong" about God and Jesus? Or am I endorsing their treating a sacred belief in one part of the world as "for entertainment purposes only" in another part of the world?

Actually, neither is the case. I see Japan's varied versions and revisions of Christianity, and our own reactions to those revisions, as examples of what Edward Said described as Giambattista Vico's concept of "the conceit of nations and of scholars". Specifically, it recognizes that the two conceits are actually the same thing happening in two very different dimensions: one mistake is brought about by space, and the other by time.

The conceit of nations is that any culture somehow is doing something unique and special in its evolution, something never done by other cultures, in the way its history progresses. Vico argued that this view is mistaken: that the progress of any culture, in a cycle from worshipping the divine—be it God or gods—to lionizing heroes to trusting in reason and rational men to understand the world and how best to function in it, is a process that happens in all cultures. Most of us tend to never see this, however, precisely because we are immersed in our own culture, and have never really had the chance to experience the culture of anyone else. Instead, we read accounts of other cultures, most often written by members of our own culture; this filter automatically becomes a built-in "proof" of the fallacy that one culture is different from, hence superior to, the other culture.

The conceit of scholars recreates the same mistake but with a different variable: time. Vico challenged the presumption that modern-day historians are essentially the same as those of the past, using the same cultural tools in the same way to perpetuate the parent culture. He argued instead that cultures evolve, challenging the belief that ways of thinking about one thing in the past—human slavery, for example—were the same ways as they are now. Cultures can and do progress, around the globe and throughout history; they can also backslide into Magical Thinking and end up having to repeat the cycle.

This is all to say that Japan's perspective on Christianity—actually several perspectives which have evolved over time—do not "prove" that they somehow "got it wrong". Japan was handed Christianity as practiced by 16th century Portuguese Jesuits and told in essence to "deal with it"—without knowing its roots or the nationalist arguments that helped shape European Christianity in decades past, much less the theological and cultural debates of centuries past. The arrival of other missionaries was an unnatural jump in the evolution, forcing changes on Japanese Christianity to happen in decades that took centuries in Europe; no surprise that the militant sectarianism of medieval Christianity was seen in Japan as destabilizing and hence dangerous.

One way for Japan to try to undo the risk to its culture is through fiction: alternate versions of history, including novels, manga and anime. They suggest major historical changes that might have happened except for one variable. What if vampires existed and the Axis powers used them to wage World War 2? What if life on other planets invaded Earth the way America invaded Japan in 1853? What if one of the heroes of the past, whether samurai Yagyu Jubei or Christian martyr Amakusa Shirō, had been born a girl? Such speculative fiction does not actually change the past, but offers a different angle from which to view it.

Manga and anime are probably better suited than any other medium to depict something that doesn't exactly match up with "real life". By definition, they are media dealing in artistic versions of whatever the subject may be, so the artistic depiction starts at a distance from reality and only moves further away, fueled by the creativity of the artists. Even if the subject is as mundane as preparing breakfast or hanging laundry, there is always a "plus" aspect just by the nature of the artistic medium.

This message may discourage some people whose beliefs are more traditional—regardless of the particular tradition—but I believe that it's a message apt for, and necessary in, our own time in the Global Village. Multiculturalism has become a fact of life since the Internet; our current cyber communications network wasn't originally intended to break down cultural barriers and connect people who would not have met otherwise, but it's where we are now. This goes for religious proselytizing as well; missionaries like Francis Xavier used to dedicate their lives and put themselves at physical risk travelling around the known world. These days, a few keystrokes can get you, or at least your blog, where you wish to go. The price, however, is equalization. The modern traveler can no longer show up offering sacred books and/or cannon fire and expect to be given a place of honor; they have to approach as equals and earn that place. Just as they can arrive with a few keystrokes, they can be "Unfriended" with a few keystrokes.

Unfortunately, cultures backslide into Magical Thinking. No culture is immune from groups such as the Branch Davidian in Texas or the Islamic State in the Middle East or the Aum Shinrikyo in Japan; countering their words and deeds, as any enlightened society must, takes a fearless application of the lessons of modernity, which can be a long game. I believe, however, that peace, like war, is cyclical; it has happened before and it can and will happen again, with a concerted effort and the use of all of the tools at our disposal—including the arts.

Even arts like comic books. Tezuka Osamu showed *Tetsuwan Atomu* (or *Astro Boy*) facing the same discrimination against robots that black people were facing in America and South Africa. Nakazawa Keiji drew *Hadashi no Gen (Barefoot Gen)* reflecting his own life as a survivor of the atomic bombing of Hiroshima. Even Hirano Kouta in his vampire fantasy *Hellsing* offers up a fictional Holy War between Protestants and Catholics as his way of saying: we don't have to go through all that again.

I was recently thinking about this, and about the anime version of Tsutsui Yasutaka's beloved science fiction novel *Toki wo Kakeru Shoujo (The Girl Who Leapt Through Time)*. This story had already been filmed when director Hosoda Mamoru, who had worked as an animation director for the *Digimon* television series, made the book the subject of his first feature film. He essentially rewrote the story so that the original "Time Leaper" appears as a secondary character, showing up to fill in a few blanks for the main character, but basically letting her figure out her Leaping for herself.

Nobody is even certain how Leaping came to be, but the central character discovers that she has been given the ability to jump herself backwards in time, sometimes a few hours, sometimes a day. Without a guide or explanation, she takes advantage of this new ability to do some trivial things, such as getting a second chance to study for a pop quiz, or take the last of the leftover pudding before her sister can get it. While she does all these little things to change her life, she doesn't see that her actions are changing the world around her in other, sometimes less benign ways. She also doesn't think about the strange tattoo-like mark that she picked up when she acquired the Leaping—until she realizes that it's essentially a counter telling her how many Leaps she has left. And she doesn't get it until she's down to her last half-dozen.

This is a lighthearted anime for the most part, but the ending has moved grown men to tears in Japan. This may be because of memories of the original book or other filmed versions, or it could be because they get the message—a message that Tsutsui could best tell allegorically, because speaking the plain truth out loud would be less interesting. It may be that Leaping was Tsutsui's metaphor for life itself: by the time we realize that we are alive, and that we have the ability to reach out to the rest of the world and allow it to reach back to us, we have already wasted so many chances on selfish or trivial choices. Getting old, or at least getting older, brings us closer to the end of life, but, as long as we aren't there yet, the magic is still there— the ability to Leap, to remake the universe, in small ways or sometimes not so small.

I don't insist that this is the only interpretation possible for *Toki wo Kakeru Shoujo*, but it is a valid interpretation given the content of the movie. In that way, I consider it to be as religious an anime as *Kaze no Tani no Nausika* with its Hollywood-inspired Messianic finale. Or the same journey of both self-discovery and community in the pastoral mysticism of Yoshitoshi ABe's *Haibane Renmei*. In Japanese arts, as in Japanese religions, there is no One True Church; nor should there be. That too would be less interesting.

References

TEXTS

Alletzhauser, Albert J. 1990. *The House of Nomura: The Rise to Power of the World's Wealthiest Company.* New York: Bloomsbury Publishing.

Aston, W. G. 1899. *A History of Japanese Literature.* Rutland, VT: Charles E. Tuttle Company.

Barrett, Gregory. 1989. *Archetypes in Japanese Film: The Sociopolitical and Religious Significance of the Principal Heroes and Heroines.* Selinsgrove: Susquehanna University Press.

Bederman, Gail. 1995. *Manliness and Civilization: A Cultural History of Gender and Race in the United States, 1880-1917.* Chicago: University of Chicago Press.

Blyth, R. H. 1949. *Senryu: Japanese Satirical Verse.* Westport, CT: Greenwood Press.

Bolton, Christopher. "The Quick and the Undead: Visual and Political Dynamics in *Blood: The Last Vampire.*" *Mechademia*, vol. 2, 2007, pp. 125-142.

Bornoff, Nicholas. 1991. *Pink Samurai: Love, Marriage and Sex in Contemporary Japan.* New York: Simon & Schuster/Pocket Books.

Boxer, C.R. 1951. *The Christian Century in Japan, 1549-1650.* Berkeley: University of California Press.

Buruma, Ian. 1984. *Behind the Mask: On Sexual Demons, Sacred Mothers, Transvestites, Gangsters, Drifters and Other Japanese Cultural Heroes.* New York: Pantheon Books.

Chinnock, Frank W. 1969. *Nagasaki: The Forgotten Bomb.* New York & Cleveland: New American Library/World Publishing Company.

Covert, Brian. 1992. "The Tezuka Controversy", *Mangajin #19*, August 10, 1992, pp. 6-10.

Draper, Robert. 2012. *Do Not Ask What Good We Do: Inside the U. S. House of Representatives.* New York: Free Press.

Drazen, Patrick. 2011. *A Gathering of Spirits: Japan's Ghost Story Tradition.* (print and e-book) Indianapolis: iUniverse.

———. 2002 (2nd edition 2014). *Anime Explosion: The What? Why? And Wow! Of Japanese Animation.* Berkeley: Stone Bridge Press.

———. 1986 (April). "Leo the (Buddhist) Lion", *Channels of Communication*, p. 10.

Drummond, Richard Henry. 1971. *A History of Christianity in Japan.* Grand Rapids: William B. Eerdmans Publishing Company.

DuBois, Thomas David. 2011. *Religion in the Making of Modern East Asia.* New York: Cambridge University Press.

Duus Masayo and Duus, Peter. 1983. *Tokyo Rose: Orphan of the Pacific.* Tokyo: Kodansha.

References

Earhart, H. Byron. 1984. *Religions of Japan: Many Traditions Within One Sacred Way*. San Francisco: Harper & Row.
Ellwood, Robert S. 1974. *The Eagle and the Rising Sun; Americans and the New Religions of Japan*. Philadelphia: Westminster Press.
Fields, Rick. 1992. *How the Swans Came to the Lake: A Narrative History of Buddhism in America*. Boston: Shambhala Publications.
Foster, Michael Dylan. 2006. "Strange Games and Enchanted Science: The Mystery of Kokkuri." *Journal of Asian Studies, vol. 65*, #2, pp. 251-275.
Franklin, H. Bruce. 1993. *M.I.A.: Mythmaking in America*. New Brunswick, NJ: Rutgers University Press.
Gunn, Geoffrey C. 2003. *First Globalization: The Eurasian Exchange, 1500 to 1800*. Lanham, MD: Rowman & Littlefield.
Hairston, Marc. 2007. "Fly Away Old Home: Memory and Salvation in *Haibane Renmei*". *Mechademia, vol. 2*, pp. 235-249.
Hane Mikiso. 1972. *Japan: A Historical Survey*. New York: Charles Scribner's Sons.
———. 1988. *Reflections on the Way to the Gallows: Portraits of Japanese Rebel Women*. New York: Pantheon.
Ink (pseudonym). "All That Jazz!" *Otaku USA*, vol. 6 #5 (April 2013) pp. 84-87.
Japan's Mass Media. *About Japan*, Series #7. Tokyo: Foreign Press Center.
LaFleur, William R. 1994. *Liquid Life: Abortion and Buddhism in Japan*. Princeton: Princeton University Press.
Lebra, Takie Sugiyama. 1984. *Japanese Women: Constraint and Fulfillment*. Honolulu: University of Hawai'i Press.
Matthew, Robert. 1989. *Japanese Science Fiction: A View of a Changing Society*. London: Routledge.
McCarthy, Helen. 1999. *Hayao Miyazaki: Master of Japanese Animation*. Berkeley: Stone Bridge Press.
McLuhan, Marshall. 1964. *Understanding Media: The Extensions of Man*. New York: McGraw-Hill.
Medved, Harry, and Randy Dreyfuss. 1978. *The Fifty Worst Films of All Time (And How They Got That Way)*. New York: Popular Library.
Morioka Kiyomi. 1975. *Religion in Changing Japanese Society*. Tokyo: University of Tokyo Press.
Ogihara-Schuck, Eriko. "The Christianizing of Animism in Manga and Anime: American Translations of Hayao Miyazaki's *Nausicaä of the Valley of the Wind.*" In Lewis, A. Davis and Kraemer, Christine Hoff, eds. 2010. *Graven Images: Religion in Comic Books and Graphic Novels*. New York: Continuum, pp. 133-146.
Ortega, Mariana. "My Father, He Killed Me; My Mother, She Ate Me: Self, Desire, Engendering, and the Mother in *Neon Genesis Evangelion.*" *Mechademia, vol. 2*, 2007, pp. 207-232.
Otmazgin, Nissim Kadosh. "Contesting soft power: Japanese popular culture in East and Southeast Asia." *International Relations of the Asia-Pacific* 2008 8(1):73-101; doi:10.1093/irap/lcm009.
Ravenscroft, Trevor. 1973. *The Spear of Destiny: The Occult Power Behind the Spear which Pierced the Side of Christ*. York Beach, ME: Samuel Weiser, Inc.
Reader, Ian. 1991. *Religion in Contemporary Japan*. Honolulu: University of Hawai'i Press.
Reischauer, Edwin O. 1965. *The United States and Japan*. Cambridge, MA: Harvard University Press.
Said, Edward W. 1978. *Orientalism*. New York: Vintage Books.
Savage, William W., Jr. 1990. *Comic Books and America 1945-1954*. Norman: University of Oklahoma Press.
Schodt, Frederik. 1983. *Manga! Manga! The World of Japanese Comics*. Tokyo and New York: Kodansha.
Seidensticker, Edward. 1990. *Tokyo Rising: The City Since the Great Earthquake*. New York: Alfred A. Knopf.
Smith, Robert J. 1983. *Japanese Society: Tradition, Self and the Social Order*. Cambridge: Cambridge University Press.

Smith, Toren. "Princess of the Manga". *Amazing Heroes* #165 (May 15, 1989), pp. 20-27.
Sugimoto Etsu Inagaki. 1925. *A Daughter of the Samurai*. New York: Doubleday Doran & Co.
Suter, Rebecca. 2015. *Holy Ghosts: The Christian Century in Modern Japanese Fiction*. Honolulu: University of Hawai'i Press.
Theroux, Paul. 1975. *The Great Railway Bazaar: By Train Through Asia*. Boston: Houghton Mifflin Company.
Tuchman, Barbara W. 1978. *A Distant Mirror: The Calamitous 14th Century*. New York: Ballantine Books.
Varley, H. Paul. 1984. *Japanese Culture* (third edition). Honolulu: University of Hawai'i Press.
Weiner, Tim. "C.I.A. spent millions to support Japanese right in 50's and 60's." *New York Times*, vol. 144, October 9, 1994, section 1, page 1.

ONLINE

Catechism of the Catholic Church. http://www.vatican.va/archive/ENG0015/_INDEX.HTM, accessed July 6, 2015.
Backlash over lesson about Islam leads to Va. school closings. Crimesider Staff AP/CBS December 17, 2015, http://www.cbsnews.com/news/backlash-over-lesson-about-islam-leads-to-virginia-school-closings/, accessed December 20, 2015.
Davidson, Danica. March 18, 2016. "Interview: Frederik L. Schodt and the Osamu Tezuka Story." *Otaku USA* website. http://otakuusamagazine.com/Manga/News1/Interview-Frederik-L-Schodt-and-The-Osamu-Tezuka-S-7572.aspx, accessed March 18, 2016.
Deacon, James. "Darani." http://www.aetw.org/jsp_darani_main.htm, accessed July 30, 2015.
"End-of-the-Year Deep Cleaning in Japan", http://resources.realestate.co.jp/living/end-of-the-year-deep-cleaning-in-japan/, accessed December 24, 2015.
Harnett, Sam. "Japan white weddings." Broadcast 12/26/2013. http://www.pri.org/stories/2012-12-26/popularity-western-style-weddings-japan-creates-demand-white-officiants, accessed August 13, 2015.
"U.S. admits CIA gave LDP money in 1950s, 1960s". *The Japan Times.* July 20, 2006. http://www.japantimes.co.jp/news/2006/07/20/national/u-s-admits-cia-gave-ldp-money-in-1950s-1960s/#.Vf3MSJeYthd, accessed September 19, 2015.
LeFebvre, Jesse. *The Rise of Wedding Churches—The "Nonreligious" Transformation of Japanese Christianity.* https://www.academia.edu/21931085/The_Rise_of_Wedding_Churches_The_Nonreligious_Transformation_of_Japanese_Christianity, accessed August 13, 2015.
"Marriage," section 3c, *The Japanese and Buddhism,* http://www.buddhanet.net/nippon/nippon_partII.html, accessed June 19, 2015.
Jones, Clayton. "Japan's Parliament Investigates Shadowy LDP Bribery Scandal". *Christian Science Monitor,* January 24, 1992. http://www.csmonitor.com/1992/0124/24012.html, accessed September 19, 2015.
Kermode, Mark. 1998. *The Exorcist – hype or horror?* http://news.bbc.co.uk/2/hi/entertainment/206337.stm, accessed August 16, 2015.
Mak Jo Si. "Taoism Exorcism vs Ghosts and Spirits". *Chi in Nature's Blog.* http://www.taoistmasterblog.com/taoism-exorcism-vs-ghosts-and-spirits/, accessed September 5, 2015.
McGray, Douglas. "Japan's Gross National Cool." *Foreign Policy*, June/July 2002, 44-54. http://www.chass.utoronto.ca/~ikalmar/illustex/japfpmcgray.htm, accessed October 24, 2015.
Parry, Richard Lloyd. "Ghosts of the Tsunami." *London Review of Books,* vol. 36 no. 3, February 6, 2014, pp. 13-17. http://www.lrb.co.uk/v36/n03/richard-lloydparry/ghosts-of-the-tsunami?src=longreads, accessed September 5, 2015.
Seiyaku.com. "Western Style Weddings in Japan". http://www.seiyaku.com/seiyaku/en/western-wedding.html, accessed August 13, 2015.
"The Imperial Hotel". http://www.mnn.com/your-home/remodeling-design/photos/6-destroyed-frank-lloyd-wright-buildings/the-imperial-hotel, accessed August 25, 2015.

Villar, Ruairidh, and Knight, Sophie. "Haunted by trauma, tsunami survivors in Japan turn to exorcists." *Reuters*, March 5, 2013, http://www.reuters.com/article/2013/03/05/us-japan-exorcist-ghosts-idUSBRE9240YZ20130305, accessed September 5, 2015.

MANGA

Arakawa Hiromu. 2001. *Fullmetal Alchemist (Hagane no Renkinjutsushi)* in 27 vols. Trans. Akira Watanabe. San Francisco: VIZ.
CLAMP (collective). 2004. *xxxHolic* in 19 vols. Trans. William Flanagan. New York: Del Rey Ballantine Books.
Fumizuki Kou. 2001. *Ai Yori Aoshi*, vol. 5. Trans. Nibley, Alethea and Nibley, Athena. Los Angeles: Tokyopop.
Hiramatsu Shinji. 1981. *Black Angels*, in 12 vols. Tokyo: Shueisha.
Hotta Yumi, and Obata Takeshi. 1998. *Hikaru no Go* in 23 vols. Tokyo: Shueisha.
———. 1998. *Hikaru no Go* in 23 vols. Trans. Andy Nakatani. San Francisco: VIZ.
Imaizumi Shinji. 1989. *Kamisama wa Sausupoo (God is a Southpaw)* in 12 vols. Tokyo: Shueisha.
Inada Shiho and Ono Fuyumi. 1998. *Ghost Hunt*, in 12 vols. Tokyo: Kodansha.
———. 2005. *Ghost Hunt*, in 12 vols, trans. Tsubasa Akira. New York: Del Rey.
Inui Haruka. "Holy Beast in Black", Trans. anon, in *Ogenki Clinic*, vol. 1, pp. 24-33. http://g.e-hentai.org/s/48ac68a93f/37060-24, accessed September 21, 2014.
Ishimori Shotaro. 1985. *Hoteru*, vol. 1-"Never Check Out". Tokyo: Shogakukan.
———. 1965. *Mutant Sab*, in 2 vols. Tokyo: Asahi Sonorama.
Kouenji H., Nagai Go and Ishikawa Ken. 1991. *Shinrei Tantei Okaruto Dan*, vol. 1. Tokyo: Taitosha.
Nakazawa Kenji. 1975. *Hadashi no Gen (Barefoot Gen)* in 10 vols. Trans: New Society Publishers. Tokyo: Shueisha.
Shiina Takashi. 1991. *Ghost Sweeper Mikami* in 39 vols. Tokyo: Shogakukan.
Takahashi Rumiko. 1989. *Ippondo no Fukuin (One Pound Gospel)* in 4 vols. Tokyo: Shogakukan.
———. 1982. *Mezon Ikkoku* in 15 vols. Tokyo: Shogakukan.
———. 1987. "Roman no akindo," pp. 35-66, in *P no higeki*. 1994. Tokyo: Shogakukan.
Takeuchi Naoko. 1997. *Seeraa Moon (Sailor Moon)*, vols. 11 & 18. Tokyo: Kodansha.
Tezuka Osamu. 1970. "Atomu Konseki Monogatari (The Story of Atom Past and Present)," in *Tetsuwan Atomu*, vols. 7-8, Tokyo: Sun Comics.
———. 1974. *Burakku Jyakku (Black Jack)*, vols. 1 & 2. Tokyo: Akita Shoten.
———. 1953. *Boku no Son Goku (My Son Goku)*, vols. 1 & 6. Manga Tezuka #12 & 17. Tokyo: Kodansha.
———. 1968. "Chitei Sensha (The Underground Tank)," pp. 93-134, in *Tetsuwan Atomu*, vol. 11, Tokyo: Sun Comics.
———. 1980. *Don Dorakyuro*, in 3 vols. Tokyo: Akita Shoten.
———. 1960. *Enzeru no Oka (Angel's Hill)*, in 2 vols. Manga Tezuka #75 & 76. Tokyo: Kodansha.
———. 1959. *Futago no Kishi*. Manga Tezuka #58. Tokyo: Kodansha.
———. 1971. *Hyaku Monogatari (One Hundred Stories)*. Tokyo: Shueisha.
———. 1959. "Iwan no Baka," pp. 35-79, in *Tetsuwan Atomu*, Manga Tezuka #226. Tokyo: Kodansha.
———. 1954. *Kei to Batsu (Crime and Punishment)*, Manga Tezuka #10. Tokyo: Kodansha.
———. 1970. *Kirihito Sanka (Ode to Kirihito)*, trans. Nieh, Camellia. New York: Vertical, Inc.
———. 1959. "Kirisuto no Me (The Eye of Christ)," pp. 7-33, in *Tetsuwan Atomu*, Manga Tezuka #226. Tokyo: Kodansha.
———. 1978. *MW*, in 3 vols. Tokyo: Shogakukan.
———. 1953. *Ribon no Kishi*, in 3 vols. Manga Tezuka #4-6. Tokyo: Kodansha.
———. 1968. "Kasei kara Kaette Kita Otoko (The Man Who Came Home from Mars)," pp. 135-199, in *Tetsuwan Atomu*, vol. 11, Tokyo: Sun Comics.

———. 1983. *Unico,* in 2 vols. Manga Tezuka #285 & 286. Tokyo: Kodansha.
Wada Shinji. 1977. *Wa ga Tomo Furankenshutain (My Friend Frankenstein).* Tokyo: Shueisha.

ANIME/FILM

Soka Jiro, Producer, and Tokiwa Kanenari, Director. 1995. *Angel of Darkness 1.*Japan: F.A.I.
Ibaraki Masahiko, Ueno Masuo, Ochi Takeshi, and Ochikoshi Takamitsu, Executive Producers, and Okamura Tensai, Director: 2011. *Ao no Ekososhisuto (Blue Exorcist).* Japan: Aniplex and A-1 Pictures.
Shimizu Yoshihiro and Matsutani Takayuki, Executive Producers, and Dezaki Osamu, Director. 1994. *Black Jack.* "Clinical Chart 5: The Owl of San Merida." Japan: Tezuka Production Co. Ltd.
Takatsuka Toshiki, Executive Producer, and Ohnuki Kenishi, Director. 1989. *Earthian.* Japan: J.C. Staff.
Takeda Seiji, Taguchi Koji, Katsumata Hideo and Minami Masahiko, Executive Producers, and Mizushima Seiji, Director. 2005. *Gehijouban Hagane no Renkinjutsushi Shanbara wo Yuku Mono (Fullmetal Alchemist the Movie: Conqueror of Shamballa).* Japan: Bones.
Ohi Mamoru and Horikiri Shinji, Producers, and Mano Akira, Director. 2006-7. *Ghost Hunt.* Japan: J.C. Staff.
Seki Hiromi, Hirao Tomoya, Kameyama Yasuo and Hatano Yoshifumi, Producers, and Umezawa Atsutoshi, Director. 1993-4. *Goosutosuiipaa Mikami (Ghost Sweeper Mikami).* Japan: Toei Animation.
Aureole Secret Factory and Fuji Television, Producers, and Tokoro Tomokazu, Director. 2003. *Haibane Renmei.* Japan: Radix.
Mukudori Nemu and Miyakawa Yasue, Producers, and Muto Yuji, Director. 1997. *Haunted Junction.* Japan: Studio DEEN.
Kawaguchi Noritaka and Shinkai Makoto, Producers, and Shinkai Makoto, Director. 2011. *Hoshi wo Ou Kodomo (Children Who Chase Lost Voices).* Japan: CoMix Wave Inc.
Kondou Michio, Hara Toru and Tokuma Yasuyoshi, Executive Producers, and Miyazaki Hayao, Director. 1984. *Kaze no Tani no Naushika (Nausicaä of the Valley of the Wind).* Japan: Topcraft.
Nomura Kazufumi and Miura Toru, Producers, and Tsukamoto Eri and Hirano Toshihiro, Directors. 1988. *Kyūketsuki Miyu (Vampire Princess Miyu).* Japan: AIC.
Yamamoto Kōji, Kobayashi Shinichiro, Tanaka Shinsaku, Kochiyama Takashi and Takeeda Yoshinori, Producers, and Yamamoto Sayo, Director. 2008-2009. *Michiko to Hatchin.* Japan: Manglobe.
Maki Taro, Executive Producer, and Kon Satoshi, Director. 2001. *Millennium Actress.* Japan: Madhouse.
Inoue Hiroaki and Sueyoshi Hirohiko, Producers, and Yamaka Hiroyugi, Director. 1987. *Ooritsu Uchuugun—Oneamise no Tsubasa (Royal Space Force—Wings of Honneamise).* Japan: Gainax.
Katayama Tetsuo, Producer, and Miyazaki Hayao, Director. 1979. *Rupan Sansei: Cariosutoro no Shiro (Lupin the Third: Castle of Cagliostro).* Japan: Tokyo Movie Shinsha.
Terada Atsushi, Shinzaka Junichi, Kitagawa Naoki, and Tomikawa Yatsuho, Executive Producers, and Watanabe Shinichiro, Director. 2012. *Sakamichi no Aporon (Kids on the Slope).* Japan: MAPPA.
Watanabe Takashi and Saito Yuichiro, Producers, and Hosoda Mamoru, Director. 2006. *Toki wo Kakeru Shoujo (The Girl Who Leapt Through Time).* Japan: Madhouse.
Kobayashi Shinichi, Takiyama Masao, and Maki Taro, Executive Producers, and Kon Satoshi, Director. 2003. *Tokyo Godfathers.* Japan: Madhouse.
Simon Channing Williams, Producer, and Mike Leigh, Director. 1999. *Topsy-Turvy.* United Kingdom/United States: Goldwyn Films, Newmarket Capital Group, The Greenlight Fund, and Thin Man Films.

Imada Chiaki, Producer, and Katsumata Tomoharu, Director. 1980. *Wa ga Seishun no Arukadia (Arcadia of my Youth)*. Japan: Toei Animation.
Matsumura Keiichi and Sugita Tsutomu, Producers, and Murase Shuko, Director. 2002. *Witch Hunter Robin*. Japan: Sunrise and Bandai Visual.
Kadokawa Tsunehiko, Executive Producer, and Rintaro, Director. 1996. *X*. Japan: Madhouse.
Inoue Hiroaki, Morijiri Kazuaki, and Morosawa Masao, Producers, and Ueda Hitoshi, Chief Animation Director. 1994-1995. *Yugen Kaisha (Phantom Quest Corp.)*. Japan: Madhouse.

Index

ABe Yoshitoshi (manga artist, b. 1971), 155, 157, 178
Ai Yori Aoshi (manga by Fumizuki Kou, 1998-2005), 83, 95–96
Aikawa Shō (screenwriter, b. 1965), 84, 143
Aizawa Kansho (spiritualist, b. 1957), 77
Akaishi Michiyo (manga artist, b. 1959), 137
Akechi Mitsuhide (samurai general, 1528-82), 12, 14, 65, 82, 87n9, 133
Akihisa Ikeda (manga artist, b. 1976), 74
Akira (manga by Otomo Katsuhiro, 1982-90), 170
Akutagawa Ryūnosuke (author, 1892-1927), 2, 138n4
Alakazam the Great!. See *My Son-Goku*
Alletzhauser, Albert J. (author, b. 1950), 89
Amakusa (island, Japan), 16, 135
Amakusa Shirō (born Masuda Shirō, Christian martyr, c. 1621-38), 16, 133, 134, 135, 135–136, 138, 138n2, 161, 176
Amaterasu (Shinto sun goddess), 70, 84, 124, 166, 172
Ammitsu-hime (manga by Kurakane Shosuke, 1949-55), 64n12
Angel of Darkness (anime dir. by Kanenari Tokiwa, 1994), 163–164, 164

Angel Sanctuary (Tenshi kinryouku) (manga by Yuki Kaori, 1994-2000), 75n3, 164–165, 166
Animage (anime magazine), 69
Anime Explosion: The What? Why? And Wow! Of Japanese Animation (history by Drazen, Patrick, 2002), vi, 75n4, 146, 172
Anime Oyako Gekijo (Anime Family Theater). See *Superbook*
Annaka, Gumma Prefecture, Japan, 23
Aquinas, Thomas (Sicilian theologian, c. 1225-74), 164
Arakawa Hiromu (Japanese manga artist, b. 1973), vi, 73, 143, 148, 159
Arcadia of My Youth (Wa ga Seishun no Arukadia) (anime dir. by Katsumata Tomoharu, 1980), 66–67
Asahi Graph (Japanese newspaper), 39, 66
Ashikaga Yoshiaki (shogun, 1537-97), 12
Asō Yutaka (cartoonist, 1898-1961), 39
Aston, William George (British literary critic, 1841-1911), 34–35, 36
Aum Shnrikyo (Buddhist cult), 177
Austen, Jane (British novelist, 1775-1817), 35

Bakin Takizawa (author, 1767-1848), 35–36
Baldwin, James (American author, essayist, 1924-1987), 2, 77

Index

Barefoot Gen (Hadashi no Gen) (manga by Nakazawa Keiji, 1973-1985), 177
Barrett, Gregory (American author, b. 1938), 2
Bederman, Gail (American historian), 128
*Battle of the Planets (*aka *Gatchaman/ Science Ninja Team Gatchaman)* (anime, 1972-74), 139
Behind the Mask: On Sexual Demons, Sacred Mothers, Transvestites, Gangsters, Drifters, and Other Japanese Cultural Heroes (cultural history by Buruma, Ian, 1985), 97n4, 152, 154, 161
Beneath the Tangles (blog), 7, 110
Black Angels (manga by Hiramatsu Shinji, 1981), 87n10, 111–114, 167–172
Blatty, William Peter (American author, 1928-2017), 85
Blood: The Last Vampire (anime dir. by Kitakubo Hiroyuki, 2000), 151
Blue Exorcist (manga by Katō Kazue, 2009-), 83–84, 119
Blyth, Reginald Horace (British author, 1898-1964), 2
Bolton, Christopher (American author), 151
The Book of Five Rings (book by Musashi Miyamoto, c. 1645), 138n5
Bornoff, Nicholas (British author, 1949-2010), 8, 161
Boxer, Charles Ralph (British author, 1904-2000), 13, 37
Branch Davidian (Christian cult), 177
Bringing Up Father (comic by George McManus, 1913-2000), 39
Bruegel, Pieter the Elder (Dutch artist, 1525-69), 155
Buonarroti, Michelangelo (Italian artist, 1475-1564), 131
Buronson (pseudonym) (manga artist, b. 1947), 111
Buruma, Ian (Dutch author, b. 1951), 97n4, 152, 154, 161
Bush, George H. W. (American President, b. 1924), 1

Campbell. Joseph (American mythologist, 1904-87), 6

Central Intelligence Agency (CIA), 22
Children Who Chase Lost Voices (Hoshi wo Ou Kodomo) (anime dir. by Shinkai Makoto, 2011), 70, 166
Chinnock, Frank W. (American author, b. 1926), 27
Christian Broadcasting Network (American television network), 139
The Christian Century in Japan, 1549-1650 (history by Boxer, C. R., 1951), 13, 37
Chrono Crusade (manga by Moriyama Daisuke, 1998-2004), 119–120
CLAMP (manga collective), 70, 72
Clarke, Arthur C. (British author, 1917-2008), 137
Coelho, Caspar (Portuguese missionary, 1530-90), 14, 115n1, 163
Confucius. *See* K'ung Fu-tzu
Corman, Roger (American movie producer/director, b. 1926), 42
Count of Monte Cristo (novel by Dumas, Alexander *pere,* 1844*)*, 33
Cowboy Bebop (anime series dir. by Watanabe Shinichirō, 1998), 140
Crime and Punishment (novel by Dostoevsky, Fyodor, 1866), 43, 54
Cromwell, Oliver (British statesman, 1599-1658), 20
Cutie Honey (manga by Ishikawa Ken and Nagai Go, 1973-74), 72, 135, 161

Darwin, Charles (British biologist, 1809-1882), 24
A Daughter of the Samurai (memoir by Sugimoto, Etsu Inagaki, 1926), 36
Davidson, Danica. (author), 40
Deacon, James (British spiritualist), 87n12
Deshima (island, Japan), 17
Dezaki Osamu (anime director, 1943-2011), 57, 58, 63
Digimon (anime series, 1999-), 177
A Distant Mirror: The Calamitous 14th Century (history by Tuchman, Barbara W., 1978), 97n2, 149, 150
Disney, Walter E. "Walt" (American animator, 1901-1966), 8, 42, 44
Dokuro kengyō (The Skull Abbot), (novel by Yokomizo Seishi, 1939), 138n3

Dōshisha University, Kyoto, 21
Dostoevsky, Fyodor (Russian author, 1821-81), 43, 54
Doyle, Sir Arthur Conan (British author, 1859-1930), 63n1
Dracula (novel by Bram Stoker, 1897), 9, 58, 75n5, 82, 148
Drazen, Patrick (American author, b. 1951), 75n4, 87n13, 133, 136, 146, 172
Drummond, Richard Henry (American author, b. 1916), 18
DuBois, Thomas David (historian, b. 1969), 20
Dumas, Alexander *père* (French novelist, 1802-70), 33, 105
"Dutch Studies" (19th century Japanese studies of western medicine), 134

Earhart, H. Byron (American scholar, b. 1935), 20, 24
Earthian (manga by Yon Kouga, 1988-94), 70–71
Edo period. *See* Tokugawa period.
Edogawa Rampo (author, pseudonym of Hirai Tarō, 1894-1965), 3
Eihei Dogen (Zen Buddhist priest, 1200-53), 156
Ellwood, Robert S. (author, b. 1933), 28
Endō Shūsaku (author, 1923-1996), 2, 31
Esper Mami (manga by Fujiko Fujio (pseudonym), 1977-82), 170
Evslin, Bernard (American author, 1922-93), 68
The Exorcist (novel by William Peter Blatty, 1971), 81, 85–86, 86, 161

Fenollosa, Ernest (American educator, 1853-1908), 24
Fields, Rick (American author, 1942-99), 24
Fillmore, Millard (American President, 1800-74), 19
Fire Force (En En no Shōbōtai, Fire Brigade of Flames) (manga by Ōkubo Atsushi, 2015-), 123–124
Fist of the North Star (Hokuto no Ken) (manga by Buronson (pseudonym), 1983-88), 111

The Flying House (anime series, 1982-83), 139
Ford, John (American director, 1894-1973), 140
Foster, Michael Dylan (American author), 170
Francis of Assisi (Italian priest, saint, born Giovanni di Bernardone, c. 1181-1226), 133, 138n1
Francis Xavier (Spanish-Basque priest, saint, 1506-1552), 11, 176
Franciscans. *See* Order of Friars Minor
Franklin, H. Bruce (American historian, b. 1934), 33
Fujin Kyōfūkai (Women's Moral Reform Society, founded 1886), 26
Fukuda Hideko (feminist author, 1865-1927), 25
Fukushima Prefecture, Tōhoku Region, Japan, 77
Fukuzawa Yukichi (author, educator, 1835-1901), 24
Fullmetal Alchemist (Hagane no Renkinjutsushi) (manga by Arakawa Hiromu, 2001-10), 73, 143, 148, 159
Fullmetal Alchemist The Movie: Conqueror of Shamballa (anime dir. by Mizushima Seiji, 2006), 82, 143, 144, 145
Fumizuki Kou (manga artist), 95

Gakko no Kaidan (School Ghost Stories) (anthology by Tsunemitsu Toru, 1990), 87n6
Galaxy Express 999 (Ginga Tetsudō 999) (manga by Matsumoto Leiji, 1977-81), 42, 72
Galilei, Galileo (Italian astronomer, mathematician, 1564-1642), 34
Gall Force (anime series, 1986-97), 122–123
A Gathering of Spirits: Japan's Ghost Story Tradition (book by Drazen, Patrick, 2011), 64n11, 87n13
Geller, Uri (Israeli psychic, b. 1946), 138n1, 170
Gemmei (empress, 661-721), 165
Getter Robo (manga by Ishikawa Ken and Nagai Gō, 1974-75), 135

Ghost Hunt (manga by Inada Shiho and Ono Fuyumi, 1998-2010), 74, 78, 79, 85, 86, 87n10, 94–95, 156
Ghost in the Shell (manga by Masamune Shirow, 1989-90), 120
Ghost Sweeper Mikami (manga by Shiina Takashi, 1991-99), 81–82, 87n9
Giant Robo (manga by Yokoyama Mitsuteru, 1967-68), 145
Gilbert, William S. (British playwright, 1836-1911), 33
Giovanni, Nikki (American poet, b. 1943), vii
The Girl Who Leapt Through Time (Toki wo Kakeru Shoujo) (novel by Tsutsui Yasutaka, 1967), 177–178
God is a Southpaw (Kamisama wa Sausupō) (manga by Imaizumi Shinji, 1989-91), 119, 146–147
Golgotha, Mount, Jerusalem, 171
Goya, Francisco (Sparish painter, 1746-1828), 131
Gundam Wing (anime dir. by Ikeda Masashi, 1995-96), 72
Gunn, Geoffrey C. (author), 19

Hachiko (dog, 1923-35), 46
Haibane Renmei (anime series created by ABe Yoshitoshi, 2002), 155–157, 178
Hairston, Marc (American author), vi, 156, 157
Hakkenden (allegorical novel by Bakin, 1814-1842), 35–36
Hana to Yume (manga magazine), 164
Hane, Mikiso (American historian, 1922-2003), 12, 13, 15, 16, 17, 25, 25–27, 27, 29n1, 167
Harano (castle, Nagasaki Prefecture, Kyushu, Japan), 133, 136
Harenchi Gakuen (Shameless School) (manga by Nagai Gō, 1968-72), 161
Harlock, Captain (manga character by Matsumoto Leiji), 42, 66
Hasegawa Machiko (manga artist, 1920-1992), 64n12
Hatori Bisco (manga artist, b. 1975), vi, 74, 87n10
Haunted Junction (manga by Mukudori Nemu, 1996-2001), 79–80

Haushofer, Karl (German educator, author, 1869-1946), 143–144
Hawaiian Islands, 25
Heart Sutra (Buddhist scripture), 86n3
Hegel, Georg Wilhelm Friedrich (German philosopher, 1770-1831), 24
Heian period (794-1185), 155
Heimin Shimbun (Commoners' News, newspaper), 25
Heiminsha (Commoners' Society), 25
Hellsing (manga by Hirano Kouta, 1997-2008), 147, 147–148, 149, 150, 177
Hepburn, James Curtis (American physician, teacher and missionary, 1815-1911), 21
Hess, Rudolf (German Nazi officer, 1894-1987), 143
Hewitt, Cindy and Donald (American translators and screenwriters), 69, 70
Hikaru no Go (manga by Obata Takeshi and Hotta Yumi, 1998-2003), 64n12, 155
Hilo, Hawai'i, 25
Himiko (empress/shamaness, c. 1st century C.E.), 168, 173n7
Hiramatsu Shinji (manga artist, b. 1955), 87n10, 111, 172
Hirano Kouta (manga artist, b. 1973), 147, 177
Hirano Toshihiro (anime director, b. 1956), 84
Hirohito (emperor during the Showa period, 1901-1989), 62
A History of Japanese Literature, (British literary history by Aston, W.G., 1899), 34
Hiwatari Saki (manga artist, b. 1961), 139
Hōchi (Japanese newspaper), 39
Hokkaido (island, Japan), 14, 19
Homer (Greek poet, c. 7th century BCE), 68
Hosoda Mamoru (anime director, b. 1967), 177
Hotel (manga by Ishinomoi Shotaro, 1985), 90
Hotta Yumi (Japanese manga writer, b. 1957), 64n12, 155

Ibuki, Mount, 135

Index

Ikeda Riyoko (manga artist, b. 1947), vi, 67
Ikkyu Sojun (Buddhist monk/poet, 1394-1481), 86n4
Imaizumi Shinji (manga artist, b. 1958), 146
Inada Shiho (manga artist), 74, 78, 85, 94
Inoue Enryō (educator, philosopher, 1858-1919), 24
Inui Haruka (manga artist, b. 1957), 162
InuYasha (manga by Takahashi Rumiko, 1996-2008), 117, 119
Ishikawa Ken (manga artist, 1948-2006), 74, 135, 161
Ishinomori Shotaro (also Ishimori Shotaro; manga artist, 1938-1998), vi, 53, 67, 90
ISIS (Muslim cult), 38n1, 177
Itō Noe (feminist, anarchist, 1895-1923), 25, 26
Izanagi (Shinto god), 161, 163, 165–166
Izanami (Shinto goddess), 161, 163, 165, 167

Japan and the Japanese (German history book by Karl Haushofer, 1933), 144
Japanese Socialist Party, 22
Jeffries, Jim (American boxer, 1875-1953), 128–129
Jesuits. *See* Society of Jesus
Jesus of Nazareth (Christian messiah), 8, 11, 16–17, 27, 46, 50, 62, 68, 73, 82, 89, 90, 97n2, 100, 105, 106, 112, 113, 131, 133, 135, 138n1, 142, 145, 151, 163, 175
Jodo Shinshu (Pure Land) Buddhism, 24, 25
Johnson, Jack (American boxer, 1878-1946), 128–129
Jones, Clayton (journalist), 22
Journey to the West (Buddhist allegory by Wu Cheng-en, c. 1592), 40, 41
Ju-On (The Grudge) (Japanese movie, 2002), 86
Jung, Carl G. (Swiss psychiatrist, 1875-1961), 6

Kagawa Toyohiko (Christian activist, 1888-1960), 26
Kanda (ward, Chiyoda District, Tokyo), 27
Kanno Sugako (feminist, journalist, 1881-1911), 25
Kanno Yoko (composer/pianist, b. 1964), 37, 107
Kansai, Japan, 79, 86n2, 94, 169
Kantō, Japan, 168, 169
Kantō Earthquake (September 1, 1923), 4, 39, 103n1
Kataoka Otogo (banker, 1880-1948), 89
Katei (poet), 2
Katō Kazue, (manga artist, b. 1980), 83
Kawabata Yasunari (author, 1899-1972), 2
Keiō University, Tokyo, 21, 24
Kekko Kamen (manga by Nagai Gō, 1974-78), 161
Kennedy, Caroline (American President's daughter, b. 1957), 160n8
Kerouac, Jack (American author, 1922-1969), 156
Key the Metal Idol (anime directed by Sato Hiroaki, 1994-97), 170
Kids on the Slope (Sakamichi no Aporon) (manga by Kodama Yuki, 2007-12), 107–108
Kiki's Delivery Service (Majo no Takkyuubin, lit. *Witch's Delivery Service)* (anime dir. by Miyazaki Hayao, 1989), 69
Kikuchi Hideyuki (author, b. 1949), 74
Kitakubo Hiroyuki (anime director, b. 1963), 151
Kitsune-onna (fox-woman), 50, 64n9
Kodama Yuki (manga artist), 107
Kojiki (Writings of Ancient Matters) (Shinto sacred text c. 711), 70, 75n3, 163, 165–166, 167
Kon Satoshi (anime director, 1963-2010), 70, 89, 91, 97n4, 140, 152
Konishi Yukinaga (general, Christian convert, 1555-1600), 135
Konno Oyuki (novelist, b. 1965), 120
Kōtoku Shūsui (anarchist, journalist, 1871-1911), 25
Kouenji Hiroshi (manga writer, b. 1941), 161
K'ung Fu-tzu (aka Confucius) (Chinese philosopher, author, 551-479 BC), 87n10, 121, 172

Kuragane Shōsuke (pseudonym) (manga artist, 1914-1973), 64n12
Kurosawa Akira (director, 1910-1998), 136
Kyoto (Japan), 12, 21, 84, 135
Kyushu (Japan), 11, 12, 18, 107, 124, 135, 136, 137

The Ladies of New Style (novel by Sudō Nansui, 1886), 34
LaFleur, William R. (American educator, 1936-2010), 18, 28, 45–46, 58
Lang, Fritz (German film director, 1890-1976), 38n5, 63n1, 143
Lebra, Takie Sugiyama (author, b. 1930), 27
Liberal Democratic Party (LDP), 22
Liliuokalani, (Queen of Hawai'ian Islands, 1838-1917), 25
Liquid Life: Abortion and Buddhism in Japan (cultural history by LaFleur, William R. 1994), 18, 19, 45–46, 58
Locke the Superman (manga by Hijiri Yuki, 1967-71), 170
Longinus (legendary Roman centurion), 82, 142, 143, 144, 145, 160n4
The Lost World (novel by Doyle, Sir Arthur Conan, 1912), 63n1
Lupin the Third: Castle of Cagliostro (anime dir. by Miyazaki Hayao, 1979), 102, 172n3

M (German film dir. by Lang, Fritz, 1931), 143
M.I.A., or, Mythmaking in America (history by Franklin, H. Bruce, 1992), 33
Macross Plus (anime dir. by Kawamori Shōji, 1994), 73, 140
Mad Max (series of Australian post-Apocalyptic movies), 169
Mai the Psychic Girl (manga by Ikegami Ryoichi and Kudō Kazuya, 1985-86), 170
Makai tenshō (Demon Resurrection) (novel by Yamada Fūtarō, 1967), 135, 138n3, 161
Manga-O (Japanese magazine), 41

Mao Zedong (Chinese ruler, 1893-1976), 22
Margaret (manga magazine), 67
Martyrdom of the 26 (Nagasaki, Japan, 1597), 15, 65, 133
Masamune Shirow (pseudonym) (manga artist, b. 1961), 120
Matthew, Robert (British author), 89
Matsudaira Nobutsuna (general, 1596-1662), 136
Matsumoto Reiji (also Leiji; manga artist, b. 1938), vi, 42, 66, 72
Matsutani Takayuki (anime producer), 62
McCarthy, Helen (British author), vi, 68
McGray, Douglas (author), 28
McLuhan, H. Marshall (Canadian media theorist, 1911-80), 2, 34
McManus, George (American cartoonist, 1884-1954), 39
Meiji era (1868-1912), 20, 21, 24, 25, 26, 28, 34, 35, 39, 94, 134, 170
Metropolis (anime, 2001), 38n5
Metropolis (German film, 1927), 38n5, 63n1, 134, 143
Mezon Ikkoku (manga by Takahashi Rumiko, 1982-88), 35, 70, 92–93, 119
Michiko to Hatchin (anime TV series, 2008-09), 105–106
The Mikado (British comic opera, 1885), 33
Millennium Actress (anime dir. by Kon Satoshi, 2003), 97n4, 152
Millennium Snow (manga by Hatori Bisco, 2001), 74
Minamoto no Yoshitsune (general, 1159-1189), 133
Mishima Yukio (author, actor, 1925-70), 2
Miyazaki Hayao (anime director, b. 1941), vi, 38n5, 42, 68, 69, 75n2, 87n10, 102, 172n1
Mochizuki Yuko (actress, 1917-77), 152
Morioka Kiyomi (author, b. 1923), 23–24
Moriyama Daisuke (manga artist, b. 1971), 119
Morse, Edward Sylvester (American zoologist, orientalist, 1838-1925), 24, 29n6
Mother Mary is Watching (Maria-sama ga Miteru) (novel series 1998-2012),

120–121, 162
Mukudori Nemu (manga artist, b. 1969), 79
Murasaki Shikibu, Lady (author, courtier, c. 973-1030), 122
Murase Shuko (anime director, b. 1964), 108, 129
Murphy, U. G. (American minister, social reformer, 1869-1967), 26
Murray, Dr. David (American educator, 1830-1905), 24
Musashi Miyamoto (samurai, author, 1584-1645), 136, 138n5
Mushi Productions (animation studio), 40, 62
Mutant Sab (manga by Ishinomori Shotaro, 1965), 53, 90
My Friend Frankenstein (Wa Ga Tomo Furankenshutain) (manga by Wada Shinji, 1977), 67–68, 153, 154
"My Johnny (Watashi no Jonii)" (manga by Satonaka Machiko, 1968), 49

Nagai Gō (manga artist, b. 1945), 72, 74, 135, 161, 162
Nagasaki (Japan), 12, 13, 15, 16, 17, 19, 20, 27, 31, 101, 135
Nakamura Hikaru (manga artist, b. 1984), 151, 152
Nakata Hideo (movie director, b. 1961), 86
Nakayoshi (manga magazine), 44, 55, 64n3, 85, 102
Nakazawa Keiji (manga artist, 1939-2012), 177
Nausicaä of the Valley of the Wind (Kaze no Tani no Naushika) (anime dir. by Miyazaki Hayao, 1984), 38n5, 42, 68–70, 163, 172n1, 178
Neon Genesis Evangelion (Shin Seiki Evangelion) (anime series, 1995), 82, 108, 130, 144–146
Nicholson, James H. (American film producer, 1916-72), 41–42
Niejima (or Niishima or Neesima), Joseph Hardy (Christian convert, 1843-90), 24
Nightow, Yasuhiro (pseudonym) (manga artist, b. 1967), 109, 110
Ninomiya Sontoku (philosopher and economist, 1787-1856), 80, 87n5

Nitobe Inazō (educator, author, 1862-1933), 26
Nobunaga the Fool (anime series dir. by Sato Eiichi, 2014), 87n9
Nobumoto Keiko (anime writer, b. 1964), 140
Nobunagun (manga by Hisa Masato, 2011), 87n9
Nonkina Tosan (Easygoing Daddy) (comic by Asō Yutaka, 1923-), 39

Ō no Yasumaro (author of *Kojiki*, d. 723), 165
Obama, Barack Hussein (American President, b. 1961), vi, 127–128, 129
Obata Takeshi (manga artist, b. 1969), vi, 64n12, 155
Occult Gang (Shinrei Tantei Okaruto Dan) (manga by Nagai Gō and Ishikawa Ken, written by Kouenji Hiroshi, 1991), 74–75, 135, 161–162
Oda Nobunaga (shogun, 1534-1582), 11–12, 13, 14, 65–66, 82, 87n9, 133
Odyssey (poem by Homer, 800 B.C.), 68
Ōe Kenzaburō (author, b. 1935), 2
Ogenki Clinic (Health Clinic) (manga by Inui Haruka, 1987-94), 162, 164
Ogihara-Schuck, Eriko (scholar), 69
Okinawa (Japan), 29n5
Ōkubo Atsushi (manga artist, b. 1979), 123
The Omen (American horror movie dir. by Donner, Richard, 1976), 53, 64n10
Ōmura Sumitada (daimyo of Nagasaki, Christian convert, 1533-87), 12
On the Waterfront (American movie dir. by Kazan, Elia, 1954), 142
One Pound Gospel (Ippondo no Fukuin) (manga by Takahashi Rumiko, 1989, 2006-08), 117–119, 147
Ono Fuyumi (novelist, manga author, b. 1960), 74, 78, 94
Order of Friars Minor/Franciscan Order, 15, 16, 17, 149
Orientalism (history by Said, Edward W., 1978), vi, 6, 9, 29, 32–33, 59, 69, 78
Orientalism (as cultural practice), 33–34, 37, 38n5, 41, 42, 70, 72, 80, 82, 84, 97n2, 114, 134, 142, 145–146, 155, 170, 172

Ortega, Mariana (author), 144–145, 152
Otmazgin, Nissim Kadosh (author), 28
Otomo Katsuhiro (manga artist, b. 1954), 170

Parry, Richard Lloyd (British journalist, author, b. 1969), 77, 78, 86n3
Perry, Matthew (American naval officer, 1794-1858), 19–20, 21, 36
Phantom Quest Corp. (Yugen Kaisha) (anime video dir. by Chigira Koichi, 1994-1995), 82
Pietà (sculpture by Buonarroti, Michelangelo), 131
Please Save My Earth (Boku no Chikyu-wo Mamotte) (manga by Hiwatari Saki, 1986-94), 139
Pokémon (anime based on video game by Tajiri Satoshi, 1997-), 66, 71
Princess Mononoke (Mononoke-hime) (anime dir. by Miyazaki Hayao, 1999), 75n2
Pure Land (Buddhist sect). *See* Jodo Shinshu

RAI (Radiotelevisione Italia, network), 62
Ranma ½ (manga by Takahashi Rumiko, 1987-1996), 117, 162
Ravenscroft, Trevor (British author, 1921-89), 144
Reader, Ian (British scholar, b. 1949), 5, 165
Recruit scandal (political bribery scandal, 1988-90), 22
Reischauer, Edwin O. (American historian, diplomat, 1910-90), 11, 13, 17, 21, 21–22, 22, 24
Rin Taro (also Rintaro; anime director, b. 1941), vi
The Ring (Ringu) (movie dir. by Nakata Hideo, 1998), 86
Robertson, Pat (American evangelist, b. 1930), 40, 63, 139
The Rosary and the Vampire (Rosario to Banpaiya) (manga by Akihisa Ikeda, 2004-07), 72, 74
Rose of Versailles (Berusai no Bara) (Japanese manga by Ikeda Riyoko, 1972-73), 67

Rowling, J. K. (British author, b. 1965), 83, 132n2
Royal Space Force: Wings of Honneamise (Oneamisu no Tsubasa) (anime dir. by Yamaga Hiroyuki, 1995), 158–159
Rurouni Kenshin (manga by Watsuki Nobuhiro, 1994-99), 110, 134
Rusoff, Lou (American screenwriter, 1911-1963), 42
Russo-Japanese War (1904-1905), 24
Ryan, Paul. American politician (b. 1970), 127
Ryūkyū Kingdom. *See* Okinawa

Said, Edward W. (Palestinian scholar, 1935-2003), vi, 6, 9, 29, 32–33, 34, 36, 37, 59, 69, 78, 175
Sailor Moon (Se-ra- Mu-n) (manga by Takeuchi Naoko, 1992-97), 66, 73, 91, 102
Saint Tail (Kaitou Saint Tail) (manga by Tachikawa Megumi, 1995-96), 124–125
Saint Young Men (Seinto Oniisan) (manga by Nakamura Hikaru, 2006-), 151–152
Sakai Toshihiko (author, socialist, 1871-1933), 25
Sakoku "Locked Country" policy, 19, 20, 21, 137
Salvation Army (evangelical organization), 26, 27, 89, 91, 96, 139, 140, 142
Samurai Spirits (videogame series), 137
Satonaka Machiko (manga artist, b. 1948), 49
Saturn Devouring His Son (painting by Goya, Francisco, c. 1820), 131
Savage, William W., Jr. (American scholar, author), 2, 64n2
Sazae-san (manga, by Hasegawa Machiko, 1946-74), 64n12
Schodt, Frederik L. (American author, b. 1950), vi, 7, 39, 40, 42, 49, 64n12, 67
Seichō no Ie (sect), 28
Seidensticker, Edward (American author, translator, 1921-2007), 4–5, 7
Sekigahara, Battle of (October 21, 1600), 15, 135
Shakespeare, William (British playwright, 1564-1616), 7, 54–55

Shibamoto Thores (illustrator), 149
Shiina Takashi (manga artist, b. 1965), vi, 81
Shikoku (island, Japan), 15
Shimabara (city, Nagasaki Prefecture, Japan), 16
Shimabara Rebellion of 1637-38, 16, 134, 136, 138, 138n2
Shimizu Takahashi (movie director, b. 1972), 86
Shinkai Makoto (anime director, b. 1973), 75n3, 166
Shonen Sunday (magazine), 54, 81
The Silence of the Lambs (American movie dir. by Demme, Jonathan, 1991), 65
Sino-Japanese War (1894-95), 24, 35
Smith, Robert (scholar, b. 1927), 17
Society of Jesus/Jesuits, 11, 13, 14, 15, 16, 17, 77, 82, 85, 115n3, 149, 176
Soka Gakkai (Buddhist sect), 8
Song of Wind and Trees (Kaze to Ki no Uta) (manga by Takemiya Keiko, 1976-84), 67, 90
Sontag, Susan (American author, 1933-2004), 2
Soul Eater (manga by Ōkubo Atsushi, 2004-14), 123
The Spear of Destiny (book by Ravenscroft, Trevor, 1972), 144
Spear of Longinus (Christian artifact), 142, 143, 144, 145
Speed Racer (Mach Go Go Go) (manga by Yoshida Tatsuo, 1966-68), 40, 139
Spencer, Herbert (British biologist, philosopher, 1820-1903), 24
Spirited Away (Sen to Chihiro no Kamikakushi, lit. *Sen and Chihiro Spirited Away)* (anime dir. by Miyazaki Hayao, 2001), 75n2, 87n10, 156
Stoker, Bram (Irish author, 1847-1912), 9, 58, 61, 75n5, 148
Sudō Nansui (novelist, journalist, 1857-1920), 34
Sugimoto Etsu Inagaki (educator, 1874-1950), 36
Sukeban Deka (manga by Wada Shinji, 1976-82), 67
Sullivan, Sir Arthur (British composer, 1842-1900), 33

Sumitomo, Japanese corporation, 40
Summa Theologica (theology by Thomas Aquinas, 1265-1274), 164
Superbook (Anime Oyako Gekijo) (anime series, 1981-82), 139
Suter, Rebecca (scholar, b. 1975), 17, 19, 29n2, 133, 135, 136–137, 137, 138n2
Suzuki Bunji (labor organizer, Christian, 1885-1946), 26
Suzuki Daisetzu (Buddhist priest, author, 1870-1966), 156
Sword Art Online (anime based on novels by Kawahara Reki, 2012-14), 91–92

Tachikawa Megumi (manga artist), 124
Taisho period (1912-26), 143
Tajiri Satoshi (videogame creator, b. 1965), 71
Takahashi Rumiko (manga artist, b. 1957), vi, 35, 70, 92, 101, 117, 119, 147, 162
Takarazuka (all-girl theatrical troupe, founded 1913), 44, 64n4
Takemiya Keiko (manga artist, b. 1950), 67, 90
Takeuchi Naoko (manga artist, b. 1967), 91, 102
Tale of Genji (Genji Monogatari) (novel by Lady Murasaki Shikibu, c. 1000), 34, 122
Tales of Earthsea (aka Gedo Senki) (anime dir. by Miyazaki Goro, 2010), 156
Tanegashima (Kagoshima Prefecture, Japan), 11
Taniguchi Masaharu (founder of Seichō no Ie, 1893-1985), 28
Tanizaki Jun'ichirō (author, 1886-1965), 2
Tatsunoko (anime studio), 63, 139
Tenchi Muyo (manga by Okuda Hitoshi, 1994-2000), 72
Tezuka Osamu (manga artist, 1928-1989), vi, 7, 9, 37, 38n5, 39–40, 42, 62, 63, 66, 67, 74, 90, 173n8, 177
Tezuka Osamu, manga by: *Angel Hill (Enzeru no Oka)* (manga, 1960-61), 55–56; *Astro Boy* (aka *Tetsuwan Atomu, The Mighty Atom*) (manga, 1952-68), 40, 46–48, 90, 173n8, 177; *Black Jack* (manga, 1973-1983), 45, 56–58, 63, 110; *Crime and Punishment*

(Kei to Batsu) (manga, 1954), 40, 42, 43, 54; *Don Dracula (Don Dorakyura)* (manga, 1980), 9, 58–62, 64n8, 64n10, 64n12, 74, 148; *Dororo* (manga, 1967-68), 63; *One Hundred Stories (Hyaku Monogatari)* (manga, 1971), 40–54; *Jungle Emperor (Janguru Taitei)* (manga, 1950-54), 40, 42; *MW* (manga, 1976-78), 51; *My Son-Goku (Boku no Son-Goku)* (manga, 1952-59), 40, 41–42; *Ode to Kirihito (Kirihito Sanka)* (manga, 1970-71), 42, 49–51; *Phoenix (Hi no Tori)* (manga, 1967-88), 42; *The Ribbon Knight (Ribon no Kishi)* (manga, 1953-56, rev. 1963-66), 40, 43–44, 64n3; *Song of Apollo (Aporo no Uta)* (manga, 1970), 40; *The Twin Knights (Futago no Kishi)* (manga, 1958-59), 44–45, 46, 64n4; *Unico* (manga, 1976-79), 42, 52–53; *The Vampyres (Banpaiya-zu)* (manga, 1966), 54–55

Tezuka Osamu no Kyūyaku Seisho Monogatari (Osamu Tezuka's Old Testament Stories), (anime, 1997), 62–63

Tezuka Pro (animation studio), 40, 57, 58

Theroux, Paul (American author, b. 1941), 3, 7

Things to Come (British film dir. by Menzies, William Cameron, 1936), 63n1

Thomas Aquinas (Italian theologian, c. 1225-74)

Three Godfathers (American film dir. by Ford, John, 1948), 140

Thule Society (German mystical cult), 144

Toei (Japanese film studio), 40, 41

Tohoku region, Honshu, Japan, 50

Tokugawa Shogunate, 13, 15, 17, 18, 19, 65, 99, 106, 123, 135, 137; Tokugawa Hidetada (1579-1632; shogun 1605-1623), 16; Tokugawa Iemitsu (1604-1651; shogun 1623-1651), 16; Tokugawa Ieyasu (1543-1616; shogun 1603-1605), 16, 17, 123, 135, 149

Tokyo Godfathers (anime dir. by Kon Satoshi, 2003), 70, 89, 91, 96, 140–142

Tokyo Tower (landmark), 82, 141

"Tokyo Rose" (legendary radio announcers), 75n1

Tokyo Sagawa Kyubin (delivery company caught in political scandal), 22

Tomi Shinzō (manga artist), 136

Topcraft (anime studio), 69

Topsy-Turvy (British film dir. by Leigh, Mike, 1999), 33

Toyotomi Hideyoshi (general, shogun, c. 1536-1598), 13, 14, 15, 15–16, 16, 29n1, 31, 65, 66, 115n1, 135, 163

Trigun (manga by Nightow Yasuhiro, 1995-97), 109–110

Trinity Blood (horror novels by Yoshida Sunao and Yasui Kentaro, 2001-05), 147, 149–150

Trump, Donald (American businessman, b. 1946), 128

Tsukimi no Sho (The Book of Gazing at the Moon) (book by Yagyu Jubei, c. 1642), 138n5

Tsutsui Yasutaka (novelist, b. 1934), 177

Tuchman, Barbara W. (American historian, 1912-89), 97n2, 149, 150

U.F.A. (German film studio), 143

Uchimura Kanzō (evangelist, 1861-1930), 25

Urakami Cathedral, Nagasaki, Japan, 27

Vampire Hunter D (novels by Hideyuki Kikuchi, 1983-), 74

Vampire Princess Miyu (Ky ū ketsuki Miyu) (anime dir. by Hirano Toshihiro, 1988), 84

Varley, H. Paul (American scholar, 1931-2015), 11, 12, 12–13, 13, 15, 19, 21, 22, 23, 149

Verbeck, Dr. Guido (Dutch educator, evangelist, 1830-98), 21

Vico, Giambattista (Italian historian, 1668-1744), 38n3, 144, 175

Video Girl Ai (Denen Shoujo) (manga by Katsura Masakazu, 1989-91), 73

Wada Shinji (manga artist, 1950-2011), 67, 153

Warring States Period (Sengoku Jidai) (1467-1573), 11, 29n1, 169

Warriors of the Wind. See *Nausicaä of the Valley of the Wind*
Waseda (university, Tokyo), 21, 28
Watsuki Nobuhiro (manga artist, b. 1970), 110, 134
Watts, Alan (American theologian, 1915-73), 156
Weiner, Tim (American journalist), 22
Wells, Herbert George (British author, 1866-1946), 63n1
Wings of Honneamise. See *Royal Space Force*
Witch Craft Works (manga by Mizunagi Ryū, 2010-13), 72
Witch Hunter Robin (anime dir. by Murase Shukō, 2002), 108–109, 129–132
Wright, Frank Lloyd (American architect, 1867-1959), 103n1

X (manga by CLAMP, 1992-2003), 72
xxxHolic (manga by CLAMP, 2003-11), 70

Yagyu Jubei (swordsman, author, 1607-50), 110, 136, 138n5, 176

Yajima Kajiko (social activist, Christian, 1833-1925), 26
Yamada Fūtarō (novelist, 1922-2001), 138n3
Yamakawa Kikue (socialist, political activist, 1890-1980), 27
Yasui Kentaro (novelist continuing the *Trinity Blood* series), 149
Yokomizo Seishi (novelist, 1902-81), 138n3
Yokota Airbase, Tokyo (American military base), 151
Yon Kouga, (manga artist), 70
Yoshida Sunao (novelist, 1969-2004), 149
Yoshihito (emperor during the Taisho period, 1879-1926), 143
Yoshitsune. *See* Minamoto no Yoshitsune
Yoshiwara (district of Tokyo), 26
Yoshiya Nobuko (author, 1896-1973), 122
Yuki Kaori (manga artist), 164–165

Zen (Japanese Buddhist sect), 156

www.ingramcontent.com/pod-product-compliance
Lightning Source LLC
Chambersburg PA
CBHW020124240426
43673CB00038B/590